Exit the King, The Killer, and Macbett

WORKS BY EUGÈNE IONESCO
PUBLISHED BY GROVE PRESS

Exit the King, The Killer, *and* Macbett

The Bald Soprano and Other Plays
(The Lesson; The Chairs; Jack, or The Submission)

Rhinoceros and Other Plays (The Leader;
The Future Is in Eggs or It Takes All Sorts to Make a World)

Three Plays (Amédée; The New Tenant; Victims of Duty)

Exit the King, The Killer, and Macbett

Three Plays by
Eugène Ionesco

**Translated from the French by
Charles Marowitz and Donald Watson**

Grove Press

New York

Published by Grove Press
841 Broadway
New York, N.Y. 10003

First Evergreen Edition 1985
ISBN: 0-8021-5110-8
Library of Congress Catalog Number: 85-81779

Manufactured in the United States of America

5 4 3

Exit the King

Exit The King was first performed on December 15, 1962 at the Théâtre de l'Alliance Française in Paris. An English version was later performed at the Edinburgh Festival in September, 1963 by the Royal Court Company.

The American première was performed by APA Repertory Company by arrangement with the APA Phoenix on September 1, 1967 in Los Angeles. It was directed by Ellis Rabb, with music by Conrad Susa, scenery design by Rouben Ter-Arutunian, lighting design by James Tilton, costumes design by Nancy Potts, and with the following cast:

BERENGER THE FIRST, *The King*	Richard Easton
QUEEN MARGUERITE, *First Wife*	Louise Latham
QUEEN MARIE, *Second Wife*	Patricia Conolly
THE DOCTOR, *who is also Surgeon, Executioner, Bacteriologist & Astrologist*	Will Geer
JULIETTE, *Domestic Help and Registered Nurse*	Pamela Payton-Wright
THE GUARD	Nicolas Martin

The photographs used throughout the text are from the APA Repertory Company production and were taken by Van Williams.

The Set

The throne room, vaguely dilapidated, vaguely Gothic. In the center of the stage, against the back wall, a few steps leading to the King's throne. On either side, downstage, two smaller thrones—those of the two QUEENS, *his wives.*

Upstage left, a small door leading to the King's apartments. Upstage right, another small door. Also on the right, downstage, a large door. Between these two doors, a Gothic window. Another small window on the left of the stage; and another small door downstage, also on the left. Near the large door, an old GUARD *with a halberd.*

Before and during the rise of the curtain, and for a few minutes afterward, you can hear a derisive rendering of regal music reminiscent of the King's Levee in the seventeenth century.

Ionesco's own suggested cuts are indicated in the text by square brackets.

GUARD (*announcing*): His Majesty the King, Berenger the First. Long live the King!

The KING *enters from the little door on the right, wearing a deep crimson cloak, with a crown on his head and a scepter in his hand, rapidly crosses the stage and goes off through the upstage door on the left.*

(*Announcing:*) Her Majesty Queen Marguerite, First Wife to the King, followed by Juliette, Domestic Help and Registered Nurse to their Majesties. Long live the Queen!

MARGUERITE, *followed by* JULIETTE, *enters through the downstage door on the left and goes out through the large door.*

(*Announcing:*) Her Majesty Queen Marie, Second Wife to the King, but first in affection, followed by Juliette, Domestic Help and Registered Nurse to their Majesties. Long live the Queen!

MARIE, *followed by* JULIETTE, *enters through the large door on the right and goes out with* JULIETTE *through the downstage door on the left.* MARIE *appears younger and more beautiful than* MARGUERITE. *She has a crown and a deep crimson cloak. She is wearing jewels. Her cloak is of more modern style and looks as if it comes from a high-class couturier. The* DOCTOR *comes in through the upstage door on the right.*

(*Announcing:*) His Notability, Doctor to the King,

7

Gentleman Court Surgeon, Bacteriologist, Executioner and Astrologist.

The DOCTOR *comes to the center of the stage and then, as though he had forgotten something, turns back the way he came and goes out through the same door. The* GUARD *remains silent for a few moments. He looks tired. He rests his halberd against the wall, and then blows into his hands to warm them.*

I don't know, this is just the time when it ought to be hot. Central heating, start up! Nothing doing, it's not working. Central heating, start up! The radiator's stone cold. It's not my fault. He never told me he'd taken away my job as Chief Firelighter. Not officially, anyway. You never know with them.

Suddenly, he picks up his weapon. QUEEN MARGUERITE *reappears through the upstage door on the right. She has a crown on her head and is wearing a deep crimson cloak that is a bit shabby. She looks rather severe. She stops in the center, downstage. She is followed by* JULIETTE.

Long live the Queen!

MARGUERITE (*to* JULIETTE, *looking around her*): There's a lot of dust about. And cigarette butts on the floor.

JULIETTE: I've just come from the stables milking the cow, your Majesty. She's almost out of milk. I haven't had time to do the living room.

MARGUERITE: This is *not* the living room. It's the throne room. How often do I have to tell you?

JULIETTE: All right, the throne room, as your Majesty wishes. I haven't had time to do the living room.

MARGUERITE: It's cold.

GUARD: I've been trying to turn the heat on, your Majesty. Can't get the system to function. The radiators won't co-operate. The sky is overcast and the clouds don't seem to want to break up. The sun's late. And yet I heard the King order him to come out.

MARGUERITE: Is that so! The sun's already deaf to his commands.

GUARD: I heard a little rumble during the night. There's a crack in the wall.

MARGUERITE: Already? Things are moving fast. I wasn't expecting this so soon.

GUARD: Juliette and I tried to patch it up.

JULIETTE: He woke me in the middle of the night, when I was sound asleep!

GUARD: And now it's here again. Shall we have another try?

MARGUERITE: It's not worth it. We can't turn the clock back. (*To* JULIETTE:) Where's Queen Marie?

JULIETTE: She must still be dressing.

MARGUERITE: Naturally!

JULIETTE: She was awake before dawn.

MARGUERITE: Oh! Well, that's something!

JULIETTE: I heard her crying in her room.

MARGUERITE: Laugh or cry, that's all she can do. (*To* JULIETTE:) Let her be sent for at once. Go and fetch her.

Just at this minute, QUEEN MARIE *appears, dressed as described above.*

GUARD (*a moment before Queen Marie's entrance*): Long live the Queen!

MARGUERITE (*to* MARIE): Your eyes are quite red, my dear. It spoils your beauty.

MARIE: I know.

MARGUERITE: Don't start crying again!

MARIE: I can't really help it.

MARGUERITE: Don't go to pieces, whatever you do. What's the use? It's the normal course of events, isn't it? You were expecting it. Or had you stopped expecting it?

MARIE: *You've* been *waiting* for it!

MARGUERITE: A good thing, too. And now the moment's arrived. (*To* JULIETTE:) Well, why don't you give her another handkerchief?

MARIE: I was still hoping . . .

MARGUERITE: You're wasting your time. Hope! (*She shrugs her shoulders.*) Nothing but hope on their lips and tears in their eyes. What a way to behave!

MARIE: Have you seen the Doctor again? What did he say?

MARGUERITE: What you've heard already.

MARIE: Perhaps he's made a mistake.

MARGUERITE: Don't start hoping all over again! The signs are unmistakable.

MARIE: Perhaps he's misinterpreted them.

MARGUERITE: There's no mistaking the signs, if you look at them objectively. And you know it!

MARIE (*looking at the wall*): Oh! That crack!

MARGUERITE: Oh! You've seen it, have you? And that's not the only thing. It's your fault if he's not prepared. It's your fault if it takes him by surprise. You let him go his own way. You've even led him astray. Oh yes! Life was very sweet. With your fun and games, your dances, your processions, your official dinners, your winning ways and your fireworks displays, your silver spoons and your honeymoons! How many honeymoons have you had?

MARIE: They were to celebrate our wedding anniversaries.

MARGUERITE: You celebrated them four times a year. "We've got to *live*" you used to say. . . . But one must never forget.

MARIE: He's so fond of parties.

MARGUERITE: People know and carry on as if they didn't. They know and they forget. But *he* is the King. *He* must not forget. He should have his eyes fixed in front of him, know every stage in the journey, know exactly how long the road, and never lose sight of his destination.

MARIE: My poor darling, my poor little King.

MARGUERITE (*to* JULIETTE): Give her another handkerchief. (*To* MARIE:) Be a little more cheerful, can't you? Tears are catching. He's weak enough already. What a pernicious influence you've had on him. But there! I'm afraid he liked you better than me! I wasn't at all jealous, I just realized he wasn't being very wise. And now you can't help him any more. Look at you! Bathed in tears. You're not defying me now. You've lost that challenging look. Where's it all gone, that brazen insolence, that sarcastic smile? Come on now, wake up! Take your proper place and try to straighten up. Think! You're still wearing your beautiful necklace! Come along! Take your place!

MARIE (*seated*): I'll never be able to tell him.

MARGUERITE: I'll see to that. I'm used to the chores.

MARIE: And don't *you* tell him either. No, no, please. Don't say a word, I beg you.

MARGUERITE: *Please* leave it to me. We'll still want you, you know, later, still need you during the ceremony. You like official functions.

MARIE: Not this one.

MARGUERITE (*to* JULIETTE): You. Spread our trains out properly.

JULIETTE: Yes, your Majesty. (JULIETTE *does so.*)

MARGUERITE: I agree it's not so amusing as all your charity balls. Those dances you get up for children, and old folks, and newlyweds. For victims of disaster or the honors lists. For lady novelists. Or charity balls for the organizers of charity balls. This one's just for the family, with no dancers and no dance.

MARIE: No, don't tell him. It's better if he doesn't notice anything.

MARGUERITE: . . . and goes out like a light? That's impossible.

MARIE: You've no heart.

MARGUERITE: Oh, yes, I have! It's beating.

MARIE: You're inhuman.

[MARGUERITE: What does that mean?

MARIE: It's terrible,] he's not prepared.

MARGUERITE: It's your fault if he isn't. He's been like one of those travelers who linger at every inn, forgetting each time that the inn is not the end of the journey. When I reminded you that in life we must never forget our ultimate fate, you told me I was a pompous bluestocking.

JULIETTE (*aside*): It *is* pompous, too!

MARIE: As it's inevitable, at least he must be told as tactfully as possible. Tactfully, with great tact.

MARGUERITE: He ought always to have been prepared for it. He ought to have thought about it every day. The time he's wasted! (*To* JULIETTE:) What's the matter with you, goggling at us like that? You're not going to break down too, I hope. You can leave us; don't go too far away, we'll call you.

JULIETTE: So I don't have to sweep the living room now?

MARGUERITE: It's too late. Never mind. Leave us.

JULIETTE *goes out on the left.*

MARIE: Tell him gently, I implore you. Take your time. He might have a heart attack.

MARGUERITE: We haven't the time to take our time. This is the end of your happy days, your high jinks, your beanfeasts and your strip tease. It's all over. You've let things slide to the very last minute and now we've not a minute to lose. Obviously. It's the last. We've a few moments to do what ought to have been done over a period of years. I'll tell you when you have to leave us alone. Then, *I'll* help him.

MARIE: It's going to be so hard, so hard.

MARGUERITE: As hard for me as for you, and for him. Stop grizzling, I say! That's a piece of advice. That's an order.

MARIE: He won't do it.

MARGUERITE: Not at first.

MARIE: I'll hold him back.

MARGUERITE: Don't you dare! It's all got to take place decently. Let it be a success, a triumph. It's a long time since he had one. His palace is crumbling. His fields lie fallow. His mountains are sinking. The sea has broken the dikes and flooded the country. He's let it all go to rack and ruin. You've driven every thought from his mind with your perfumed embrace. Such bad taste! But that was him all over! Instead of conserving the soil, he's let acre upon acre plunge into the bowels of the earth.

MARIE: Expert advice on how to stop an earthquake!

MARGUERITE: I've no patience with you! . . . He could still have planted conifers in the sand and cemented the threatened areas. But no! Now the kingdom's as full of holes as a gigantic Gruyère cheese.

MARIE: We couldn't fight against fate, against a natural phenomenon like erosion.

MARGUERITE: Not to mention all those disastrous wars. While his drunken soldiers were sleeping it off, at night or after a lavish lunch in barracks, our neighbors were pushing back our frontier posts. Our national boundaries were shrinking. His soldiers didn't want to fight.

MARIE: They were conscientious objectors.

MARGUERITE: We called them conscientious objectors here at home. The victorious armies called them cowards and deserters, and they were shot. You can see the result: towns razed to the ground, burnt-out swimming pools, abandoned bistros. The young are leaving their homeland in hordes. At the start of his reign there were nine thousand million inhabitants.

MARIE: Too many. There wasn't room for them all.

MARGUERITE: And now only about a thousand old people left. Less. Even now, while I'm talking, they're passing away.

MARIE: There are forty-five *young* people too.

MARGUERITE: No one else wants *them. We* didn't want them either; we were forced to take them back. Anyway, they're aging fast. Repatriated at twenty-five, two days later and they're over eighty. You can't pretend that's the normal way to grow old.

MARIE: But the king, *he's* still young.

MARGUERITE: He *was* yesterday, he *was* last night. You'll see in a moment.

GUARD (*announcing*): His Notability, the Doctor, has returned. His Notability, His Notability!

The DOCTOR *enters through the large door on the right, which opens and closes by itself. He looks like an astrologer and an executioner at one and the same time. On his head he is wearing a pointed hat with stars. He is dressed in red with a hood hanging from the collar, and holding a great telescope.*

DOCTOR (*to* MARGUERITE): Good morning, your Majesty. (*To* MARIE:) Good morning, your Majesty. I hope your Majesties will forgive me for being rather late. I've come straight from the hospital, where I had to perform several surgical operations of the greatest import to science.

MARIE: You can't operate on the King!

MARGUERITE: You can't *now,* that's true.

DOCTOR (*looking at* MARGUERITE, *then at* MARIE): I know. Not his Majesty.

MARIE: Doctor, is there anything new? He *is* a little better, isn't he? Isn't he? He *could* show *some* improvement, couldn't he?

DOCTOR: He's in a typically critical condition that admits no change.

MARIE: It's true, there's no hope, no hope. (*Looking at* MARGUERITE.) She doesn't want me to hope, she won't allow it.

MARGUERITE: Many people have delusions of grandeur, but you're deluded by triviality. There's never been a queen like you! You make me ashamed for you. Oh! She's going to cry again.

DOCTOR: In point of fact, there *is,* if you like, *something* new to report.

MARIE: What's that?

DOCTOR: Something that merely confirms the previous symptoms. Mars and Saturn have collided.

MARGUERITE: As we expected.

DOCTOR: Both planets have exploded.

MARGUERITE: That's logical.

DOCTOR: The sun has lost between fifty and seventy-five percent of its strength.

MARGUERITE: That's natural.

DOCTOR: Snow is falling on the North Pole of the sun. The Milky Way seems to be curdling. The comet is exhausted, feeling its age, winding its tail around itself and curling up like a dying dog.

MARIE: It's not true, you're exaggerating. You must be. Yes, you're exaggerating.

DOCTOR: Do you wish to look through this telescope?

MARGUERITE (*to* DOCTOR): There's no point. We believe you. What else?

DOCTOR: Yesterday evening it was spring. It left us two hours and thirty minutes ago. Now it's November. Outside our frontiers, the grass is shooting up, the trees are turning green. All the cows are calving twice a day. Once in the morning and again in the afternoon about five, or a quarter past. Yet in our own country, the brittle leaves are peeling off. The trees are sighing and dying. The earth is quaking rather more than usual.

GUARD (*announcing*): The Royal Meteorological Institute calls attention to the bad weather conditions.

MARIE: I can feel the earth quaking, I can hear it. Yes, I'm afraid I really can.

MARGUERITE: It's that crack. It's getting wider, it's spreading.

DOCTOR: The lightning's stuck in the sky, the clouds are raining frogs, the thunder's mumbling. That's why we can't hear it. Twenty-five of our countrymen have been liquefied. Twelve have lost their heads. Decapitated. This time, without my surgical intervention.

MARGUERITE: Those are the signs all right.

DOCTOR: Whereas . . .

MARGUERITE (*interrupting him*): No need to go on. It's what always happens in a case like this. We know.

GUARD (*announcing*): His Majesty, the King!

Music.

Attention for His Majesty! Long live the King!

The KING *enters through the upstage door on the left. He has bare feet.* JULIETTE *comes in behind the* KING.

MARGUERITE: Now where has he scattered his slippers?

JULIETTE: Sire, they are here.

MARGUERITE: It's a bad habit to walk about barefoot.

MARIE (*to* JULIETTE): Put his slippers on. Hurry up! He'll catch cold!

MARGUERITE: It's no longer of any importance if he catches cold. It's just that it's a bad habit.

While JULIETTE *is putting the King's slippers on and*

MARIE *moves toward him, the royal music can still be heard.*

DOCTOR *(with a humble and unctuous bow)*: May I be allowed to wish your Majesty a good day. And my very best wishes.

MARGUERITE: That's nothing now but a hollow formality.

KING *(to* MARIE, *and then to* MARGUERITE*)*: Good morning, Marie. Good morning, Marguerite. Still here? I mean, you're here already! How do you feel? *I* feel awful! I don't know quite what's wrong with me. My legs are a bit stiff. I had a job to get up, and my feet hurt! I must get some new slippers. Perhaps I've been growing! I had a bad night's sleep, what with the earth quaking, the frontiers retreating, the cattle bellowing and the sirens screaming. There's far too much noise. I really must look into it. We'll see what we can do. Ouch, my ribs! *(To* DOCTOR:*)* Good morning, Doctor. Is it lumbago? *(To the others:)* I'm expecting an engineer . . . from abroad. Ours are no good nowadays. They just don't care. Besides, we haven't any. Why did we close the Polytechnic? Oh yes! It fell through a hole in the ground. And why should we build more when they all disappear through a hole? On top of everything else, I've got a headache. And those clouds . . . I thought I'd banished the clouds. Clouds! We've had enough rain. Enough, I said! Enough rain. Enough, I said! Oh! Look at that! Off they go again! There's an idiotic cloud that can't restrain itself. Like an old man, weak in the bladder. *(To* JULIETTE:*)* What are you staring at me for? You look very red today. My bedroom's full of cobwebs. Go and brush them away.

JULIETTE: I removed them all while your Majesty was still

asleep. I can't think where they spring from. They keep on coming back.

DOCTOR (*to* MARGUERITE): You see, your Majesty. This, too, confirms my diagnosis.

KING (*to* MARIE): What's wrong with you, my love?

MARIE (*stammering*): I don't know . . . nothing . . . nothing wrong.

KING: You've got rings around your eyes. Have you been crying? Why?

MARIE: Oh God!

KING (*to* MARGUERITE): I won't have anyone upset her. And why did she say, "Oh God?"

MARGUERITE: It's an expression. (*To* JULIETTE:) Go and get rid of those cobwebs again.

KING: Oh yes! Those cobwebs, disgusting! They give you nightmares!

MARGUERITE (*to* JULIETTE): Hurry up, don't dawdle! Have you forgotten how to use a broom?

JULIETTE: Mine's all worn away. I need a new one. I could really do with twelve brooms.

JULIETTE *goes out.*

KING: Why are you all staring at me like this? Is there something abnormal about me? Now it's so normal to be abnormal, there's no such thing as abnormality. So that's straightened that out.

MARIE (*rushing toward the* KING): My dear King, you're limping!

KING (*taking two or three paces with a slight limp*): Limping? *I'm* not limping. I *am* limping a little.

MARIE: Your leg hurts. I'm going to help you along.

KING: It doesn't hurt. Why should it hurt? Why, yes, it *does* just a little. It's nothing. (*To* MARIE:) I don't need anyone to help me. Though I like being helped by you.

MARGUERITE (*moving toward the* KING): Sire, I have some news for you.

MARIE: No, be quiet!

MARGUERITE (*to* MARIE): Keep quiet yourself!

MARIE (*to the* KING): What she says isn't true.

KING: News about what? *What* isn't true? Marie, why do you look so sad! What's the matter with you?

MARGUERITE (*to the* KING): Sire, we have to inform you that you are going to die.

DOCTOR: Alas, yes, your Majesty.

KING: But I know that, of course I do! We *all* know it! You can remind me when the time comes. Marguerite, you have a mania for disagreeable conversation early in the morning.

MARGUERITE: It's midday already.

KING: It's not midday. Why yes, it is! It doesn't matter. For me, it's the morning. I haven't eaten anything yet. Let my breakfast be brought. To be honest, I'm not very hungry. Doctor, you'll have to give me some pills to stimulate my appetite and shake up my liver. My tongue's all coated, isn't it?

He shows his tongue to the DOCTOR.

DOCTOR: Yes, indeed, your Majesty.

KING: My liver's all choked up. I had nothing to drink last night, but I've a nasty taste in my mouth.

DOCTOR: Your Majesty, Queen Marguerite has spoken the truth. You *are* going to die.

KING: What, again? You get on my nerves! I'll die, yes, I'll die all right. In forty, fifty, three hundred years. Or even later. When I want to, when I've got the time, when I make up my mind. Meanwhile, let's get on with affairs of state. (*He climbs the steps of the throne.*) Ouch! My legs! My back! I've caught a cold. This palace is so badly heated, full of draughts and gales. What about those broken windowpanes? Have they replaced those tiles on the roof? No one works any more. I shall have to see to it myself, but I've had other things to do. You can't count on anyone. (*To* MARIE, *who is trying to support him:*) No, I can manage. (*He helps himself up with his scepter, using it as a stick.*) There's some use in this scepter yet. (*He manages to sit down, painfully, helped after all by* MARIE.) No, I say, no, I can do it. That's it! At last! This throne's got very hard! We ought to have it upholstered. And how is my country this morning?

MARGUERITE: What remains of it . . .

KING: There are still a few tidbits left. We've got to keep an eye on them, anyhow. And it'll give you something else to think about. Let us send for all our ministers.

JULIETTE *appears.*

Go and fetch the ministers. I expect they're still fast

asleep. They imagine there's no more work to be done.

JULIETTE: They've gone off on their holidays. Not very far, because now the country's all squashed up. It's shrunk. They're at the opposite end of the kingdom, in other words, just around the corner at the edge of the wood beside the stream. They've gone fishing. They hope to catch a few to feed the population.

KING: Go to the wood and fetch them.

JULIETTE: They won't come. They're off duty. But I'll go and see if you like. (*She goes to look through the window.*)

KING: No discipline!

JULIETTE: They've fallen into the stream.

MARIE: Try and fish them out again.

JULIETTE *goes out.*

KING: If the country could produce any other political experts, I'd give those two the sack.

MARIE: We'll find some more.

DOCTOR: We won't find any more, your Majesty.

MARGUERITE: You won't find any more, Berenger.

MARIE: Yes we will, among the school children, when they're grown up. We've a little time to wait, but once these two have been fished out, they can keep things going for a while.

DOCTOR: The only children you find in the schools today are a few congenital mental defectives, Mongoloids and hydrocephalics with goiters.

KING: I see the nation's not very fit. Try and cure them, Doctor, or improve their condition a bit. So at least they can learn the first four or five letters of the alphabet. In the old days, we used to kill them off.

DOCTOR: His Majesty could no longer allow himself that privilege! Or he'd have no more subjects left.

KING: Do something with them, anyway!

MARGUERITE: We can't improve anything now. We can't cure anyone. Even *you* are incurable now.

DOCTOR: Sire, you are now incurable.

KING: I am not ill.

MARIE: He feels quite well. (*To the* KING:) Don't you?

KING: A little stiffness, that's all. It's nothing. It's a lot better now, anyway.

MARIE: He says it's all right, you see, you see.

KING: Really, I feel fine.

MARGUERITE: You're going to die in an hour and a half, you're going to die at the end of the show.

KING: What did you say, my dear? That's not funny.

MARGUERITE: You're going to die at the end of the show.

MARIE: Oh God!

DOCTOR: Yes, Sire, you are going to die. You will not take your breakfast tomorrow morning. Nor will you dine tonight. The chef has shut off the gas. He's handing in his apron. He's putting the tablecloths and napkins away in the cupboard, forever.

MARIE: Don't speak so fast, don't speak so loud.

KING: And who can have given such orders, without my consent? I'm in good health. You're teasing me. Lies. (*To* MARGUERITE:) You've always wanted me dead. (*To* MARIE:) She's always wanted me dead. (*To* MARGUERITE:) I'll die when I want to. I'm the king. I'm the one to decide.

DOCTOR: You've lost the power to decide for yourself, your Majesty.

MARGUERITE: And now you can't even help falling ill.

KING: I'm *not* ill! (*To* MARIE:) Didn't you just say I wasn't ill? I'm still handsome.

MARGUERITE: And those pains of yours?

KING: All gone.

MARGUERITE: Move about a bit. You'll see!

KING (*who has just sat down again, tries to stand up*): Ouch! . . . That's because I wasn't mentally prepared. I didn't have time to think! I think and I am cured. The king can cure himself, but I was too engrossed in ruling my kingdom.

MARGUERITE: Your kingdom! What a state *that's* in! You can't govern it now. Really, you *know* you can't, but you won't admit it. You've lost your power now, over yourself and over the elements. You can't stop the rot and you've no more power over us.

MARIE: You'll always have power over me.

MARGUERITE: Not even you.

JULIETTE *enters.*

JULIETTE: It's too late to fish the ministers out now. The

stream they fell into, with all its banks and willows, has vanished into a bottomless pit.

KING: I see. It's a plot. You want me to abdicate.

MARGUERITE: That's the best way. A voluntary abdication.

DOCTOR: Abdicate, Sire. That would be best.

KING: Abdicate? Me?

MARGUERITE: Yes. Abdicate governmentally! And morally!

DOCTOR: And physically!

MARIE: Don't give your consent! Don't listen to them!

KING: They're mad. Or else they're traitors.

JULIETTE: Sire, Sire, my poor lord and master, Sire.

MARIE (*to the* KING): You must have them arrested.

KING (*to the* GUARD): Guard! Arrest them!

MARIE: Guard! Arrest them! (*To the* KING:) That's it. Give orders!

KING (*to the* GUARD): Arrest them all! Lock them up in the tower! No, the tower's collapsed. Take them away, and lock them up in the cellar, in the dungeons, or in the rabbit hutch. Arrest them, all of them! That's an order!

MARIE (*to the* GUARD): Arrest them!

GUARD (*without moving*): In the name of His Majesty . . . I . . . I . . . arrest . . . you.

MARIE (*to the* GUARD): Get moving, then!

JULIETTE: He's the one who's arrested.

KING (*to the* GUARD): Do it, then, Guard! Do it!

MARGUERITE: You see, now he can't move. He's got gout and rheumatism.

DOCTOR (*indicating the* GUARD): Sire, the army is paralyzed. An unknown virus has crept into his brain to sabotage his strong points.

MARGUERITE (*to the* KING): Your Majesty, you can see for yourself, it's your own orders that paralyze him.

MARIE (*to the* KING): Don't you believe it! She's trying to hypnotize you. [It's a question of will power. You can control the whole situation by will power.]

GUARD: I you . . . in the name of the King . . . I you . . . (*He stops speaking, his mouth wide open.*)

KING (*to the* GUARD): What's come over you? Speak! Advance! Do you think you're playing statues?

MARIE (*to the* KING): Don't ask him questions! Don't argue! Give orders! Sweep him off his feet in a whirlwind of will power!

DOCTOR: You see, your Majesty, he can't move a muscle. He can't say a word, he's turned to stone. He's deaf to you already. It's a characteristic symptom. Very pronounced, medically speaking.

KING: Now we'll see if I've still any power or not.

MARIE (*to the* KING): Prove that you have! You can if you want to.

KING: I'll prove that I want to, I'll prove I can.

MARIE: Stand up, first!

KING: I stand up. (*He makes a great effort, grimacing.*)

MARIE: You see how easy it is!

KING: You see, both of you, how easy it is! You're a pair of humbugs! Conspirators, Bolsheviks! (*He walks to* MARIE, *who tries to help him.*) No, no, alone . . . because I can, all by myself.

He falls. JULIETTE *rushes forward to pick him up.*

I can get up by myself. (*He does indeed get up by himself, but with difficulty.*)

GUARD: Long live the King!

The KING *falls down again.*

The King is dying.

MARIE: Long live the King!

The KING *stands up with difficulty, helping himself with his scepter.*

GUARD: Long live the King!

The KING *falls down again.*

The King is dead!

MARIE: Long live the King! Long live the King!

MARGUERITE: What a farce!

The KING *stands up again, painfully.*

JULIETTE (*who has disappeared, reappears*): Long live the King!

She disappears again. The KING *falls down again.*

GUARD: The King is dying!

MARIE: No! Long live the King! Stand up! Long live the King!

JULIETTE (*appearing, then disappearing again, while the* KING *stands up*): Long live the King!

This scene should be played like a tragic Punch and Judy show.

GUARD: Long live the King!

MARIE: You see, he's better now.

MARGUERITE: It's his last burst of energy, isn't it, Doctor?

DOCTOR (*to* MARGUERITE): Just a final effort before his strength gives out.

KING: I tripped, that's all. It can happen to anyone. It does happen, you know. My crown!

The crown had fallen to the ground when the KING *collapsed.* MARIE *puts it back on his head again.*

That's a bad omen.

MARIE: Don't you believe it!

The King's scepter falls.

KING: That's another bad omen.

MARIE: Don't you believe it! (*She gives him his scepter.*) Hold it firmly in your hand! Clench your fist!

GUARD: Long live . . . Long live . . . (*Then he falls silent.*)

DOCTOR (*to the* KING): Your Majesty . . .

MARGUERITE (*to the* DOCTOR, *indicating* MARIE): We must keep that woman quiet! She says anything that comes into her head. She's not to open her mouth again without our permission.

MARIE *is motionless.*

(*To the* DOCTOR, *indicating the* KING:) Now, try and make him understand.

DOCTOR (*to the* KING): Your Majesty, several decades or even three days ago, your empire was flourishing. In three days, you've lost all the wars you won. And those you lost, you've lost again. [While our harvests rotted in the fields and our continent became a desert, our neighbors' land turned green again. And it was a wilderness last Thursday!] The rockets you want to fire can't even get off the ground. Or else they leave the pad and drop back to earth with a thud.

KING: A technical fault.

DOCTOR: There weren't any in the past.

MARGUERITE: Your triumphs are all over. You've got to realize that.

DOCTOR: Your pains, your stiffness . . .

KING: I've never had them before. This is the first time.

DOCTOR: Exactly. That's the sign. It really has happened all at once, hasn't it?

MARGUERITE: You should have expected it.

DOCTOR: It's happened all at once and you're no longer your own master. You must have noticed, Sire. Try and have the courage to look facts in the face! Just try!

KING: I picked myself up. You're lying. I *did* pick myself up.

DOCTOR: You're a very sick man, and you could never make that effort again.

MARGUERITE: Of course not. It won't be long now. (*To the* KING:) What can you still *do?* Can you give an order that's obeyed? Can you change anything? Just try and you'll see.

KING: It's because I never used my will power that everything went to pieces. Sheer neglect. It can all be put right. It will all be restored and look like new. You'll soon see what I can do. Guard, move, approach!

MARGUERITE: He can't. He can only obey other people now. Guard, take two paces forward!

The GUARD *advances two paces.*

Guard, two paces back!

The GUARD *takes two paces back.*

KING: Off with that guard's head, off with his head!

The Guard's head leans a little to the right, a little to the left.

His head's toppling! It's going to fall!

MARGUERITE: No, it isn't. It wobbles a bit, that's all. No worse than it was before.

KING: Off with that doctor's head, off with it at once! Right now, off!

MARGUERITE: The Doctor has a sound head on his shoulders. He's got it screwed on all right!

DOCTOR: I'm sorry, Sire, as you see, I feel quite ashamed.

KING: Off with Marguerite's crown! Knock it on the floor!

It is the King's crown which again falls to the floor. MARGUERITE *picks it up.*

MARGUERITE: All right, I'll put it on again.

KING: Thank you. What *is* all this? Witchcraft? How have I lost my power over you? Don't imagine I'll let things go on like this. I'm going to get to the bottom of this. There must be rust in the machine. It stops the wheels from turning.

MARGUERITE (*to* MARIE): You can speak now. We give you permission.

MARIE (*to the* KING): Tell me to do something and I'll do it! Give me an order! Command me, Sire, command me! I'll obey you.

MARGUERITE (*to the* DOCTOR): She thinks what she calls love can achieve the impossible. Sentimental superstition. Things have changed. That's out of the question now. We're past that stage already. A long way past.

MARIE (*who has retreated backward to the left and is now near the window*): Your orders, my King. Your orders, my love. See how beautiful I am! Smell my perfume! Order me to come to you, to kiss you!

KING (*to* MARIE): Come to me, kiss me!

MARIE *does not move.*

Can you hear me?

MARIE: Why yes, I can hear you. I'll do it.

KING: Come to me, then!

MARIE: I'd like to. I'm going to. I want to do it. But my arms fall to my side.

KING: Dance, then!

MARIE *does not move.*

Dance! Or at least, turn your head, go to the window, open it and close it again!

MARIE: I can't!

KING: I expect you've got a stiff neck. You must have a stiff neck. Step forward, come closer to me!

MARIE: Yes, Sire.

KING: Come closer to me!

MARIE: Yes, Sire.

KING: And smile!

MARIE: I don't know what to do, how to walk. I've suddenly forgotten.

MARGUERITE: Take a few steps nearer!

MARIE *advances a little in the direction of the* KING.

KING: You see, she's coming!

MARGUERITE: Because she listened to *me.* (*To* MARIE:) Stop! Stand still!

MARIE: Forgive me, your Majesty. It's not my fault.

MARGUERITE (*to the* KING): Do you need any more proof?

KING: I order trees to sprout from the floor. (*Pause.*) I order the roof to disappear. (*Pause.*) What? Nothing? I order rain to fall. (*Pause—still nothing happens.*) I order a thunderbolt, one I can hold in my hand. (*Pause.*) I order leaves to grow again. (*He goes to the window.*) What? Nothing? I order Juliette to come in through the great door.

JULIETTE *comes in through the small door upstage left.*

Not that way, this way! Go out by that door. (*He indicates the large door.*)

JULIETTE *goes out by the small door on the left, opposite.*

(*To* JULIETTE:) I order you to stay.

JULIETTE *has gone out.*

I order bugles to sound. I order bells to ring! A salute from a hundred and twenty-one guns in my honor. (*He listens.*) Nothing! . . . Wait! Yes! . . . I can hear something.

DOCTOR: It's only the buzzing in your ears, your Majesty.

MARGUERITE (*to the* KING): Don't try any more! You're making a fool of yourself.

MARIE (*to the* KING): You're—you're getting too tired, my dear little King. Don't despair! You're soaked in perspiration. Rest a little! After a while, we'll start again. Wait for an hour and then we'll manage it.

MARGUERITE (*to the* KING): In one hour and twenty-five minutes, you're going to die.

DOCTOR: Yes, Sire. In one hour, twenty-four minutes and fifty seconds.

KING (*to* MARIE): Marie!

MARGUERITE: In one hour, twenty-four minutes and forty-one seconds. (*To the* KING:) Prepare yourself!

MARIE: Don't give in!

MARGUERITE (*to* MARIE): Stop trying to distract him! [Don't open your arms to him! He's slipping away already.]

You can't hold him back now. The official program must be followed, in every detail.

GUARD (*announcing*): The ceremony is about to commence!

General commotion. They all take up their positions, as if for some solemn ceremony. The KING *is seated on his throne, with* MARIE *at his side.*

KING: Let time turn back in its tracks.

MARIE: Let us be as we were twenty years ago.

KING: Let it be last week.

MARIE: Let it be yesterday evening. Turn back, time! Turn back! Time, stop!

MARGUERITE: There is no more time. Time has melted in his hands.

DOCTOR (*to* MARGUERITE, *after looking heavenward through his telescope*): If you look through this telescope, which can see through roofs and walls, you will notice a gap in the sky that used to house the Royal Constellation. In the annals of the universe, his Majesty has been entered as deceased.

GUARD: The King is dead! Long live the King!

MARGUERITE (*to the* GUARD): Idiot! Can't you keep quiet!

DOCTOR: He is, indeed, far more dead than alive.

KING: I'm not. I don't want to die. Please don't let me die! Be kind to me, all of you, don't let me die! I don't want to.

[MARIE (*helplessly*): How can I give him the strength to resist? I'm weakening, myself. He doesn't believe *me* any more, he only believes *them*. (*To the* KING:) But don't give up hope, there's still hope!

MARGUERITE (*to* MARIE): Don't confuse him! You'll only make things worse for him now.]

KING: I don't want to, I don't want to.

DOCTOR: The crisis I was expecting. It's perfectly normal. The first breach in his defenses, already.

MARGUERITE (*to* MARIE): The crisis will pass.

GUARD (*announcing*): The King is passing!

DOCTOR: We shall miss your Majesty greatly! And we shall say so publicly. That's a promise.

KING: I don't want to die.

MARIE: Oh dear, look! His hair has suddenly gone white.

The King's hair has indeed turned white. The wrinkles are spreading across his forehead, over his face. All at once, he looks fourteen centuries older.

DOCTOR: Antiquated. And so suddenly, too!

KING: Kings ought to be immortal.

MARGUERITE: They are. Provisionally.

KING: They promised me *I* could choose the time when I would die.

MARGUERITE: That's because they thought you'd have chosen long ago. But you acquired a taste for authority. Now you must be *made* to choose. You got stuck in the mud of life. You felt warm and cozy. (*Sharply.*) Now you're going to freeze.

KING: I've been trapped. I should have been warned, I've been trapped.

MARGUERITE: You were often warned.

KING: You warned me too soon. I won't die. . . . I don't want to. Someone must save me, as I can't save myself.

MARGUERITE [It's your fault if you've been taken unawares, you ought to have been prepared. You never had the time.] You'd been condemned, and you should have thought about that the very first day, and then day after day, five minutes every day. It wasn't much to give up. Five minutes every day. Then ten minutes, a quarter, half an hour. That's the way to train yourself.

KING: I *did* think about it.

MARGUERITE: Not seriously, not profoundly, never with all your heart and soul.

MARIE: He was alive.

MARGUERITE: Too much alive. (*To the* KING:) You ought to have had this thought permanently at the back of your mind.

DOCTOR: He never looked ahead, he's always lived from day to day, like most people.

MARGUERITE: You kept on putting it off. At twenty you said you'd wait till your fortieth year before you went into training. At forty . . .

KING: I was in such good health, I was so young!

MARGUERITE: At forty: why not wait till you were fifty? At fifty . . .

KING: I was full of life, wonderfully full of life!

MARGUERITE: At fifty, you wanted first to reach your sixties. And so you went on, from sixty to ninety to a hundred and twenty-five to two hundred, until you were four hundred years old. Instead of putting things off for ten years at a time, you put them off for fifty. Then you postponed them from century to century.

KING: But I was just about to start. Oh! If I could have a whole century before me, perhaps then I'd have time!

DOCTOR: All you have now is one hour, Sire. You must do it all in an hour.

MARIE: He'll never have enough time, it's impossible. He must be given more.

MARGUERITE: That *is* impossible. But an hour gives him all the time he needs.

DOCTOR: A well spent hour's better than whole centuries of neglect and failure. Five minutes are enough, ten fully conscious seconds. We're giving him an hour! Sixty minutes, three thousand and six hundred seconds. He's in luck.

MARGUERITE: He's lingered too long by the wayside.

[MARIE: We've been ruling the kingdom. *He's* been working.

GUARD: The Labors of Hercules.

MARGUERITE: Pottering about.]

Enter JULIETTE.

JULIETTE: Poor Majesty, my poor master's been playing truant.

KING: I'm like a schoolboy who hasn't done his homework and sits for an exam without swatting up the papers.

MARGUERITE: Don't let that worry you!

KING: . . . like an actor on the first night who doesn't know his lines and who dries, dries, dries. Like an orator pushed onto a platform who's forgotten his speech and has no idea who he's meant to be addressing. I don't know this audience, and I don't want to. I've nothing to say to them. What a state I'm in!

GUARD (*announcing*): The King has just alluded to his State.

MARGUERITE: A state of ignorance.

JULIETTE: He'd like to go on playing truant for centuries to come.

KING: I'd like to re-sit the exam.

MARGUERITE: You'll take it now. No re-sits are allowed.

DOCTOR: There's nothing you can do, your Majesty. Neither can we. We only practice medical science, we can't perform miracles.

KING: Do the people know the news? Have you warned them? I want everyone to know that the King is going to die. (*He makes a rush to open the window, with a great effort, for his limp is getting worse.*) My good people, I am going to die! Hear me! Your King is going to die!

MARGUERITE (*to the* DOCTOR): They mustn't hear him. Stop him shouting!

KING: Hands off the King! I want everyone to know I'm going to die! (*He shouts.*)

DOCTOR: Scandalous!

KING: People, I've got to die!

MARGUERITE: What was once a king is now a pig that's being slaughtered.

MARIE: He's just a king. He's just a man.

DOCTOR: Your Majesty, think of the death of Louis XIV, of Philip II, or of the Emperor Charles V, who slept in his own coffin for twenty years. It is your Majesty's duty to die with dignity.

KING: Die with dignity? (*At the window.*) Help! Your King is going to die!

MARIE: Poor dear King, my poor little King!

JULIETTE: Shouting won't help.

A feeble echo can be heard in the distance: "The King is going to die."

KING: Hear that?

MARIE: I hear, I can hear.

KING: They've answered me. Perhaps they're going to save me.

JULIETTE: There's no one there.

The echo can be heard: "Help!"

DOCTOR: It's only the echo, a bit late in answering.

MARGUERITE: Late as usual, like everything else in this country. Nothing functions properly.

KING (*leaving the window*): It's impossible. (*Going back to the window:*) I'm frightened. It's impossible.

MARGUERITE: He imagines no one's ever died before.

MARIE: No one *has* died before.

MARGUERITE: It's all very painful.

JULIETTE: He's crying! Just like anyone else!

MARGUERITE: What a commonplace reaction! I hoped terror would have produced some fine ringing phrases. (*To the* DOCTOR:) I must put you in charge of the chronicles. We'll attribute to him the fine words spoken by others. We'll invent some new ones, if need be.

DOCTOR: We'll credit him with some edifying maxims. (*To* MARGUERITE:) We'll watch over his legend. (*To the* KING:) We'll watch over your legend, your Majesty.

KING (*at the window*): People, help! . . . Help, people!

MARGUERITE: Haven't you had enough, your Majesty? It's a waste of effort.

KING (*at the window*): Who will give me his life? Who will give his life for the King's? His life for the good old King's, his life for the poor old King's?

MARGUERITE: It's indecent!

MARIE: Let him try everything once.

JULIETTE: As there's no one left in the country to hear, why not? (*She goes out.*)

[MARGUERITE: The spies are still with us.

DOCTOR: Enemy ears listening at the frontiers.

MARGUERITE: He'll disgrace us all, panicking like this.]

DOCTOR: The echo's stopped answering. His voice doesn't

carry any more. He can shout as much as he likes. It won't even reach as far as the garden wall.

MARGUERITE (*while the* KING *is wailing*): He's moaning.

DOCTOR: We're the only ones who can hear him now. He can't even hear himself.

The KING *turns around and takes a few steps toward the center of the stage.*

KING: I'm cold, I'm frightened, I'm crying.

MARIE: His legs are all stiff.

DOCTOR: He's riddled with rheumatism. (*To* MARGUERITE:) An injection to quiet him?

JULIETTE *appears with an invalid chair on wheels, which has a crown and royal emblems on the back.*

KING: I won't have an injection.

MARIE: No injection.

KING: I know what they mean! I've had injections given to other people before! (*To* JULIETTE:) I never told you to bring that chair. I'm going for a walk, I want to take the air.

JULIETTE *leaves the chair in a corner of the stage on the left and goes out.*

MARGUERITE: Sit down in that chair or you'll fall.

The KING *is, in fact, staggering.*

KING: I won't give in! I intend to stay on my feet.

JULIETTE *returns with a blanket.*

JULIETTE: You'd feel much better, Sire, much more comfortable with a blanket over your knees and a hot water bottle. (*She goes out.*)

KING: No, I want to stay on my feet. I want to scream. I want to scream. (*He screams.*)

GUARD (*announcing*): His Majesty is screaming!

DOCTOR (*to* MARGUERITE): He won't scream for long. I know the symptoms. He'll get tired. He'll stop and then he'll listen to us.

JULIETTE *comes in, bringing more warm clothing and a hot water bottle.*

KING (*to* JULIETTE): I won't have them!

MARGUERITE: Sit down quickly, sit down.

KING: I refuse! (*He tries to climb the steps of the throne and fails. He goes and sits down all the same, collapsing on the Queen's throne to the right.*) I can't help it, I nearly fell over.

JULIETTE, *after following the* KING *with the objects mentioned above, goes and puts them on the invalid chair.*

MARGUERITE (*to* JULIETTE): Take his scepter, it's too heavy for him.

KING (*to* JULIETTE, *who is returning to him with a nightcap*): I won't wear that!

JULIETTE: It's a sort of crown, but not so heavy.

KING: Let me keep my scepter!

MARGUERITE: You've no longer the strength to hold it.

DOCTOR: It's no good trying to lean on it now. We'll carry you. We'll wheel you along in the chair.

KING: I want to keep it.

MARIE (*to* JULIETTE): Leave him his scepter! He wants it.

JULIETTE *looks to* MARGUERITE *for her instructions.*

MARGUERITE: After all, I don't see why not.

JULIETTE *gives the scepter back to the* KING.

KING: Perhaps it's not true. Tell me it's not true. Perhaps it's a nightmare.

The others are silent.

Perhaps there's a ten to one chance, one chance in a thousand.

The others are silent. The KING *is sobbing.*

I often used to win the sweepstakes!

DOCTOR: Your Majesty!

KING: I can't listen to you any more, I'm too frightened. (*He is sobbing and moaning.*)

MARGUERITE: You must listen, Sire.

KING: I *won't* hear what you're saying. Your words frighten me. I won't hear any more talk. (*To* MARIE, *who is trying to approach him:*) Don't you come any nearer either. You frighten me with your pity. (*He moans again.*)

[MARIE: He's like a small child. He's a little boy again.

MARGUERITE: An ugly little boy, with a beard and wrinkles. You're too lenient with him!

JULIETTE (*to* MARGUERITE): You don't try and put yourself in his place.]

KING: No, speak to me! I didn't mean it, speak to me! Stand by me, hold me! Help me up! No, I want to run away. (*He rises painfully to his feet and goes to sit down on the other small throne on the left.*)

JULIETTE: His legs can hardly carry him.

KING: It hurts to move my arms, too. Does that mean it's starting? No. Why was I born if it wasn't forever? Damn my parents! What a joke, what a farce! I came into the world five minutes ago. I got married three minutes ago.

MARGUERITE: Two hundred and eighty-three years.

KING: I came to the throne two and a half minutes ago.

MARGUERITE: Two hundred and seventy-seven years and three months.

KING: Never had time to say knife! Never had time to get to know life.

MARGUERITE: He never even tried.

MARIE: It was like a brisk walk through a flowery lane, a promise that's broken, a smile that fades.

MARGUERITE (*to the* DOCTOR, *continuing*): Yet he had the greatest experts to tell him all about it. Theologians, people of experience, and books he never read.

KING: I never had the time.

MARGUERITE: You used to say you had all the time in the world.

KING: I never had the time, I never had the time, I never had the time!

[JULIETTE: He's going back to that again.

MARGUERITE (*to the* DOCTOR): All the time it's the same old story.]

DOCTOR: I'd say things were looking up. However much he moans and groans, he's started to reason things out. He's complaining, protesting, expressing himself. That means he's begun to resign himself.

KING: I shall never resign myself.

DOCTOR: As he says he won't, it's a sign that he *will*. He's posing the problem of resignation, raising the question.

MARGUERITE: At last!

DOCTOR: Your Majesty, you have made war one hundred and eighty times. You have led your armies into two thousand battles. First, on a white horse with a conspicuous red-and-white plume, and you never knew fear. Then, when you modernized the army, you would stand on top of a tank, or on the wing of a fighter plane leading the formation.

MARIE: He was a hero.

DOCTOR: You have come near death a thousand times.

KING: I only came *near* it. I could tell it wasn't meant for me.

MARIE: You were a hero, do you hear? Remember that.

MARGUERITE: Aided and abetted by this doctor here, the executioner, you ordered the assassination . . .

KING: Execution, not assassination.

DOCTOR (*to* MARGUERITE): Execution, your Majesty, not assassination. I was only obeying orders. I was a mere instrument, just an executor, not an executioner. It was all euthanasia to me. Anyhow, I'm sorry. Please forgive me.

MARGUERITE (*to the* KING): I tell you, you had my parents butchered, your own brothers, your rivals, our cousins and great-grandcousins, and all their families, friends and cattle. You massacred the lot and scorched all their lands.

DOCTOR: His Majesty used to say they were going to die one day, anyway.

KING: That was for reasons of State.

MARGUERITE: You're dying too because of your state.

KING: But I *am* the State.

JULIETTE: And what a state the poor man's in!

MARIE: He was the law, above the law.

[KING: I'm not the law any more.

DOCTOR: He admits it. Better and better.

MARGUERITE: That makes things easier.]

KING (*groaning*): I'm not above the law any more, not above the law any more.

GUARD (*announcing*): The King is no more above the law.

JULIETTE: The poor old boy's no more above the law. He's just like us and not unlike my granddad!

MARIE: Poor little chap, poor child!

KING: Child! A child? Then I can make a fresh start! I want to start again. (*To* MARIE:) I want to be a baby and you can be my mother. Then they won't come for me. I

still don't know my reading, writing and arithmetic.
I want to go back to school and be with all my play-
mates. What do two and two make?

JULIETTE: Two and two make four.

MARGUERITE (*to the* KING): You knew that already.

KING: She was only prompting me. . . . Oh dear, it's no good
trying to cheat! Oh dear, oh dear! There are so many
people being born at this moment, numberless babies
all over the world.

MARGUERITE: Not in *our* country.

DOCTOR: The birth rate's down to zero.

JULIETTE: Not a lettuce, not a grass that grows.

MARGUERITE: Utter sterility, because of you!

MARIE: I won't have you blaming him!

JULIETTE: Perhaps everything will grow again.

MARGUERITE: When he's accepted the inevitable. When he's
gone.

KING: When I've gone, when I've gone. They'll laugh and
stuff themselves silly and dance on my tomb. As if I'd
never existed. Oh, please make them all remember
me! Make them weep and despair and perpetuate my
memory in all their history books. Make everyone
learn my life by heart. Make them all live it again. Let
the schoolchildren and the scholars study nothing else
but me, my kingdom and my exploits. Let them burn
all the other books, destroy all the statues and set mine
up in all the public squares. My portrait in every Min-
istry, my photograph in every office of every Town
Hall, including Rates and Taxes, and in *all* the hos-

pitals. Let every car and pushcart, flying ship and steamplane be named after me. Make them forget all other captains and kings, poets, tenors and philosophers, and fill every conscious mind with memories of me. Let them learn to read by spelling out my name: B, E, BE for Berenger. Let my likeness be on all the ikons, me on the millions of crosses in all our churches. Make them say Mass for me and let *me* be the Host. Let all the windows light up in the shape and color of my eyes. And the rivers trace my profile on the plains! Let them cry my name throughout eternity, and beg me and implore me.

MARIE: Perhaps you'll come back again?

KING: Perhaps I will come back. Let them preserve my body in some palace, on a throne, and let them bring me food. Let musicians play for me and virgins grovel at my ice-cold feet.

The KING *has risen in order to make this speech.*

JULIETTE (*to* MARGUERITE): He's raving, Ma'am.

GUARD (*announcing*): His Majesty the King is delirious.

MARGUERITE: Not yet. There's too much sense in what he says. Too much, and not enough.

DOCTOR (*to the* KING): If such be your will, your Majesty, we will embalm your body and preserve it.

JULIETTE: As long as we can.

KING: Horror! I don't want to be embalmed. I want nothing to do with that corpse. I don't want to be burnt. I don't want to be buried, I don't want to be thrown to the wild beasts or the vultures. I want to feel arms around me, warm arms, cool arms, soft arms, strong arms.

JULIETTE: He's not too sure what he *does* want.

MARGUERITE: We'll make his mind up for him. (*To* MARIE:) Now don't faint!

JULIETTE *is weeping.*

And there's another one! They're always the same!

KING: If I *am* remembered, I wonder for how long? Let them remember me to the end of time. And beyond the end of time, in twenty thousand years, in two hundred and fifty-five thousand million years . . . There'll be no one left to think of anyone then. They'll forget before that. Selfish, the lot of them. They only think of their own little lives, of their own skins. Not of *mine*. If the whole earth's going to wear out or melt away, it will. If every universe is going to explode, explode it will. It's all the same whether it's tomorrow or in countless centuries to come. What's got to finish one day is finished now.

MARGUERITE: Everything is yesterday.

JULIETTE: Even "today" will be "yesterday."

DOCTOR: All things pass into the past.

MARIE: My darling King, there is no past, there is no future. Remember, there's only a present that goes right on to the end, everything is present. Be present, be the present!

KING: Alas! I'm only present in the past.

MARIE: No, you're not.

MARGUERITE: That's right, Berenger, try and get things straight.

MARIE: Yes, my King, get things straight, my darling! Stop torturing yourself! "Exist" and "die" are just words, figments of our imagination. Once you realize that, nothing can touch you. [Forget our empty clichés. We can never know what it really means, "exist" or "die." Or if we think we do, our knowledge has deceived us. Stand firm, get a grip on yourself! Never lose sight of yourself again! Sweep everything else into oblivion! *Now* you exist, you *are*. Forget the rest. That's the only truth.] Just be an eternal question mark: what ...? why...? how...? And remember: that you can't find the answers is an answer in itself. It's you, all the life in you, straining to break out. Dive into an end-less maze of wonder and surprise, then you too will have no end, and can exist forever. Everything is strange and undefinable. Let it dazzle and confound you! Tear your prison bars aside and batter down the walls! Escape from definitions and you will breathe again!

DOCTOR: He's choking!

MARGUERITE: Fear cramps his vision.

MARIE: Open the floodgates of joy and light to dazzle and confound you. Illuminating waves of joy will fill your veins with wonder. If you want them to.

JULIETTE: You bet he does.

MARIE (*in a tone of supplication*): I implore you to remember that morning in June we spent together by the sea, when happiness raced through you and inflamed you. You knew then what joy meant: rich, changeless and undying. If you knew it once, you can know it now. You found that fiery radiance within you. If it *was* there *once*, it is *still* there *now*. Find it again. Look for it, in yourself.

KING: I don't understand.

MARIE: You don't understand any more.

MARGUERITE: He never did understand himself.

MARIE: Pull yourself together!

KING: How do I manage that? No one can or will help me. And *I* can't help myself. Oh help me, sun! Sun, chase away the shadows and hold back the night! Sun, sun, illumine every tomb, shine into every hole and corner, every nook and cranny! Creep deep inside me! Ah! Now my feet are turning cold. Come and warm me, pierce my body, steal beneath my skin, and blaze into my eyes! Restore their failing light, and let me see, see, see! Sun, sun, will you miss me? Good little sun, protect me! And if you're in need of some small sacrifice, then parch and wither up the world. Let every human creature die provided *I* can live forever, even alone in a limitless desert. I'll come to terms with solitude. I'll keep alive the memory of others, and I'll miss them quite sincerely. But I can live in the void, in a vast and airy wasteland. It's better to miss one's friends than to be missed oneself. Besides, one never is. Light of our days, come and save me!

DOCTOR (*to* MARIE): This is not the light *you* meant. [This is not the timeless waste you wanted him to aim for: He didn't understand you, it's too much for his poor brain.]

MARGUERITE (*to* MARIE, *or referring to* MARIE): Love's labors lost. You're on the wrong track.

KING: Let me go on living century after century, even with a raging toothache. But I fear what must end one day has ended now.

[DOCTOR: Well, Sire, what are you waiting for?]

MARGUERITE: It's only his speeches that are never ending! (*Indicating* MARIE *and* JULIETTE.) And these two weeping women. They only push him deeper in the mire, trap him, bind him and hold him up.

KING: No, there's not enough weeping, not enough lamentation. Not enough anguish. (*To* MARGUERITE:) Don't stop them weeping and wailing and pitying their King, their young King, old King, poor little King. *I* feel pity when I think how they'll miss me, never see me again, and be left behind all alone. I'm still the one who thinks about others, about everyone. All the rest of you, be me, come inside me, come beneath my skin. I'm dying, you hear, I'm trying to tell you. I'm dying, but I can't express it, unless I talk like a book and make literature of it.

[MARGUERITE: Is that what·it is!

DOCTOR: It's not worth recording his words. Nothing new.

KING: They're all strangers to me. I thought they were my family. I'm frightened, I'm sinking, I'm drowning, I've gone blank, I've never existed. I'm dying.

MARGUERITE: Now that *is* literature!]

DOCTOR: And that's the way it goes on, to the bitter end. As long as we live we turn everything into literature.

MARIE: If only it could console him!

GUARD (*announcing*): The King finds some consolation in literature!

KING: No, no. I know, nothing can console me. It just wells up inside me, then drains away. Oh dear, oh dear, oh dear, oh dear, oh dear! (*Lamentations—then without declamation, he goes on moaning gently to himself.*) Help me, you countless thousands who died before me! Tell me how you managed to accept death and die. Then teach me! Let your example be a consolation to me, let me lean on you like crutches, like a brother's arms. Help me to cross the threshold you have crossed! Come back from the other side a while and help me! Assist me, you who were frightened and did not want to go! What was it like? Who held you up? Who dragged you there, who pushed you? Were you afraid to the very end? And you who were strong and courageous, who accepted death with indifference and serenity, teach me your indifference and serenity, teach me resignation!

The following dialogue should be spoken and acted as though it were ritual, with solemnity, almost chanted, accompanied by various movements, with the actors kneeling, holding out their arms, etc.

JULIETTE: You statues, you dark or shining phantoms, ancients and shades . . .

MARIE: Teach him serenity.

GUARD: Teach him indifference.

DOCTOR: Teach him resignation.

MARGUERITE: Make him see reason and set his mind at rest.

KING: You suicides, teach me how to feel disgust for life! Teach me lassitude! What drug must I take for that?

DOCTOR: I could prescribe euphoric pills or tranquilizers.

MARGUERITE: He'd vomit them up!

JULIETTE: You remembrances . . .

GUARD: You pictures of days gone by . . .

JULIETTE: . . . which no longer exist but in our memories of memories . . .

GUARD: Recollections of recollections . . .

MARGUERITE: He's got to learn how to let go and then surrender completely.

GUARD: . . . we invoke you.

MARIE: You morning mists and dews . . .

JULIETTE: You evening smoke and clouds . . .

MARIE: You saints, you wise and foolish virgins, help him! For *I* cannot.

JULIETTE: Help him!

KING: You who died blissfully, who looked death in the face, who remained conscious of your end . . .

JULIETTE: Help him!

MARIE: Help him all of you, help him, I beg you!

KING: You who died happy, what face did you see close to yours? What smile gave you ease and made *you* smile? What were the last rays of light that brushed your face?

JULIETTE: Help him, you thousand millions of the dead!

GUARD: Oh you, great Nothing, help the King!

KING: Thousands and millions of the dead. They multiply my anguish. I am the dying agony of all. My death is manifold. So many worlds will flicker out in me.

MARGUERITE: Life is exile.

KING: I know, I know.

DOCTOR: In short, Majesty, you will return to your own country.

MARIE: You'll go back where you came from when you were born. Don't be so frightened, you're sure to find something familiar there.

[KING: I like exile. I ran away from my homeland and I don't want to go back. What *was* that world like?

MARGUERITE: Try and remember.

KING: I can see nothing, I can see nothing.

MARGUERITE: Remember! Come along, think! Think carefully! Think, just think! You've never thought!

DOCTOR: He's never given it a second thought since then!]

MARIE: Other world, lost world, buried and forgotten world, rise again from the deep!

JULIETTE: Other plains, other valleys, other mountain chains . . .

MARIE: Remind them of your name.

[KING: No memories of that distant land.

JULIETTE: He can't remember his homeland.

DOCTOR: He's in no state to do so, he's too weak.

KING: No nostalgia, however dim or fleeting.]

MARGUERITE: Plunge into your memories, dive through the gaps in your memory into a world beyond memory. (*To the* DOCTOR:) *This* is the only world he really misses!

MARIE: Memories immemorial, appear before him! Help him!

[DOCTOR: You see, it's quite a problem to get him to take the plunge.

MARGUERITE: He'll have to do it.

GUARD: His Majesty's never been down in a diving bell.

JULIETTE: Pity he never had the training.

MARGUERITE: It's a job he'll have to learn.]

KING: When faced with death, even a little ant puts up a fight. Suddenly, he's all alone, torn from his companions. In him, too, the universe flickers out. It's not natural to die, because no one ever wants to. I want to exist.

JULIETTE: That's all he knows. He wants to exist forever.

[MARIE: It seems to him he always *has*.

MARGUERITE: He'll have to stop looking about him, stop clinging to pictures of the outside world. He must shut himself up and lock himself in. (*To the* KING:) Not another word, be quiet, stay inside! Stop looking around and it'll do you good!

KING: Not the sort of good *I* want.

DOCTOR (*to* MARGUERITE): We haven't quite got to that stage. He still can't manage that. Your Majesty should encourage him, of course, but don't push him too far —not yet.

MARGUERITE: It won't be easy, but we can be patient and wait.

DOCTOR: We're sure of the final result.]

KING: Doctor, Doctor, am I in the throes of death already? ... No, you've made a mistake ... not yet ... not yet. (*A kind of sigh of relief.*) It hasn't started yet. I exist, I'm still here. I can see. There are walls and furniture here, there's air to breathe, I can watch people watching me and catch their voices. I'm alive, I can think, I can see, I can hear, I can still see and hear. A fanfare!

A sort of fanfare can be heard far away in the distance. He starts walking.

GUARD: The King is walking! Long live the King!

The KING *falls down.*

JULIETTE: He's down!

GUARD: The King is down! The King is dying!

The KING *gets up.*

MARIE: He's up again!

GUARD: The King is up! Long live the King!

MARIE: He's up again!

GUARD: Long live the King!

The KING *falls down.*

The King is dead!

MARIE: He's up again!

The KING *does indeed get up again.*

He's still alive!

GUARD: Long live the King!

The KING *makes for his throne.*

JULIETTE: He wants to sit on his throne.

MARIE: The King still reigns! The King still reigns!

DOCTOR: And now for the delirium.

MARIE (*to the* KING, *who is trying to totter up the steps of his throne*): Don't let go, hang on! (*To* JULIETTE, *who is trying to help the* KING:) Leave him alone! He can do it alone!

The KING *fails to climb the steps of the throne.*

[KING: And yet I've still got my legs!

MARIE: Try again!]

MARGUERITE: We've got thirty-two minutes and thirty seconds left.

KING: I can still stand up.

DOCTOR (*to* MARGUERITE): It's the last convulsion but one.

The KING *falls into the invalid chair, which* JULIETTE *has just brought forward. They cover him up and give him a hot water bottle, while he is still saying:*

KING: I can still stand up.

The hot water bottle, the blankets, etc., are gradually brought into the following scene by JULIETTE.

MARIE: You're out of breath, you're tired. Have a rest and you can stand up again later.

MARGUERITE (*to* MARIE): Don't lie! That doesn't help him!

KING (*in his chair*): I used to like Mozart. I'll never hear that music again.

MARGUERITE: You'll forget all about it.

KING (*to* JULIETTE): Did you mend my trousers? Or do you think now it's not worth the trouble? There was a hole in my red cloak. Have you patched it? Have you sewn those buttons on my pajamas? Have you had my shoes resoled?

JULIETTE: I never gave it another thought.

KING: You never gave it another thought! What *do* you think about? Talk to me! What does your husband do?

JULIETTE *has now put on, or is putting on, her nurse's cap and white apron.*

JULIETTE: I'm a widow.

KING: What do you think about when you do the housework?

JULIETTE: Nothing, your Majesty.

KING: Where do you come from? What's your family?

MARGUERITE (*to the* KING): You never took any interest before.

MARIE: He's never had time to ask her.

MARGUERITE (*to the* KING): And you're not really interested now.

DOCTOR: He wants to gain time.

KING (*to* JULIETTE): Tell me how you live. What sort of life do you have?

JULIETTE: A bad life, Sire.

KING: Life can never be bad. It's a contradiction in terms.

JULIETTE: Life's not very beautiful.

KING: Life is life.

JULIETTE: When I get up in the winter, it's still dark. And I'm cold as ice.

KING: So am I. But it's not the same cold. You don't like feeling cold?

JULIETTE: When I get up in the summer, it's only just beginning to get light. A pale sort of light.

KING (*rapturously*): A *pale* light! There are all sorts of light: blue and pink and white and green, and *pale!*

JULIETTE: I do all the palace laundry in the wash house. It hurts my hands and cracks my skin.

KING (*rapturously*): And it hurts! One can feel one's skin! Haven't they bought you a washing machine yet? Marguerite! A palace, and no washing machine!

MARGUERITE: We had to pawn it to raise a State loan.

JULIETTE: I empty the chamber pots. I make the beds.

KING: She makes the beds! Where we lie down and go to sleep and then wake up again. Did you ever realize that every day you woke up? To wake up every day . . . Every morning one comes into the world.

JULIETTE: I polish the parquet floors, and sweep, sweep, sweep! There's no end to it.

KING (*rapturously*): There's no end to it!

JULIETTE: It gives me the backache.

KING: That's right. She has a back! We've all got backs!

JULIETTE: Pains in the kidneys.

KING: And kidneys too!

JULIETTE: And now we've no gardeners left, I dig and rake and sow.

KING: And then things grow!

JULIETTE: I get quite worn out, exhausted!

KING: You ought to have told us.

JULIETTE: I *did* tell you.

KING: That's true. Such a lot has escaped my notice. [I never got to know everything. I never went everywhere I could. My life could have been so full.]

JULIETTE: There's no window in my room.

KING (*rapturously again*): No window! You go out in search of light. You find it and then you smile. To go out, you turn the key in the door, open it, then close it again and turn the key to lock it. Where do you live?

JULIETTE: In the attic.

KING: To come down in the morning, you take the stairs, you go down one step, then another, down a step, down a step, down a step. And when you get dressed, you put on first your stockings, then your shoes.

JULIETTE: Down at heel!

KING: And a dress. It's amazing . . .

JULIETTE: A cheap one. A tatty old thing!

KING: You don't know what you're saying! It's beautiful, a tatty old dress!

JULIETTE: Once I had an abscess in the mouth and they pulled out one of my teeth.

KING: You're in terrible pain. But it starts to ease off, and then disappears. It's a tremendous relief, it makes you feel wonderfully happy.

JULIETTE: I feel tired, tired, tired!

KING: So you take a rest. That's good.

JULIETTE: Not enough time off for that!

KING: You can still hope you'll have some, one day. . . . You go out with a basket and do the shopping. You say good day to the grocer.

JULIETTE: He's enormous! Hideously fat! So ugly he frightens the birds and the cats away.

KING: Marvelous! You take out your purse, you pay, and get your change. The market's a medley of green lettuce, red cherries, golden grapes and purple eggplants . . . all the colors of the rainbow! . . . It's extraordinary! Incredible! Like a fairy tale!

JULIETTE: And then I go home . . . the same way I came.

KING: You take the same road twice a day! With the sky above you! You can gaze at it twice a day. And you breathe the air. You never realize you're breathing. You must think about it. Remember! I'm sure it never crosses your mind. It's a miracle!

JULIETTE: And then, then I do the washing up from the day before. Plates smothered in sticky fat! And then I have the cooking to do.

KING: Sublime!

JULIETTE: You're wrong. It's a bore. It makes me sick!

KING: It's a bore! Some people one can *never* understand! It's wonderful to feel bored and *not* to feel bored, too, to lose one's temper, and *not* to lose one's temper, to be *dis*contented and to be content. To practice resignation and to insist on your rights. You get excited, you talk and people talk to you, you touch and they touch you. All this is magical, like some endless celebration.

JULIETTE: You're right there. There's no end to it! After that, I still have to wait at table.

KING (*still rapturously*): You wait at table! You wait at table! What do you serve at table?

JULIETTE: The meal I've just prepared.

KING: What, for example?

JULIETTE: I don't know, the main dish. Stew!

KING: Stew! Stew! (*Dreamily.*)

JULIETTE: It's a meal in itself.

KING: I used to be so fond of stew, with vegetables and potatoes, cabbage and carrots all mixed up with butter, crushed with a fork and mashed together.

JULIETTE: We could bring him some.

KING: Send for some stew!

MARGUERITE: No.

JULIETTE: But if he likes it.

DOCTOR: Bad for his health. He's on a diet.

KING: I want some stew.

DOCTOR: It's not what the doctor orders for a dying man.

MARIE: But if it's his last wish . . .

MARGUERITE: He must detach himself.

KING: Gravy . . . hot potatoes . . . and carrots to lead me by the nose . . .

JULIETTE: He's still making jokes.

KING (*wearily*): Till now, I'd never noticed how beautiful carrots were. (*To* JULIETTE:) Quick! Go and kill the two spiders in my bedroom! I don't want them to survive me. No, don't kill them! Perhaps in *them* there's something still of *me* . . . it's dead, that stew . . . vanished from the universe. There never was such a thing as stew.

GUARD (*announcing*): Stew has been banished from the length and breadth of the land.

MARGUERITE: At last, something achieved! At least he's given *that* up! Of all the things we crave for, the minor ones go first. Now we can begin. Gently, as you remove a dressing from an open sore, first lifting the corners, because they're furthest from the center of the wound. (*Approaching the* KING.) Juliette, wipe the sweat from his face, he's dripping wet. (*To* MARIE:) No, not you!

DOCTOR (*to* MARGUERITE): It's panic oozing through his pores.

He examines the sick man, while MARIE *might kneel for a moment, covering her face with her hands.*

You see, his temperature's gone down, though there's not much sign of goose flesh. His hair was standing on end before. Now it's resting and lying flat. He's not used to being so terrified yet, oh no! But now he can see the fear inside him; that's why he's dared to close his eyes. He'll open them again. He still looks tense, but see how the wrinkles of old age are settling on his face. Already he's letting things take their course. He'll still have a few setbacks. It's not as quick as all that. But he won't have the wind up any more. That would have been too degrading. He'll still be subject to fright, but pure fright, without abdominal complications. We can't hope this death will be an example to others. But it will be fairly respectable. His *death* will kill him now, and not his fear. We'll have to help him all the same, your Majesty, he'll need a lot of help, till the very last second, till he's drawn his very last breath.

MARGUERITE: I'll help him. I'll drive it out of him. I'll cut him loose. I'll untie every knot and ravel out the tangled skein. I'll separate the wheat from the tenacious tares that cling to him and bind him.

[DOCTOR: It won't be easy.

MARGUERITE: Where on earth did he pick up all these weeds, these trailing creepers?

DOCTOR: They've grown up slowly, through the years.

MARGUERITE: You've settled down nicely now, your Majesty. Don't you feel more peaceful?

MARIE (*standing up, to the* KING): Until Death comes, you are still *here*. When Death is here, *you* will have gone. You won't meet her or see her.

MARGUERITE: The lies of life, those old fallacies! We've heard them all before. Death has always been here, present in the seed since the very first day. She is the shoot that grows, the flower that blows, the only fruit we know.

MARIE (*to* MARGUERITE): That's a basic truth too, and we've heard *that* before!

MARGUERITE: It's a basic truth. And the ultimate truth, isn't it, Doctor?

DOCTOR: What you both say is true. It depends on the point of view.

MARIE (*to the* KING): You used to believe me, once.

KING: I'm dying.

DOCTOR: He's changed *his* point of view. He's shifted his position.

MARIE: If you've to look at it from both sides, look at it from my side too.

KING: I'm dying. I can't. I'm dying.

MARIE: Oh! My power over him is going.]

MARGUERITE (*to* MARIE): Neither your charm nor your charms can bewitch the King any more.

GUARD (*announcing*): The Charm of Queen Marie no longer casts its spell over the King.

MARIE (*to the* KING): You used to love me, you love me still, as I have always loved you.

MARGUERITE: She thinks of no one but herself.

JULIETTE: That's human nature.

MARIE: I've always loved you, I love you still.

KING: I don't know why, but that doesn't seem to help.

DOCTOR: Love is mad.

MARIE (*to the* KING): Love *is* mad. And if you're mad with love, if you love blindly, completely, death will steal away. If you love me, if you love everything, love will consume your fear. Love lifts you up, you let yourself go and fear lets go of you. The whole universe is one, everything lives again and the cup that was drained is full.

KING: I'm full all right, but full of holes. I'm a honeycomb of cavities that are widening, deepening into bottomless pits. It makes me dizzy to look down the gaping gulfs inside me. I'm coming to an end.

MARIE: There is no end. Others will take your place and gaze at the sky for *you*.

KING: I'm dying.

MARIE: Become these other beings, and live in them. There's always something here . . . something . . .

KING: What's that?

MARIE: Something that exists. *That* never perishes.

KING: And yet there's still . . . there's still . . . there's still so little left.

MARIE: The younger generation's expanding the universe.

KING: I'm dying.

MARIE: Conquering new constellations.

KING: I'm dying.

MARIE: Boldly battering at the gates of Heaven.

KING: They can knock them flat for all I care!

DOCTOR: They've also started making elixirs of immortality.

KING (*to the* DOCTOR): Incompetent fool! Why didn't *you* discover them before?

MARIE: New suns are about to appear.

KING: It makes me wild!

MARIE: Brand-new stars. Virgin stars.

KING: They'll fade away. Anyhow, I don't care!

GUARD (announcing): Constellations old or new no longer interest His Majesty, King Berenger!

MARIE: A new science is coming into being.

KING: *I'm* dying.

[MARIE: A new wisdom's taking the place of the old, a stupidity and ignorance greater than before, different of course but still the same. Let that console you and rejoice your heart.

KING: I'm frightened, I'm dying.

MARIE: You laid the foundations for all this.

KING: I didn't do it on purpose.]

MARIE: You were a pioneer, a guide, a harbinger of all these new developments. You count. And you will be counted.

KING: I'll never be the accountant. I'm dying.

MARIE: Everything that has been will be, everything that will be is, everything that will be has been. You are inscribed forever in the annals of the universe.

KING: Who'll look up those old archives? I die, so let everything die! No, let everything stay as it is! No, let everything die, if my death won't resound through worlds without end! Let everything die! No, let everything remain!

GUARD: His Majesty the King wants the remains to remain.

KING: No, let it all die!

GUARD: His Majesty the King wants it all to die!

KING: Let it all die with me! No, let it all survive me! No, let it all stay, let it all die, stay, die!

MARGUERITE: He doesn't know *what* he wants.

JULIETTE: I don't think he knows what he wants *any more*.

DOCTOR: He no longer *knows* what he wants. His brain's degenerating, he's senile, gaga.

GUARD (*announcing*): His Majesty has gone ga . . .

MARGUERITE (*to the* GUARD, *interrupting him*): Idiot, be quiet! We want no more doctors' bulletins given to the press. [People would only laugh, those who are still here to laugh and to listen. The rest of the world can pick up your words by radio, and they're quite jubilant.]

GUARD (*announcing*): Doctors' bulletins suspended by order of Her Majesty Queen Marguerite.

MARIE (*to the* KING): My King, my little King. . . .

KING: When I had nightmares and cried in my sleep, you would wake me up, kiss me and smooth away my fears.

MARGUERITE: She can't do that now!

KING: When I had sleepless nights and wandered out of my room, you would wake up too. In your pink-flowered dressing gown, you'd come and find me in the throne room, take me by the hand and lead me back to bed.

JULIETTE: It was just the same with my husband.

KING: I used to share my colds with you and the flu.

MARGUERITE: You won't catch colds now!

KING: In the morning we used to open our eyes at the very same moment. I shall close them alone, or not have *you* beside me. We used to think the same things at the same time. And you'd finish a sentence I'd just started in my head. I'd call you to rub my back when I was in the bath. And you'd choose my ties for me. Though I didn't always like them. We used to fight about that. No one knew, and no one ever will.

[DOCTOR: A storm in a teacup.

MARGUERITE: How suburban! We'll have to draw a veil over *that*!

KING (*to* MARIE): You'd hate my hair to be untidy. You used to comb it for me.

JULIETTE: It's so romantic, all this.

MARGUERITE: You hair won't be untidy now!

JULIETTE: But it's really very sad.

KING: Then you'd dust my crown and polish the pearls to make them shine.]

MARIE (*to the* KING): Do you love me? Do you love me? I've always loved *you*. Do you still love *me?* He *does* still love me. Do you love me today? Do you love me this minute? Here I am. . . . Here. . . . I'm here. . . .

Look! Look! . . . Take a good look! . . . Well, *look* at me!

KING: I've always loved myself, at least I can still love myself, feel myself, see myself, contemplate myself.

[MARGUERITE (*to* MARIE): That's enough! (*To the* KING:) You must stop looking back. That's a piece of advice. Or hurry and get it over. Soon this will be an order. (*To* MARIE:) I've told you before. From now on you can't do him anything but harm.]

DOCTOR (*looking at his watch*): He's running late . . . he's turned back in his tracks.

MARGUERITE: It's not serious. Don't worry, Doctor, Executioner. His little tricks, these kicks against the pricks . . . it was all to be expected, all part of the program.

DOCTOR: If this was a good old heart attack, we wouldn't have had so much trouble.

MARGUERITE: Heart attacks are reserved for businessmen.

DOCTOR: . . . or even double pneumonia!

MARGUERITE: That's for the poor, not for kings.

KING: I could decide not to die.

JULIETTE: You see, he's not cured yet.

KING: What if I decided to stop wanting things, to just stop wanting, and decided not to decide!

[MARGUERITE: We could decide for you.

GUARD (*announcing*): The Queen and the Doctor no longer owe the King obedience.

DOCTOR: We owe him *dis*obedience.

KING: Who except the King can release you from your duty to the King?

MARGUERITE: Force can do that, the force of events. First principles dictate their own commandments.

DOCTOR (*to* MARGUERITE): First principles and commandments are now invested in us.]

GUARD (*while* JULIETTE *starts pushing the* KING *around the stage in his invalid chair*): It was His Majesty, my Commander in Chief, who set the Thames on fire. It was he who invented gunpowder and stole fire from the gods. He nearly blew the whole place up. But he caught the pieces and tied them together again with string. I helped him, but it wasn't so easy. *He* wasn't so easy either. He was the one who fitted up the first forges on earth. He discovered the way to make steel. He used to work eighteen hours a day. And he made *us* work even harder. He was our chief engineer. As an engineer he made the first balloon, and then the zeppelin. And finally, with his own hands, he built the first airplane. At the start it wasn't a success. The first test pilots, Icarus and the rest, all fell into the sea. Till eventually he piloted the plane himself. I was his mechanic. Long before that, when he was only a little prince, he'd invented the wheelbarrow. I used to play with him. Then rails and railways and automobiles. He drew up the plans for the Eiffel Tower, not to mention his designs for the sickle and the plough, the harvesters and the tractors.

KING: Tractors? Good Heavens, yes! I'd forgotten.

GUARD: He extinguished volcanoes and caused new ones to erupt. He built Rome, New York, Moscow and Geneva. He *founded* Paris. He created revolutions, counter-revolutions, religion, reform and counter-reform.

JULIETTE: You wouldn't think so to look at him.

KING: What's an automobile?

JULIETTE (*still pushing him in his wheel chair*): It runs along by itself.

GUARD: He wrote tragedies and comedies, under the name of Shakespeare.

JULIETTE: Oh, so that's who Shakespeare was!

DOCTOR (*to the* GUARD): You ought to have told us before! Think how long we've been racking our brains to find out!

GUARD: It was a secret. He wouldn't let me. He invented the telephone and the telegraph, and fixed them up himself. He did everything with his own hands.

JULIETTE: He was never any good with his hands! He used to call the plumber at the slightest sign of a leak!

GUARD: My Commander in Chief was a very handy man!

JULIETTE: Now he can't even get his shoes on. Or off!

GUARD: Not so long ago he managed to split the atom.

JULIETTE: Now he can't even turn the light off. Or on!

GUARD: Majesty, Commander in Chief, Master, Managing Director . . .

MARGUERITE (*to the* GUARD): We know all about his earlier exploits. We don't need an inventory.

The GUARD *returns to his post.*

KING (*while he is being pushed around*): What's a horse?

. . . Those are windows, those are walls and this is the floor. I've done such things! What do they say I did? I don't remember what I did. I forget, I forget. (*While he is still being pushed around*:) And that's a throne.

MARIE: Do you remember me? I'm here, I'm here.

KING: I'm here. I exist.

JULIETTE: He doesn't even remember what a horse is.

KING: I remember a little ginger cat.

MARIE: He remembers a cat.

KING: I used to have a little ginger cat. We called him our wandering Jew. I had found him in a field, stolen from his mother, a real wildcat. He was two weeks old, or a little more, but he knew how to scratch and bite. He was quite fierce. I fed him and stroked him and took him home and he grew into the gentlest of cats. Once, Madame, he crept into the coat sleeve of a lady visitor. He was the politest of creatures, a natural politeness, like a prince. When we came home in the middle of the night he used to come and greet us with his eyes full of sleep. Then he'd stumble off back to his box. In the morning he'd wake us up to crawl into our bed. [One day we'd shut the bedroom door. He tried so hard to open it, shoving his little behind against it. He got so angry and made a terrible row; he sulked for a week.] He was scared stiff of the vacuum cleaner. A bit of a coward really, that cat; defenseless, a poet cat. We bought him a clockwork mouse. He started by sniffing it anxiously. When we wound it up and the mouse began to move, he spat at it, then took to his heels and crouched under the wardrobe. [When he'd grown up, his lady friends would pace round the house, courting and calling him. It used to frighten him silly and he wouldn't move.] We tried to introduce him to the outside world. We put him down on the pavement near the window. He was terrified, afraid of the pigeons that hopped all around him. There he was, pressed against the wall, miaowing and crying to me in desperation. To him, other animals and cats were strange creatures he mistrusted or enemies he feared. He only felt at home with us. [We were his family. He was not afraid of men. He'd jump on their shoulders without warning, and lick their hair.] He thought *we* were cats and cats were something else. And yet one fine day he must have felt the urge to go out on his own. The neighbor's big dog killed him. And there he was, like a toy cat, a twitching marionette with one eye gone and a paw torn off, yes, like a doll destroyed by a sadistic child.

[MARIE (*to* MARGUERITE): You shouldn't have left the door open; I warned you.

MARGUERITE: I hated that sentimental, timorous beast.

KING: How I missed him! He was good and beautiful and wise, all the virtues. He loved me, he loved me. My poor little cat, my one and only cat.]

The lines about the cat should be spoken with as little emotion as possible: to say them, the KING *should rather give an impression of being dazed, in a kind of dreamy stupor, except perhaps in this very last speech, which expresses a certain sorrow.*

[DOCTOR: I tell you he's running late.

MARGUERITE: I'm watching it. The timetable allows for holdups. Some delays were expected, you know.]

KING: I used to dream about him . . . that he was lying in the grate, on the glowing embers, and Marie was surprised he didn't burn. I told her, "Cats don't burn, they're fireproof." He came miaowing out of the fireplace in a cloud of thick smoke. But it wasn't him any more. What a transformation! It was a different cat, fat and ugly. An enormous she-cat. Like his mother, the wildcat. A bit like Marguerite.

For a few moments JULIETTE *leaves the* KING *in his wheelchair downstage in the center, facing the audience.*

JULIETTE: It's a great pity, I must say, a real shame! He was such a good king.

DOCTOR: Far from easy to please. Really quite wicked. Revengeful and cruel.

MARGUERITE: Vain.

JULIETTE: There have been worse.

MARIE: He was gentle, he was tender.

GUARD: We were rather fond of him.

DOCTOR (*to the* GUARD *and to* JULIETTE): You both complained about him, though.

JULIETTE: That's forgotten now.

[DOCTOR: Several times I had to intervene on your behalf.

MARGUERITE: He only listened to Queen Marie.

DOCTOR: He was hard and severe, and not even just.

JULIETTE: We saw him so little. And yet we *did* see him, we saw him quite often really.

GUARD: He was strong. It's true he cut a few heads off.

JULIETTE: Not many.

GUARD: All for the public good.

DOCTOR: And the result? We're surrounded by enemies.

MARGUERITE: You can hear us crumbling away. We've lost our frontiers already, only an ever widening gulf cuts us off from our neighbors.

JULIETTE: It's better that way. Now they can't invade us.

MARGUERITE: We're poised over a gaping chasm. Nothing but a growing void all around us.

GUARD: We're still clinging to the earth's crust.

MARGUERITE: Not for long!

MARIE: Better to perish with him!

MARGUERITE: There's nothing but the crust left. We'll soon be adrift in space.]

DOCTOR: And it's all his fault! He never cared what came after him. He never thought about his successors. After him the deluge. Worse than the deluge, after him there's nothing! Selfish bungler!

JULIETTE: *De mortuis nihil nisi bene.* He was king of a great kingdom.

MARIE: He was the heart and center of it.

JULIETTE: Its royal residence.

GUARD: A kingdom that stretched for thousands of miles around. You couldn't even glimpse its boundaries.

JULIETTE: Boundless in space.

MARGUERITE: But bounded in time. At once infinite and ephemeral.

JULIETTE: He was its Prince, its First Gentleman, he was its father and its son. He was crowned King at the very moment of his birth.

MARIE: He and his kingdom grew up together.

MARGUERITE: And vanish together.

[JULIETTE: He was the King, master of all the universe.

DOCTOR: An unwise master, who didn't know his own kingdom.

MARGUERITE: He knew very little of it.

MARIE: It was too extensive.

JULIETTE: The earth collapses with him. The suns are growing dim. Water, fire, air, ours and every universe, the whole lot disappears. In what warehouse or cellar, junkroom or attic will there ever be room to store all this? It'll take up space all right!]

DOCTOR: When kings die, they clutch at the walls, the trees, the fountains, the moon. They pull themselves up. . . .

MARGUERITE: But it all crashes down.

GUARD: And disintegrates.

DOCTOR: It melts and evaporates, till there's not a drop left, not a speck of dust, not the faintest shadow.

[JULIETTE: He drags it all with him into the abyss.

MARIE: He'd organized his world so well. He hadn't quite become master of it. But he would have been. He's dying too soon. He'd divided the year into four seasons. He was really getting on very nicely. He'd thought up the trees and the flowers, all the perfumes and colors.

GUARD: A world fit for a king.

MARIE: He'd invented the oceans and the mountains: nearly sixteen thousand feet for Mont Blanc.

GUARD: Over twenty-nine thousand for the Himalayas.

MARIE: The leaves fell from the trees, but they grew again.

JULIETTE: That was clever.]

MARIE: The very day he was born, he created the sun.

JULIETTE: And that wasn't enough. He had to have fire made too.

MARGUERITE: And there were wide-open spaces, and there were stars, and the sky and oceans and mountains; and there were plains, there were cities, and people and faces and buildings and rooms and beds; and the light and the night; and there were wars and there was peace.

GUARD: And a throne.

MARIE: And his fingers.

MARGUERITE: The way he looked and the way he breathed.

JULIETTE: He's still breathing now.

MARIE: He's still breathing, because I'm here.

MARGUERITE (*to the* DOCTOR): Is he still breathing?

JULIETTE: Yes, your Majesty. He's still breathing, because we're here.

DOCTOR (*examining the invalid*): Yes, yes, no doubt about it. He's still breathing. His kidneys have stopped functioning, but the blood's still circulating. Going round and round. His heart is sound.

MARGUERITE: It'll have to stop soon. What's the good of a heart that has no reason to beat?

DOCTOR: You're right. His heart's gone berserk. D'you hear?

You can hear the frantic beatings of the King's heart.

There it is, racing away, then it slows down, then it's off again, as fast as it can go.

The beatings of the King's heart shake the house. The crack in the wall widens and others appear. A stretch of wall could collapse or vanish from sight.

JULIETTE: Good God! Everything's falling to pieces!

MARGUERITE: A mad heart, a madman's heart!

DOCTOR: A heart in a panic. It's infectious. Anyone can catch it.

MARGUERITE (*to* JULIETTE): It'll all be quiet in a moment.

DOCTOR: We know every phase of the disease. It's always like this when a universe snuffs out.

MARGUERITE (*to* MARIE): It proves his universe is not unique.

JULIETTE: That never entered his head.

MARIE: He's forgetting me. At this very moment he's forgetting me. I can feel it, he's leaving me behind. I'm nothing if he forgets me. I can't go on living if I don't exist in his distracted heart. Hold tight, hold firm! Clench your fists with all your strength! Don't let go of me!

JULIETTE: Now his strength has left him.

MARIE: Cling to me, don't let go! It's I who keep you alive. I keep *you* alive, you keep *me* alive. D'you see, d'you understand? If you forget me, if you abandon me, I no longer exist, I am nothing.

DOCTOR: He will be a page in a book of ten thousand pages in one of a million libraries which has a million books.

JULIETTE: It won't be easy to find that page again.

[DOCTOR: Oh yes, you'll find it catalogued by subject matter, in alphabetical order . . . until the day comes when the paper's turned to dust . . . unless it's destroyed by fire. Libraries often go up in smoke.]

JULIETTE: He's clenching his fists. He's hanging on. He's still resisting. He's coming back to consciousness.

MARIE: He's not coming back to me.

JULIETTE (*to* MARIE): Your voice is waking him up, his eyes are open. He's looking at you.

DOCTOR: Yes, his heart's ticking over again.

[MARGUERITE: He's in a fine state! A dying man trapped in a thicket of thorns. A thicket of thorns! How can we pull him out? (*To the* KING:) You're stuck in the mud, caught in the brambles.

JULIETTE: And when he does get free, he'll leave his shoes behind.]

MARIE: Hold me tight, as I hold you! Look at me, as I look at you!

The KING *looks at her.*

MARGUERITE: She's getting you all mixed up. Forget about her and you'll feel better.

DOCTOR: Give in, your Majesty. Abdicate, Majesty.

JULIETTE: You'd better abdicate, if you must.

JULIETTE *pushes him round in his chair again and stops in front of* MARIE.

KING: I can hear, I can see, who are you? Are you my mother? My sister? My wife? My daughter? My niece? My cousin? . . . I know *you* . . . I'm sure I *do* know you.

They turn him to face MARGUERITE.

You hateful, hideous woman! Why are you still with me? Why are you leaning over me? Go away, go away!

MARIE: Don't look at her! Turn your eyes on me, and keep them wide open! Hope! I'm here. Remember who you are! I'm Marie.

KING (*to* MARIE): Marie!?

MARIE: If you don't remember, gaze at me and learn again that I am Marie. Look at my eyes, my face, my hair, my arms! And learn me off by heart!

MARGUERITE: You're upsetting him. He's past learning anything now.

MARIE (*to the* KING): If I can't hold you back, at least turn and look at me! I'm here! Keep this picture of me in your mind and take it with you!

MARGUERITE: He could never drag that around, he hasn't got the strength. It's too heavy for a ghost, [and we can't let other ghosts oppress him. He'd collapse under the weight. His ghost would bleed to death. He wouldn't be able to move.] He's got to travel light. (*To the* KING:) Throw everything away, lighten the load.

DOCTOR: [It's time he began to get rid of the ballast.] Lighten the load, your Majesty.

The KING *rises to his feet, but he has a different way of moving, his gestures are jerky, he already begins to look rather like a sleepwalker. The movements of a sleepwalker will become more and more pronounced.*

KING: Marie?

MARGUERITE (*to* MARIE): You see, your name means nothing to him now.

GUARD: Marie's name now means nothing to the King.

KING: Marie! (*As he pronounces this name, he can stretch out his arms and then let them fall again.*)

MARIE: He's said it.

DOCTOR: Repeated it, but without understanding.

JULIETTE: Like a parrot. Sounds that are dead.

KING (*to* MARGUERITE, *turning toward her*): I don't know you, I don't love you.

JULIETTE: He knows what not knowing means.

MARGUERITE (*to* MARIE): He'll start his journey with a picture of *me* in his mind. That won't get in his way. [It will leave him when it has to.] It's fitted with a gadget that's worked by remote control. (*To the* KING:) Have another look!

The KING *turns toward the audience.*

MARIE: He can't see you.

MARGUERITE: He won't see *you* any more.

By some theatrical trick, MARIE *suddenly disappears.*

JULIETTE: He can't see any more.

DOCTOR (*examining the* KING): That's true, he's lost his sight.

He has been moving his finger in front of the King's eyes; or perhaps a lighted candle or a match or a cigarette lighter held in front of Berenger's eyes. They stare out vacantly.

JULIETTE: He can't see any more. The Doctor has made an official pronouncement.

GUARD: His Majesty is officially blind.

[MARGUERITE: He'll see better if he looks inside himself.

KING: I can see things and faces and towns and forests, I can see space, I can see time.

MARGUERITE: Look a little further.

KING: I can't see any further.

JULIETTE: His horizon's closing in, blocking his view.

MARGUERITE: Cast your eyes beyond what you can see. Behind the road, through the mountain, away beyond that forest, the one you never cleared for cultivation.

KING: The ocean, I daren't go any further, I can't swim.

DOCTOR: Not enough exercise!

MARGUERITE: That's only the surface of things. Look deep inside them.]

KING: There's a mirror in my entrails where everything's reflected, I can see more and more, I can see the world, I can see life slipping away.

MARGUERITE: Look beyond the reflection.

KING: I see myself. Behind everything, I exist. Nothing

but me everywhere. [I am the earth, I am the sky, I am the wind, I am the fire;] am I in every mirror or am I the mirror of everything?

JULIETTE: He loves himself too much.

DOCTOR: A well-known disease of the psyche: narcissism.

[MARGUERITE: Come nearer.

KING: There isn't a path.

JULIETTE: He can hear. He's turning his head as he speaks, he's trying to listen, he's stretching out an arm, and now the other.]

GUARD: What's he trying to take hold of?

JULIETTE: He wants something to lean on.

For a few moments the KING *has been advancing like a blind man, with very unsteady steps.*

KING: Where are the walls? Where are the arms? Where are the doors? Where are the windows?

JULIETTE: The walls are here, your Majesty, we are all here. Here's an arm for you.

JULIETTE *leads the* KING *to the left, and helps him touch the wall.*

KING: The wall is here. The scepter!

JULIETTE *gives it to him.*

JULIETTE: Here it is!

KING: Guard, where are you? Answer me!

GUARD: Still yours to command, your Majesty. Yours to command.

The KING *takes a few steps toward the* GUARD. *He touches him.*

Yes, yes, I'm here. Yes, yes, I'm here.

JULIETTE: Your apartments are this way, your Majesty.

GUARD: I swear we'll never leave you, Majesty.

The GUARD *suddenly disappears.*

JULIETTE: We're here beside you, we'll stay with you.

JULIETTE *suddenly disappears.*

KING: Guard! Juliette! Answer me! I can't hear you any more. Doctor, Doctor, am I going deaf?

DOCTOR: No, your Majesty, not yet.

KING: Doctor!

DOCTOR: Forgive me, your Majesty, I must go. I'm afraid I have to. I'm very sorry, please forgive me.

The DOCTOR *retires. He goes out bowing, like a marionette, through the upstage door on the right. He has gone out backward, with much bowing and scraping, still excusing himself.*

KING: His voice is getting faint and the sound of his footsteps is fading, he's gone!

MARGUERITE: He's a doctor, with professional obligations.

Before she left, JULIETTE *must have pushed the wheel chair into a corner so it is not in the way.*

KING (*stretching out his arms*): Where are the others? (*The* KING *reaches the downstage door on the right, then makes for the downstage door on the left.*) They've gone and they've shut me in.

MARGUERITE: They were a nuisance, all those people. They were in your way, hanging around you, getting under your feet. Admit they got on your nerves!

The KING *is walking rather more easily.*

KING: I need their services.

MARGUERITE: I'll take their place. I'm the queen of all trades.

KING: I didn't give anyone leave to go. Make them come back, call them.

[MARGUERITE: They've been cut off. It's what you wanted.

KING: It's not what I wanted.]

MARGUERITE: They could never have gone away if you hadn't wanted them to. You can't go back on your decision now. You've dropped them.

KING: Let them come back!

MARGUERITE: You've even forgotten their names. What were they called?

The KING *is silent.*

How many were there?

KING: Who do you mean? . . . I don't like being shut in. Open the doors.

MARGUERITE: A little patience. The doors will soon be open wide.

KING (*after a silence*): The doors . . . the doors . . . what doors?

MARGUERITE: Were there once some doors? Was there once a world, were you ever alive?

KING: I am.

MARGUERITE: Keep still. Moving tires you.

The KING *does as she says.*

KING: I am. . . . Sounds, echoes, coming from a great distance, fainter and fainter, dying away. I am deaf.

MARGUERITE: You can still hear *me,* you'll hear me all the better.

The KING *is standing motionless, without a word.*

Sometimes you have a dream. And you get involved, you believe in it, you love it. In the morning, when you open your eyes, the two worlds are still confused. The brilliance of the light blurs the faces of the night. You'd like to remember, you'd like to hold them back. But they slip between your fingers, the brutal reality of day drives them away. What did I dream about, you ask yourself? What was it happened? Who was I kissing? Who did I love? What was I saying and what was I told? Then you find you're left with a vague regret for all those things that were or seemed to have been. You no longer know what it was that was there all around you. You no longer know.

KING: I no longer know what was there all around me. I know I was part of a world, and this world was all about me. I know it was me and what else was there, what else?

MARGUERITE: There are still some cords that bind you which I haven't yet untied. Or which I haven't cut. There are still some hands that cling to you and hold you back. (*Moving around the* KING, MARGUERITE *cuts the space, as though she had a pair of invisible scissors in her hand.*)

KING: Me. Me. Me.

MARGUERITE: This you is not the real you. It's an odd collection of bits and pieces, horrid things that live on you like parasites. The mistletoe that grows on the bough is not the bough, the ivy that climbs the wall is not the wall. You're sagging under the load, your shoulders are bent, that's what makes you feel so old. And it's that ball and chain dragging at your feet which make it so difficult to walk. (MARGUERITE *leans down and removes an invisible ball and chain from the King's feet, then as she gets up she looks as though she were making a great effort to lift the weight.*) A ton weight, they must weigh at least a ton. (*She pretends to be throwing them in the direction of the audience; then, freed of the weight, she straightens up.*) That's better! How did you manage to trail them around all your life?

The KING *tries to straighten up.*

And I used to wonder why you were so round-shouldered! It's because of that sack! (MARGUERITE *pretends to be taking a sack from the King's shoulders and throws it away.*) And that heavy pack. (MARGUERITE *goes through the same motions for the pack.*) And that spare pair of army boots.

KING (*with a sort of grunt*): No.

MARGUERITE: Don't get so excited! You won't need an extra pair of boots any more. Or that rifle, or that machine gun. (*The same procedure as for the pack.*) Or that tool box. (*Same procedure: protestations from the* KING.) He seems quite attached to it! A nasty rusty old saber. (*She takes it off him, although the* KING *tries grumpily to stop her.*) Leave it all to me and be a good boy. (*She taps on the King's hand.*) You don't need self-defense any more. No one wants to hurt you now. All those thorns and splinters in your cloak, those creepers and seaweed and slimy wet leaves. How they stick to you! I'll pick them off, I'll pull them away. What dirty marks they make! (*She goes through the motions of picking and pulling them off.*) The dreamer comes out of his dream. There you are! Now I've got rid of all those messy little things that worried you. Now your cloak's more beautiful, we've cleaned you up. You look much better for it. Now have a little walk. Give me your hand, give me your hand then! Don't be afraid any more, let yourself go! I'll see you don't fall. You don't dare!

KING (*in a kind of stammer*): Me.

MARGUERITE: Oh no! He imagines he's *everything!* He thinks *his* existence is *all* existence. I'll have to drive *that* out of his head! (*Then, as if to encourage him:*) Nothing will be forgotten. It's all quite safe in a mind that needs no memories. A grain of salt that dissolves in water doesn't disappear: it makes the water salty. Ah, that's it! Straighten up! Now you're not round-shouldered, no more pains in your back, no more stiffness! Wasn't it a heavy weight to bear? Now you feel better. You can go forward now, go on! Come along, give me your hand!

The King's shoulders are slowly rounding again.

Don't hunch your shoulders, you've no more loads to bear. . . . Oh, those conditioned reflexes, so hard to shake off! . . . You've no more weight on your shoulders, I tell you. Stand up straight! (*She helps him to straighten up.*) Your hand! . . .

The KING is undecided.

How disobedient he is! Don't clench your fists like that! Open your fingers out! What are you holding? (*She unclenches his fingers.*) He's holding the whole kingdom in his hand. In miniature: on microfilm . . . in tiny grains. (*To the* KING:) That grain won't grow again, it's bad seed! They're all moldy! Drop them! Unclasp your fingers! I order you to loosen those fingers! Let go of the plains, let go of the mountains! Like this. They were only dust. (*She takes him by the hand and drags him away, in spite of some slight resistance still from the* KING.) Come along! Still trying to resist! Where does he find all this will power? No, don't try to lie down! Don't sit down either! No reason why you should stumble. I'll guide you, don't be frightened! (*She guides him across the stage, holding him by the hand.*) You can do it now, can't you? It's easy, isn't it? I've had a gentle slope made for you. It gets steeper later on, but that doesn't matter. You'll have your strength back by then. Don't turn your head to see what you'll never see again, think hard, concentrate on your heart, keep right on, you must!

KING (*advancing with his eyes closed, still held by the hand*): The Empire . . . has there ever been another Empire like it? With two suns, two moons and two heavens to light it. And there's another sun rising, and there's another! A third firmament appearing, shooting up and fanning out! As one sun sets, others are rising . . . dawn and twilight all at once. . . . Beyond the seven hundred and seventy-seven poles.

MARGUERITE: Go further, further, further. Toddle on, toddle on, go on!

KING: Blue, blue.

MARGUERITE: He can still distinguish colors. (*To the* KING:)
Give up this Empire too! And give your colors up!
They're leading you astray, holding you back. You
can't linger any longer, you can't stop again, you
mustn't! (*She moves away from the* KING.) Walk by
yourself! Don't be frightened! Go on! (MARGUERITE,
from one corner of the stage, is directing the KING *at
a distance.*) It's not the day now or the night, there's
no more day and no more night. Try and follow that
wheel that's spinning around in front of you! Don't
lose sight of it, follow it! But not too close, it's all in
flames, you might get burnt. Go forward! I'll move
the undergrowth aside. Watch out! Don't bump into
that phantom on your right . . . clutching hands, im-
ploring hands, pitiful arms and hands, don't you come
back, away with you! Don't touch him, or I'll strike
you! (*To the* KING:) Don't turn your head! Skirt the
precipice on your left, and don't be afraid of that
howling wolf . . . his fangs are made of cardboard,
he doesn't exist. (*To the wolf*:) Wolf, cease to exist!
(*To the* KING:) Don't be afraid of the rats now either!
They can't bite your toes. (*To the rats*:) Rats and
vipers, cease to exist! (*To the* KING:) And don't start
pitying that beggar who's holding out his hand! . . .
Beware of that old woman coming toward you! . . .
Don't take that glass of water she's offering! You're
not thirsty. (*To the imaginary old woman*:) He has no
need to quench his thirst, my good woman, he's not
thirsty. Don't stand in his way! Vanish! (*To the* KING:)
Climb over the fence . . . that big truck won't run
you over, it's a mirage . . . cross now. . . . Why no,
daisies don't sing, even in the spring. I'll smother
their cries. I'll obliterate them! . . . And stop listening

to the babbling of that brook! It's not real anyway, it's deceiving you . . . false voices, be still! (*To the* KING:) No one's calling you now. Smell that flower for the last time, then throw it away! Forget its perfume! Now you've lost the power of speech. Who's left for you to talk to? Yes, that's right. Put your best foot forward! Now the other! There's a footbridge. No, you won't feel giddy.

The KING *is advancing toward the steps of the throne.*

Hold yourself straight! You don't need your stick, besides you haven't got one. Don't bend down and whatever you do, don't fall! Up, up you go!

The KING *starts to climb the three or four steps to the throne.*

Higher, up again, up you go, still higher, higher, higher!

The KING *is quite close to the throne.*

Now turn and face me! Look at me! Look right through me! Gaze into my unreflecting mirror and stand up straight! . . . Give me your legs! The right one! Now the left!

As she gives him these orders, the KING *stiffens his legs.*

Give me a finger! Give me two fingers . . . three, four . . . five . . . all ten fingers! Now let me have your right arm! Your left arm! Your chest, your two shoulders and your stomach!

The KING *is motionless, still as a statue.*

There you are, you see! Now you've lost the power of speech, there's no need for your heart to beat, no more need to breathe. It was a lot of fuss about nothing, wasn't it? Now you can take your place.

Sudden disappearance of QUEEN MARGUERITE *on the left. The* KING *is seated on his throne. During this final scene, the doors, windows and walls of the throne room will have slowly disappeared. This part of the action is very important.*

Now there is nothing on the stage except the KING *on his throne in a grayish light. Then the* KING *and his throne also disappear.*

Finally, there is nothing but the gray light.

This disappearance of the windows, the doors and the walls, the KING *and the throne must be very marked, but happen slowly and gradually. The* KING *sitting on his throne should remain visible for a short time before fading into a kind of mist.*

THE KILLER

TRANSLATOR'S NOTE

An attempt has been made to reach a compromise between American and British English, but in the event of production, producers should feel themselves free to change any word that would obviously offend an audience.

Two cases in point would be: elevator/lift and prefect/monitor.

THE KILLER

First produced in Paris by José Quaglio at the Théâtre Récamier, the 27th February, 1959.

CHARACTERS, VOICES, SILHOUETTES
(in order of appearance):

BÉRENGER, an average, middle-aged citizen.

THE ARCHITECT, of ageless, bureaucratic age.

DANY, young typist, conventional pin-up.

THE CLOCHARD, drunk.

THE OWNER OF THE BISTRO, middle-aged, fat, dark and hairy.

ÉDOUARD, 35, thin, nervous, darkly dressed, in mourning.

THE CONCIERGE (preceded by THE VOICE OF THE CONCIERGE), typical concierge.

VOICE OF THE CONCIERGE'S DOG.

A MAN'S VOICE.

SECOND MAN'S VOICE.

TRUCK DRIVER'S VOICE.

CAR DRIVER'S VOICE.

FIRST OLD MAN.

SECOND OLD MAN.

THE GROCER.

SCHOOLMASTER'S VOICE.

FIRST VOICE FROM THE STREET.

SECOND VOICE (GRUFF) FROM THE STREET.

THIRD VOICE (PIPING) FROM THE STREET.

FOURTH VOICE FROM THE STREET.

FIRST VOICE FROM BELOW.

SECOND VOICE FROM BELOW.

VOICE FROM THE RIGHT.

Voice from Above.

Voice from the Left.

Second Voice from the Left.

Woman's Voice from the Entrance.

Silhouette of a Motorcyclist on his Bicycle.

Postman's Voice (preceding the Postman himself, if
  desired).

Mother Peep.

Voices of the Crowd.

The Drunk in Top Hat and Tails.

The Old Gentleman with the Little White Beard.

First Policeman.

Second Policeman.

The Echo.

The Killer.

STAGE DIRECTIONS

Several of these parts may be played by the same actors. More-
over, it is probable that all the voices in the second act will not
be heard. Any cuts required may be made in the first half of
Act II: it will all depend on the effectiveness of these voices and
their absurd remarks. The director can choose those he likes.
He should, however, try if possible to obtain stereophonic sound
effects. In the second act it is also better to have the greatest possible number of figures appearing in silhouette the other side of
the window, as on a stage behind the stage. In any case, after the
curtain has risen on the second act, some voices and sounds
around the empty stage are indispensable, at least for a few
minutes, in order to continue and in a way intensify the visual
and aural atmosphere of street and city; this is first created at the
end of Act I, fades after the arrival of Bérenger and returns again
in force at the start of Act III to die right away at the end.

A few cuts could also be made in Act I, according to the power of the actor playing the part and his natural capacity to 'put it over'.

Bérenger's speech to the Killer at the end of the play is one short act in itself. The text should be interpreted in such a way as to bring out the gradual breaking-down of Bérenger, his falling apart and the vacuity of his own rather commonplace morality, which collapses like a leaking balloon. In fact Bérenger finds within himself, in spite of himself and against his own will, arguments in favour of the Killer.

ACT ONE

No decor. An empty stage when the curtain rises. Later there will only be, on the left of the stage, two garden chairs and a table, which the ARCHITECT will bring on himself. They should be near at hand in the wings.

The atmosphere for Act I will be created by the lighting only. At first, while the stage is still empty, the light is grey, like a dull November day or afternoon in February. The faint sound of wind; perhaps you can see a dead leaf fluttering across the stage. In the distance the noise of a tram, vague outlines of houses; then, suddenly, the stage is brilliantly lit; a very bright, very white light; just this whiteness, and also the dense vivid blue of the sky. And so, after the grisaille, the lighting effects should simply be made up of white and blue, the only elements in the decor. The noise of the tram, the wind and the rain will have stopped at the very moment the light changes. The blue, the white, the silence and the empty stage should give a strange impression of peace. The audience must be given time to become aware of this. Not until a full minute has passed should the characters appear on the scene.

BÉRENGER comes on first, from the left, moving quickly. He stops

in the centre of the stage and turns round briskly to face the
ARCHITECT, *who has followed him more slowly.* BÉRENGER *is*
wearing a grey overcoat, hat and scarf. The ARCHITECT *is in a*
summer-weight jacket, light trousers, open-necked shirt and with-
out a hat; under his arm he is carrying a briefcase, rather thick and
heavy, like the one ÉDOUARD *has in Act II.*

BÉRENGER: Amazing! Amazing! It's extraordinary! As far as I
can see, it's a miracle... [*Vague gesture of protest from the*
ARCHITECT.]... A miracle, or, as I don't suppose you're a
religious man, you'd rather I called it a marvel! I congratulate
you most warmly, it's a marvel, really quite marvellous,
you're a marvellous architect!...

ARCHITECT: Oh... you're very kind...

BÉRENGER: No, no. I *want* to congratulate you. It's absolutely incredible, you've achieved the incredible! The real thing is
quite beyond imagination.

ARCHITECT: It's the work I'm commissioned to do, part of my
normal duties, what I specialize in.

BÉRENGER: Why, yes, of course, to be sure, you're an architect, a
technician and a conscientious civil servant at one and the
same time... Still, that doesn't explain everything. [*Looking*
round him and staring at several fixed points on the stage:] Beautiful,
what a magnificent lawn, that flower-bed!... Oh, what
flowers, appetizing as vegetables, and what vegetables, fragrant
as flowers... and what a blue sky, what an amazingly blue
sky. How wonderful it is! [*To the* ARCHITECT:] In all the
cities of the world, all cities of a certain size, I'm sure there are
civil servants, municipal architects like you, with the same
duties as you, earning the same salary. But they're nowhere
near achieving the same results. [*Gesture of the hand.*] Are you
well paid? I'm sorry, perhaps I'm being indiscreet...

ARCHITECT: Please don't apologize... I'm fairly well paid, the
scale is laid down. It's reasonable... It's all right.

BÉRENGER: But ingenuity like yours is worth its weight in gold. And what's more, I mean the price gold fetched before 1914... the real thing.

ARCHITECT: [*with a modestly disclaiming gesture*] Oh...

BÉRENGER: Oh yes it is... You're the town architect, aren't you?... *Real* gold... After all, today, gold has been devalued, like so many other things, it's paper gold...

ARCHITECT: Your surprise, your...

BÉRENGER: Call it my admiration, my enthusiasm!

ARCHITECT: Very well, your enthusiasm, then, touches me very deeply. I feel I must thank you, dear Monsieur... Bérenger. [*The* ARCHITECT *bows in thanks, after first searching one of his pockets for a card which doubtless bears the name of* BÉRENGER, *and as he bows he reads the name off the card.*]

BÉRENGER: Genuinely enthusiastic, quite genuinely. I'm not the flattering kind, I can tell you.

ARCHITECT: [*ceremoniously, but unimpressed*] I am very highly honoured.

BÉRENGER: It's magnificent! [*He looks about him.*] I'd been told all about it, you see, but I didn't believe it... or rather I wasn't told a thing about it, but I *knew*, I knew that somewhere in our dark and dismal city, in all its mournful, dusty, dirty districts, there was one that was bright and beautiful, this neighbourhood beyond compare, with its sunny streets and avenues bathed in light... this radiant city within a city which you've built...

ARCHITECT: It's a nucleus which is, or rather was, in theory meant to be extended. I planned it all by order of the City Council. I don't allow myself any personal initiative...

BÉRENGER: [*continuing his monologue*] I believed in it, without believing, I knew without knowing! I was afraid to hope... hope, that's not a French word any more, or Turkish, or Polish... Belgian perhaps... and even then...

ARCHITECT: I see, I understand.

BÉRENGER: And yet, *here* I am. Your radiant city is *real*. No doubt of that. You can touch it with your fingers. The blue brilliance of it looks absolutely natural... blue and green... oh, that grass, those rose-pink flowers...

ARCHITECT: Yes, those pink flowers really are roses.

BÉRENGER: Real roses? [*He walks about the stage, pointing, smelling the flowers, etc.*] More blue and more green things too... the colours of joy. And what peace, what peace!

ARCHITECT: That's the rule here, Monsieur... [*He reads off the card*:]... Bérenger. It's all calculated, all intentional. Nothing was to be left to chance in this district, the weather here is always fine. ... And so the building plots always fetch... or rather... always used to fetch a high price... the villas are built of the best materials... built to last, built with care.

BÉRENGER: I don't suppose it ever rains in these houses?

ARCHITECT: Definitely not! That's the least you can expect. Does it rain in yours?

BÉRENGER: Yes, I'm afraid it does.

ARCHITECT: It oughtn't to, even in your district. I'll send a man round.

BÉRENGER: Well, I suppose it doesn't really rain *inside*. Only in a manner of speaking. It's so damp, it's as if it *was* raining.

ARCHITECT: I see. Morally speaking. In any case, here in this district it never rains at all. And yet all the walls and all the roofs of the buildings you can see are damp-proof. It's a habit, a matter of form. Quite unnecessary, but it keeps up an old tradition.

BÉRENGER: You say it *never* rains? And all these things growing? This grass? And not a dead leaf on the trees, not a faded flower in the garden!

ARCHITECT: They're watered from below.

BÉRENGER: A technical marvel! Forgive me for being so astonished, a layman like me... [*With his handkrcheief he is mopping the sweat from his brow.*]

ARCHITECT: Why don't you take your overcoat off? Carry it on your arm, you're too hot.

BÉRENGER: Why yes... I'm not at all cold any more... Thank you, thanks for the suggestion. [*He takes off his overcoat and puts it over his arm; he keeps his hat on his head. He looks up, with a gesture:*] The leaves on the trees are small enough for the light to filter through, but not too big, so as not to darken the front of the houses. I must say it's amazing to think that in all the rest of the town the sky's as grey as the hair on an old woman's head, that there's dirty snow at the pavements' edge, and the wind blowing there. When I woke up this morning I was very cold. I was frozen. The radiators work so badly in my block of flats, especially on the ground-floor. They work even worse when they don't make up the fire... So I mean to say...

[*A telephone bell rings, coming from the* ARCHITECT's *pocket; the* ARCHITECT *takes a receiver from it and listens; the telephone wire ends in his pocket.*]

ARCHITECT: Hullo?

BÉRENGER: Forgive me, Monsieur, I'm keeping you from your work...

ARCHITECT: [*to telephone*] Hullo? [*To* BÉRENGER:] Not a bit... I've kept an hour free to show you the district. No trouble at all. [*To telephone:*] Hullo? Yes. I know about that. Let the assistant manager know. Right. Let him hold an investigation if he insists. *He* can make the official arrangements. I'm with Monsieur Bérenger, for the visit to the radiant city. [*He puts the machine back in his pocket. To* BÉRENGER, *who has taken a few steps away, lost in admiration:*] You were saying? Hey, where are you?

BÉRENGER: Here. I'm sorry. What was I saying? Oh yes... Oh, it doesn't really matter now.

ARCHITECT: Go ahead. Say it anyway.

BÉRENGER: I was saying... oh yes... in my district, especially where I live, everything is damp; the coal, the bread, the wind, the wine, the walls, the air, and even the fire. What a job I had this morning, getting up, I had to make a big effort.

It was really painful. I'd never have made up my mind if the sheets hadn't been damp too. I never imagined that, suddenly, as if by magic, I should find myself in the midst of spring, in the middle of April, the April of my dreams... my earliest dreams...

ARCHITECT: Dreams! [Shrugging his shoulders.] Anyhow, it would have been better if you'd come sooner, come before...

BÉRENGER: [interrupting him] Ah yes, I've lost a lot of time, that's true...

[BÉRENGER and the ARCHITECT go on walking about the stage. BÉRENGER should give the impression he is walking through tree-lined avenues and parks. The ARCHITECT follows him, more slowly. At times BÉRENGER will have to turn round to speak to the ARCHITECT in a louder voice. He should appear to be waiting for the ARCHITECT to come closer. Pointing to empty space:]

BÉRENGER: There's an attractive house! The façade is delightful, such a wonderfully pure style. 18th century? No, 15th or the end of the 19th? It's classical anyway, and then it's so neat, so smart... Ah yes, I've lost a lot of time, is it too late?... No... Yes... No, it may not be too late, what do you think?

ARCHITECT: I haven't given the matter much thought.

BÉRENGER: I'm thirty-five years old, Monsieur, thirty-five... Actually to tell the truth, I'm forty, forty-five, perhaps a little more.

ARCHITECT: [consulting the card] We know. Your age is on the card. We have files on everyone.

BÉRENGER: Really? Oh!

ARCHITECT: It's quite usual, we have to have them for the record, but don't worry, the code provides no penalties for that kind of prevarication, not for vanity.

BÉRENGER: Thank goodness for that! Anyway, if I only admit to thirty-five, it's certainly not to deceive my fellow citizens, what's it matter to them? It's to deceive myself. In this way I act on myself by suggestion, I believe myself to be younger, I cheer myself up...

ARCHITECT: It's only human, only natural. [*The pocket telephone rings; the* ARCHITECT *takes it out again.*]

BÉRENGER: Oh, what nice little stones on the paths!

ARCHITECT: [*to telephone*] Hullo?... A woman? Take a description of her. Enter it up. Send it to the statistics department...

BÉRENGER: [*pointing to the corner of the stage on the left*] What's that over there?

ARCHITECT: [*to telephone*] No, no, no, nothing else to report. All the time *I'm* here, nothing else *can* happen. [*He puts the receiver back in his pocket. To* BÉRENGER:] I'm sorry, I'm listening now.

BÉRENGER: [*as before*] What's that over there?

ARCHITECT: Oh, that... It's a greenhouse.

BÉRENGER: A greenhouse?

ARCHITECT: Yes. For the flowers that can't get used to a temperate climate, the flowers that like the cold. We've created a wintry climate for them. Now and again we have a little storm...

BÉRENGER: Ah, everything's been thought of... yes, Monsieur, I could be sixty years old, seventy, eighty, a hundred and twenty, how do I know?

ARCHITECT: Morally speaking!

BÉRENGER: It can be interpreted physically too. It's psychosomatic... Am I talking nonsense?

ARCHITECT: Not particularly. Like everyone else.

BÉRENGER: I feel old. Time is above all subjective. Or rather I *used* to feel old. Since this morning I'm a new man. I'm sure I'm becoming myself again. The world's becoming itself again; it's all thanks to *your* power. Your magic light...

ARCHITECT: My electric light!

BÉRENGER: ... Your radiant city. [*He points quite near.*] It's the power of those immaculate walls covered with roses, your masterpiece! Ah, yes, yes, yes!... nothing's really lost, I'm sure of that now... Now, in fact, I *do* remember, two or three people did tell me about the smiling city; some said it was quite near, others that it was far away, that it was easy to get to, hard to find, that it was a district specially reserved...

ARCHITECT: Not true!

BÉRENGER: ... That there was no means of transport...

ARCHITECT: Nonsense. There's a tram stop over there, at the end of the main thoroughfare.

BÉRENGER: Yes, of course, of course! I know *now*. For a long time, I tell you, I tried consciously or unconsciously to find the way. I would walk right to the end of a street, and then realize it was a dead end. I'd follow a wall or a fence until I reached the river far from the bridge, away beyond the market and the gates of the town. Or else I'd meet some friends on the way, who hadn't seen me since our army days; I'd be forced to stop and chat to them until it was too late and I had to go home. Still, what does it matter now? I'm *here*. My worries are over.

ARCHITECT: It was really so simple. You only had to drop me a line, write an official letter to the municipal offices, and one of my departments would have sent you all the necessary information by registered post.

BÉRENGER: Why yes, I only needed to think of that! Oh well, no good crying over lost years...

ARCHITECT: How did you set about finding the way today?

BÉRENGER: Pure accident. I just took the tram.

ARCHITECT: What did I tell you?

BÉRENGER: Took the wrong tram, I meant to take another, I was sure it wasn't going the right way, and yet it *was*, by mistake, a lucky mistake...

ARCHITECT: Lucky?

BÉRENGER: No? Not lucky? But it *was*. Very, very lucky.

ARCHITECT: Oh well, you'll see for yourself, later.

BÉRENGER: I've seen already. I'm firmly convinced.

ARCHITECT: Anyway, remember you must always go as far as the terminus. Whatever the circumstances. All trams lead this way: it's the depot.

BÉRENGER: I know. The tram brought me here, to this stop. Although I hadn't been here before, I recognized everything at once; the avenues and the houses all blossoming, and you, looking as if you expected me.

ARCHITECT: I'd been informed.

BÉRENGER: It's such a transformation! It's as though I was far away in the South, two or three thousand miles away. Another universe, a world transfigured! And just that very short journey to get here, a journey that isn't *really*, since you might say it takes place in the same place... [*He laughs; then embarrassed:*] Forgive me, that wasn't very funny.

ARCHITECT: Don't look so upset. I've heard worse. I'll put it down to your state of bliss...

BÉRENGER: I've no mind for science. I suppose that's why in spite of your very pertinent explanations, *I* can't explain how the weather can always be fine here! Perhaps—this may have made it easier for you—perhaps it's a more sheltered spot? And yet it's not surrounded by hills to protect it from bad weather! Besides, hills don't chase the clouds away or stop it raining, everyone knows that. Is it that there are bright warm waves of air coming from a fifth point of the compass or some third stratum of the upper air? No, I suppose there aren't. Everyone would know about it. I'm really stupid. There's no breeze, although the air smells good. I must say it's odd, Monsieur, it's very odd!

ARCHITECT: [*giving the authoritative information*] I tell you there's nothing unusual about it, it's a technical matter! So try and understand. You ought to have taken an Adult Education Course. It's just that this is a little island... with concealed ventilators I copied from the ones in those oases that crop up all over the place in the desert, where suddenly out of the dry sand you see amazing cities rising up, smothered with dewy roses, girdled with springs and rivers and lakes...

BÉRENGER: Oh yes... That's true. You mean those cities that are also called mirages. I've read explorers' tales about them.

You see, I'm not completely uneducated. Mirages... there's
nothing more real than a mirage. Flowers on fire, trees in
flame, pools of light, that's all there really is that matters. I'm
sure of it. And over there? What's that?

ARCHITECT: Over where? Where? Oh, over there?

BÉRENGER: Looks like an ornamental pool.

[*By means of the lighting, the vague outline of an ornamental pool
appears at the back of the stage just as he says these words.*]

ARCHITECT: Er... yes, it *is* a pool. You recognized it. It's a pool,
all right. [*He consults his watch.*] I think I still have a few minutes.

BÉRENGER: Can we go and see?

ARCHITECT: You want to have a closer look? [*He appears to
hesitate.*] Very well. If you insist, I'll have to show it you.

BÉRENGER: Or instead... I don't know what to choose... It's all
so beautiful... I like ornamental pools, but I rather like the
look of that flowering hawthorn too. If you don't mind, we can
look at the pool later...

ARCHITECT: As you like.

BÉRENGER: I love hawthorn bushes.

ARCHITECT: You've only to make up your mind.

BÉRENGER: Yes, yes, let's go over to the hawthorn.

ARCHITECT: I'm completely at your service.

BÉRENGER: One can't see everything at once.

ARCHITECT: True enough.

[*The pool disappears. They walk a few steps.*]

BÉRENGER: What a sweet smell! You know, Monsieur, I...
forgive me for talking about myself... one can say anything
to an architect, he understands everything.

ARCHITECT: Do please carry on. Don't be shy.

BÉRENGER: Thank you! You know, I do so need another life, a
new life. Different surroundings, a different setting. A different
setting, you'll think that's not much to ask, and that... with
money, for example..

ARCHITECT: No, not at all...

BÉRENGER: Yes, yes, you're too polite... A setting, *that's* just superficial, an artistic consideration, unless it's, how shall I say, a setting, a background that would answer some profound need inside, which would be somehow...

ARCHITECT: I see, I see...

BÉRENGER: ... the projection, the continuation of the universe inside you. Only, to project this universe within, some outside help is needed: some kind of material, physical light, a world that is objectively new. Gardens, blue sky, or the spring, which corresponds to the universe inside and offers a chance of recognition, which is like a translation or an anticipation of that universe, or a mirror in which its own smile could be reflected... in which it can find itself again and say: that's what I am in reality and I'd forgotten, a smiling being in a smiling world... Come to think of it, it's quite wrong to talk of a world within and a world without, separate worlds; there's an initial impulse, of course, which starts from us, and when it can't project itself, when it can't fulfil itself objectively, when there's not total agreement between myself inside and myself outside, then it's a catastrophe, a universal contradiction, a schism.

ARCHITECT: [scratching his head] What a vocabulary you have. We don't talk the same language.

BÉRENGER: I felt I couldn't go on living, and yet I couldn't die. Luckily it's all going to be different now.

ARCHITECT: Don't get too excited!

BÉRENGER: I'm sorry. I get carried away.

ARCHITECT: That's characteristic of you. You're one of those poetic personalities. As they exist, I suppose they must be necessary.

BÉRENGER: Year after year of dirty snow and bitter winds, of a climate indifferent to human beings... streets and houses and whole districts of people who aren't really unhappy, but worse, who are neither happy nor unhappy, people who are ugly because they're neither ugly nor beautiful, creatures that are dismally neutral, who long without longings as though they're unconscious, unconsciously suffering from being alive. But *I* was aware of the sickness of life. Perhaps because I'm more intelligent, or just the opposite, *less* intelligent, not so wise, not so resigned, not so patient. Is that a fault or a virtue?

ARCHITECT: [*giving signs of impatience*] Depends.

BÉRENGER: You can't tell. The winter of the soul! I'm not expressing myself clearly, am I?

ARCHITECT: I'm not capable of judging. It's not one of my duties. The logic department sees to that.

BÉRENGER: Perhaps you don't appreciate my lyrical side?

ARCHITECT: [*dryly*] Why yes, of course!

BÉRENGER: Well, you see: once upon a time there was a blazing fire inside me. The cold could do nothing against it, a youthfulness, a spring no autumn could touch; a source of light, glowing wells of joy that seemed inexhaustible. Not happiness, I mean joy, felicity, which made it possible for me to live...

[*The telephone rings in the* ARCHITECT's *pocket.*]

There was enormous energy there...

[*The* ARCHITECT *takes the telephone from his pocket.*]

A force... it must have been the life force, mustn't it?

ARCHITECT: [*holding the receiver to his ear*] Hullo?

BÉRENGER: And then it grew weaker and all died away.

ARCHITECT; [*to the telephone*] Hullo? Fine, fine, fine!... Don't tell me that only happened yesterday!

BÉRENGER: [*continuing his monologue*] Oh it must go back... I don't know how long... a long, long time ago...

[*The* ARCHITECT *puts the receiver back in his pocket and shows fresh signs of impatience; he goes into the wings on the left and brings on a chair, which he sets down in the left-hand corner, where the greenhouse was supposed to be.*]

Must be centuries ago... or perhaps only a few years, perhaps it was yesterday...

ARCHITECT: I must ask you to excuse me, I'm afraid I must go to my office. I've some urgent matters to attend to. [*He goes off left for a moment.*]

BÉRENGER: [*alone*] Oh... Monsieur, really, I'm so sorry, I...

ARCHITECT: [*coming back with a small table, which he sets in front of the chair; he sits down, takes the telephone from his pocket, puts it on the table and lays his briefcase open before him*] It's for me to apologize.

BÉRENGER: Oh, no! I feel terrible about it!

ARCHITECT: Don't let it upset you too much. I have two ears; one for duty, and the other I reserve for you. One eye too, for you. The other's for the borough.

BÉRENGER: It won't tire you too much?

ARCHITECT: Don't worry. I'm used to it. All right, carry on... [*He takes from his briefcase, or pretends to, some files which he lays out on the table and opens.*] I'm attending to my files, and to you too... You were saying you didn't know how long ago it was this force died away!

BÉRENGER: It certainly wasn't yesterday. [*He goes on walking, from now on, round and round the* ARCHITECT, *who is plunged in his files.*] It's such an old story, I've almost forgotten, it might have been an illusion; and yet it can't be an illusion when I still feel the loss of it so badly.

ARCHITECT: [*in his files*] Go on.

BÉRENGER: I can't analyse the feeling, I don't even know if the experience I had can be communicated. It wasn't very frequent. It happened, five or six, ten times perhaps in my life. Often enough, though, to fill to overflowing Heaven knows what secret reservoirs of my mind with joy and conviction. When I was in a gloomy mood, the memory of that dazzling radiance, that glowing feeling, gave fresh life to the force within me, to those reasonless reasons for living and loving... loving what?... Loving everything wholeheartedly...

ARCHITECT: [*to the telephone*] Hullo, the supplies have run out!

BÉRENGER: Yes, I'm afraid they have, Monsieur.

ARCHITECT: [*who has hung up*] I wasn't saying that to you, it's about my files.

BÉRENGER: It's true for me too, Monsieur, the reservoirs are empty. I'm not economically sound any more. My supplies of light have run out. I'll try and explain... I'm not imposing on you?

ARCHITECT: It's going in the record. That's my job. Carry on, don't mind me.

BÉRENGER: It happened as spring was ending, or perhaps in the very first days of summer, just before midday; it all came about in a way that was perfectly simple and perfectly unexpected as well. The sky was as pure as the one you've managed to cover your radiant city with, Monsieur. Yes, it happened in extraordinary silence, in a long, long second of silence...

ARCHITECT: [*still in his files*] Right. Fine.

BÉRENGER: The last time I must have been seventeen or eighteen, and I was in a little country town... which one?... I wonder which it was?... Somewhere in the South, I think... It's of no importance anyway, the place hardly counts. I was walking along a narrow street, which was both old and new, with low houses on either side, all white and tucked away in courtyards or little gardens, with wooden fences, painted... pale yellow, was it pale yellow? I was all alone in the street. I was walking along by the fences and the houses, and it was fine, not too hot, with the sun above, high above my head in the blue of the sky. I was walking fast, but where was I going? I don't remember. I was deeply aware of the unique joy of being alive. I'd forgotten everything, all I could think of was those houses, that deep sky and that sun, which seemed to be coming nearer, within my grasp, in a world that was made for me.

ARCHITECT: [*consulting his watch*] She's not here yet! Late again!

BÉRENGER: [*continuing*] Suddenly the joy became more intense, breaking all bounds! And then, oh what indescribable bliss took hold of me! The light grew more and more brilliant, and still lost none of its softness, it was so dense you could almost breathe it, it had become the air itself, you could drink it like clear water... How can I convey its incomparable brilliance?.... It's as if there were four suns in the sky...

ARCHITECT: [*speaking into the telephone*] Hullo? Have you seen my
secretary today? There's a pile of work waiting. [*He hangs up
angrily.*]

BÉRENGER: The houses I was passing were like immaterial shades
ready to melt away in that mightier light which governed all.

ARCHITECT: I'll make her pay a nice fat fine!

BÉRENGER: [*to* ARCHITECT] You see what I mean?

ARCHITECT: [*vaguely*] More or less. Your story seems clearer now.

BÉRENGER: Not a man in the street, not a cat, not a sound, there
was only me.

[*The telephone bell rings.*]

And yet I didn't suffer from being alone, I didn't feel lonely.

ARCHITECT: [*to the telephone*] Well, has she arrived?

BÉRENGER: My own peace and light spread in their turn throughout the world, I was filling the universe with a kind of ethereal
energy. Not an empty corner, everything was a mingling of
airiness and plenitude, perfectly balanced.

ARCHITECT: [*to the telephone*] At last! Put her on the line.

BÉRENGER: A song of triumph rose from the depths of my being:
I *was*, I realized I had always *been*, that I was no longer going
to die.

ARCHITECT: [*on the telephone, mastering his irritation*] I must say
I'm very pleased to hear your voice, Mademoiselle. It's about
time. What?

BÉRENGER: Everything was virgin, purified, discovered anew. I
had a feeling of inexpressible surprise, yet at the same time it
was all quite familiar to me.

ARCHITECT: [*on the telephone*] What do you mean by that,
Mademoiselle?

BÉRENGER: That's *it* all right, I said to myself, that's *it*, all right...
I can't tell *you* what I mean by 'it', but I promise you, Monsieur
I understood quite well what I meant.

ARCHITECT: [*on the telephone*] I don't understand you, Mademoiselle. You've no reason to be dissatisfied with us, I should

say the boot's on the other foot.

BÉRENGER: I felt I was there at the gates, at the very centre of the universe... That must seem contradictory to you?

ARCHITECT: [*on the telephone*] One moment, please. [*To* BÉRENGER:] I follow you, I follow you, don't worry, I get the general idea. [*On the telephone :*] Hullo, yes?

BÉRENGER: I walked and ran and cried: I *am*, I *am*, *everything* is, everything *is!*... Oh, I'm sure I could have flown away, I'd lost so much weight, I was lighter than the blue sky I was breathing... The slightest effort, the tiniest little leap would have been enough... I should have taken off... I'm sure I should.

ARCHITECT: [*on the telephone, banging his fist on the table*] Now that's going too far! What's made you feel like this?

BÉRENGER: If I didn't do it, it's because I was too happy, it didn't even enter my head.

ARCHITECT: [*on the telephone*] You want to leave the Service? Think carefully before you resign. Without any good reason you're abandoning a brilliant career! After all, with us your future is insured, *and* your life... your life! You aren't afraid of the danger!

BÉRENGER: And suddenly, or rather gradually... no, it was all at once, I don't know, I only know that everything went grey and pale and neutral again. Not really, of course, the sky was still pure, but it wasn't the same purity, it wasn't the same sun, the same morning, the same spring. It was like a conjuring trick. The light was the same as on any other day, ordinary daylight.

ARCHITECT: [*on the telephone*] You can't stand the situation any longer? That's childish. I refuse your resignation. Come and clear up the day's mail anyway, and you can explain yourself. I'm waiting for you. [*He hangs up.*]

BÉRENGER: There was a kind of chaotic vacuum inside me, I was overcome with the immense sadness you feel at a moment of tragic and intolerable separation. The old gossips came out of their courtyards and split my eardrums with their screeching voices, the dogs barked, and I felt lost among all those people, all those *things*...

ARCHITECT: She's a stupid girl. [*He stands up.*] Still, it's her own affair. There are thousands more after her job... [*He sits down again.*]... and a life without peril.

BÉRENGER: And since then, it's been perpetual November, perpetual twilight, twilight in the morning, twilight at midnight, twilight at noon. The light of dawn has gone! And to think we call this civilization!

ARCHITECT: We're still waiting!

BÉRENGER: It's only the memory of what happened that's helped me to go on living in this grey city.

ARCHITECT: [*to* BÉRENGER] You got over it, just the same, this... melancholy?

BÉRENGER: Not entirely. But I promised myself I wouldn't forget. I told myself that on the days I felt sad and nervous, depressed and anxious, I would always remember that glorious moment. It would help me to bear everything, give me a reason for living, and be a comfort to me. For years I felt sure...

ARCHITECT: Sure of what?

ᴇNGER: Sure I'd been sure... but the memory wasn't strong nough to stand the test of time.

ᴄHITECT: But it seems to me...

ᴇʀᴇNGER: You're wrong, Monsieur. The memory I've kept is nothing now but the memory of a memory, like a thought grown foreign to me, like a tale told by another, a faded picture whose brightness I could no longer restore. The water in the well had dried up and I was dying of thirst... But *you* must understand me perfectly, this light is in *you* too, it's the same as mine, because [*A broad gesture taking in empty space.*] you have obviously recreated and materialized it. This radiant district must have sprung from you... You've given me back that forgotten light... almost. I'm terribly grateful to you. In my name and in the name of all who live here, I thank you.

ARCHITECT: Why yes, of course.

BÉRENGER: And with you, it's not the unreal product of an over-
heated imagination. These are real houses and stones and bricks
and cement. [*Touching empty space.*] It's concrete, solid,
tangible. Yours is the right system, your methods are rational.
[*He still appears to be feeling the walls.*]

ARCHITECT: [*also feeling the invisible walls, after leaving his corner*]
It's brick, yes, and good brick too. Cement, the best quality.

BÉRENGER: [*as before*] No, no, it's not just a dream, this time.

ARCHITECT: [*still feeling the invisible walls, then stopping with a
sigh*] Perhaps it would have been better if it had been a dream.
It's all the same to me. I'm a civil servant. But for a lot of other
people, reality, unlike dreams, can turn into a nightmare...

BÉRENGER: [*who also stops feeling the invisible walls, greatly surprised*] Why, what do you mean?

[*The* ARCHITECT *returns to his files.*]

In any case, I'm glad my memory is real and I can feel it with
my fingers. I'm as young as I was a hundred years ago. I can
fall in love again... [*Calling to the wings on the right:*] Mademoiselle, oh, Mademoiselle, will you marry me?

[*Just as he finishes this last sentence,* DANY *comes in from the right.
She is the* ARCHITECT's *blonde secretary.*]

ARCHITECT: [*to* DANY *as she enters*] Oh, so there you are! I've
got something to say to you!

DANY: [*To* BÉRENGER] Do give me time to think it over!

ARCHITECT: [*to* BÉRENGER] My secretary, Mademoiselle Dany.
[*To* DANY:] Monsieur Bérenger.

DANY: [*absentmindedly, rather nervously, to* BÉRENGER] Pleased to
meet you.

ARCHITECT: [*to* DANY] In the Civil Service we don't like people
to be late, Mademoiselle, or impulsive either.

BÉRENGER: [*to* DANY, *who goes and sets her typewriter on the table,
and fetches a chair from the wings on the left*] Mademoiselle Dany,
what a lovely name! Have you thought it over yet? The

answer's 'Yes' isn't it?

DANY: [*to the* ARCHITECT] I've made up my mind to leave, Monsieur, I need a holiday, I'm tired.

ARCHITECT: [*sweetly*] If that's all it is, you should have told me. We can arrange something. Would you like three days off?

BÉRENGER: [*to* DANY] It is Yes, isn't it? Oh, you're so beautiful.

DANY: [*to* ARCHITECT] I must have a much longer rest than that.

ARCHITECT: [*to* DANY] I'll apply to the Departmental Board, I can get you a week—half-pay.

DANY: [*to* ARCHITECT] I need a permanent rest.

BÉRENGER: [*to* DANY] I like fair girls, with glowing faces, bright eyes and long legs!

ARCHITECT: Permanent? I see!...

DANY: [*to* ARCHITECT] I simply must do some different work. I can't stand the situation any longer.

ARCHITECT: Oh, so that's it.

DANY: [*to* ARCHITECT] Yes, Monsieur.

BÉRENGER: [*to* DANY, *enthusiastically*] You said Yes! Oh, Mademoiselle Dany...

ARCHITECT: [*to* BÉRENGER] She's talking to me, not to you.

DANY: [*to* ARCHITECT] I always hoped things might change, but they're still the same. I don't see any chance of improvement.

ARCHITECT: Now think, I'm telling you again, think carefully! If you no longer belong to our organization, the Civil Service can no longer take you under its wing. Do you realize? Are you fully aware of the dangers that lie in wait?

DANY: Yes, Monsieur, no one's in a better position than I am to know about that.

ARCHITECT: You're willing to take the risk?

DANY: [*to* ARCHITECT] I am, yes, Monsieur.

BÉRENGER: [*to* DANY] Say Yes to me too. You say it so nicely.

ARCHITECT: [*to* DANY] Then I refuse all responsibility. You have been warned.

DANY: [*to* ARCHITECT] I'm not deaf, I understand, you needn't repeat yourself!

BÉRENGER: [*to* ARCHITECT] Isn't she sweet! Delightful. [*To* DANY:] Mademoiselle, Mademoiselle, we'll live here, in this district, in this villa! We'll be happy at last.

ARCHITECT: [*to* DANY] So you really won't change your mind? It's a crazy, headstrong thing to do!

DANY: [*to* ARCHITECT] No, Monsieur.

BÉRENGER: [*to* DANY] Oh, you didn't say No?

ARCHITECT: [*to* BÉRENGER] She said No to *me*.

BÉRENGER: Ah, that's all right, then!

DANY: [*to* ARCHITECT] I hate the Civil Service, I detest your beautiful district, I can't stand any more, I can't bear it!

ARCHITECT: [*to* DANY] It's not *my* district.

BÉRENGER: [*to* DANY, *who is not listening*] Give me your answer, beautiful Demoiselle, Dany the magnificent, Dany the sublime... May I call you Dany?

ARCHITECT: [*to* DANY] I can't stop you resigning, so you'd better go, but keep a sharp look-out. That's a piece of friendly advice I'm giving you, fatherly advice.

BÉRENGER: [*to* ARCHITECT] Were you decorated for your achievements in urban development? You should have been.

DANY: [*to* ARCHITECT] If you like, I'll finish typing the letters before I go.

BÉRENGER: [*to* ARCHITECT] If I'd been the Mayor, I'd have decorated you all right.

ARCHITECT: [*to* BÉRENGER] Thank you. [*To* DANY:] You needn't bother, thank you. I'll manage.

BÉRENGER: [*smelling imaginary flowers*] What a lovely smell! Are they lilies?

ARCHITECT: No, violets.

DANY: [*to* ARCHITECT] I was only trying to be helpful.

BÉRENGER: [*to* ARCHITECT] May I pick some for Dany?

ARCHITECT: If you like.

BÉRENGER: [*to* DANY] You don't know, my dear, dear Dany, dear fiancée, how I've longed for you.

DANY: If that's how you take it... [*In some irritation she briskly puts her things in order and picks up her typewriter.*]

BÉRENGER: [*to* DANY] We'll live in a wonderful flat, full of sunshine.

DANY: [*to* ARCHITECT] Surely you can understand I can't go on sharing the responsibility. It's too much for me.

ARCHITECT: The Civil Service is not responsible for that.

DANY: [*to* ARCHITECT] You ought to be able to realize...

ARCHITECT: [*to* DANY] It's not for you to give *me* advice. That's *my* business. But I warn you again; watch your step.

DANY: [*to* ARCHITECT] I'm not taking advice from you either. It's *my* business too.

ARCHITECT: [*to* DANY] All right, all right!

DANY: Au revoir, Monsieur.

ARCHITECT: Goodbye.

DANY: [*to* BÉRENGER] Au revoir, Monsieur.

BÉRENGER: [*running after* DANY, *who is making for the exit on the right*] Dany, Mademoiselle, don't go before you've given me an answer... At least, please take these violets.

[DANY *goes out.* BÉRENGER *stands near the exit, his arms hanging loosely.*]

Oh... [*To* ARCHITECT:] You understand the human heart; when a woman doesn't answer Yes or No, it means Yes, doesn't it? [*Calling towards the wings on the right:*] You'll be my inspiration, my Muse. I'll really *work*. [*While a slight echo is heard repeating the previous words,* BÉRENGER *moves two paces nearer the* ARCHITECT *and indicates the empty space:*] I'll not give up. I'm settling down here with Dany. I'll buy that white house, with the trees and grass all round, the one that looks abandoned by the builders... I haven't much money, you'll let me pay in instalments.

ARCHITECT: If you really want to! If you're not going to change your mind.

BÉRENGER: I'm determined. Why should I change my mind? With your permission, I want to be a citizen of the radiant city. I'll move in tomorrow, even if the house isn't quite ready yet.

ARCHITECT: [*looking at his watch*] Twenty-five to one.

[*Suddenly, there is the noise of a stone falling a few paces from* BÉRENGER, *between him and the* ARCHITECT.]

BÉRENGER: Oh! [*Starts back a little.*] A stone!

ARCHITECT: [*impassively, without surprise*] Yes, a stone!

BÉRENGER: [*leans forward and picks up the stone, then straightens up and inspects it in his hand*] It *is* a stone!

ARCHITECT: Haven't you seen one before?

BÉRENGER: Yes... of course... What? They're throwing stones at us?

ARCHITECT: *A* stone, just one stone, not stones!

BÉRENGER: I understand, they threw a stone at us.

ARCHITECT: Don't worry. They're not really going to stone you. It didn't touch you, did it?

BÉRENGER: It could have.

ARCHITECT: No, no, of course it couldn't. It *cannot* touch you. It's only teasing.

BÉRENGER: Oh, I see!... If it's only teasing, then I suppose I can take a joke! [*He drops the stone.*] I don't easily take offence. Especially in these surroundings it takes a lot to upset you. She will write to me, won't she? [*He casts a rather anxious look about him.*] It's so restful here, and intended to be that way. Almost a little too restful, don't you think? Why can't you see a single soul in the streets? We really are the only people out!... Oh yes, of course, it must be because it's lunchtime. Everyone's eating. But why can't we hear any laughter at table, any clinking of glasses? Not a sound, not a whisper, not a voice singing. And all the windows are shut! [*He looks round the empty stage, surprised.*] I didn't notice before. It would be understandable in a dream, but not when it's real.

ARCHITECT: I'd have thought it was obvious.

[*The sound of broken window-panes is heard.*]

BÉRENGER: What's happening now?

ARCHITECT: [*taking the telephone from his pocket again; to* BÉRENGER]

That's easy. You don't know what it is? A window's been smashed. It must have been broken by a stone.

[*The noise of another window being smashed;* BÉRENGER *starts back more violently. On the telephone:*] Two broken windows.

BÉRENGER: What's it all about? A joke, I suppose? Two jokes! [*Another stone knocks his hat off; he picks the hat up quickly and puts it back on his head.*] Three jokes!

ARCHITECT: [*putting the telephone back in his pocket and frowning*] Now listen, Monsieur. You and I are not business men. We're civil servants, bureaucrats. So I must tell you officially, bureaucratically, that the house that looked abandoned really has been abandoned by the builders. The police have suspended all construction work. I knew this before, but I've just had it confirmed by phone.

BÉRENGER: What?... Why?

ARCHITECT: It's an unnecessary step to take anyway. You're the only one wants to buy any property now. I don't suppose you know what it's all about...

BÉRENGER: What *is* it all about?

ARCHITECT: Actually, the people who live in this district want to leave it...

BÉRENGER: Leave the radiant district? The people want to leave it...

ARCHITECT: Yes. They've no other homes to go to. Otherwise they'd *all* have packed their bags. Perhaps too they make it a point of honour not to run away. They'd rather stay and hide in their beautiful flats. They only come out when they really have to, in groups of ten or fifteen at a time. And even that doesn't make for safety...

BÉRENGER: What's so dangerous? Just another joke, isn't it! Why are you looking so serious? You're clouding the whole place over! You're trying to frighten me!...

ARCHITECT: [*solemnly*] A civil servant doesn't make jokes.

BÉRENGER: [*terribly upset*] What are you talking about? You're really upsetting me! It's you who just threw that stone at me...

Morally speaking of course! Oh dear, and I already felt I'd taken root in these surroundings! Now all the brilliance they offer is dead, and they're nothing more than an empty frame... I feel shut out!

ARCHITECT: I'm very sorry. Steady there!

BÉRENGER: I've a horrible premonition.

ARCHITECT: I'm so sorry, so sorry.

[During the previous dialogue and what comes after, the acting should never lose a touch of irony, which should especially balance the pathetic moments.]

BÉRENGER: I can feel the darkness spreading inside me again!

ARCHITECT: [dryly] Sorry, very sorry, so sorry.

BÉRENGER: Please, you must explain. I was so hoping to spend a nice day!... I was so happy a few moments ago.

ARCHITECT: [pointing] You see this ornamental pool?

[The pool reappears, clearly this time.]

BÉRENGER: It's the same one we went past already, just now!

ARCHITECT: I wanted to show you then... You preferred the hawthorns... [He points to the pool again :] It's there in the pool every day, that two or three people are found, drowned.

BÉRENGER: Drowned?

ARCHITECT: Come and look if you don't believe me. Come on, come closer!

BÉRENGER: [accompanying the ARCHITECT to the place indicated or right to the front of the stage, while the objects referred to appear as they are mentioned] Go nearer!

ARCHITECT: Look! What do you see?

BÉRENGER: Oh, Heavens!

ARCHITECT: Come on now, no fainting, be a man!

BÉRENGER: [with an effort] I can see... it's not true... Yes, I can see, on the water, the dead body of a little boy, floating in his hoop... a little chap of five or six... He's clutching the stick in his hand... Next to him the bloated corpse of an officer in the engineers in full uniform...

ARCHITECT: There are even three today. [Pointing] Over there!

BÉRENGER: It's a plant in the water!

ARCHITECT: Look again.

BÉRENGER: Good God!... Yes... I see! It's red hair streaming up from the bottom, stuck to the marble edge of the pool. How horrible! It must be a woman.

ARCHITECT: [*shrugging his shoulders*] Obviously. And one's a man. And the other's a child. *We* don't know any more than that, either.

BÉRENGER: Perhaps it's the boy's mother! Poor devils! Why didn't you tell me before?

ARCHITECT: But I told you! You were always stopping me, always admiring the beautiful surroundings.

BÉRENGER: Poor devils! [*Violently*] Who did it?

ARCHITECT: The murderer, the thug. Always the same elusive character.

BÉRENGER: But our lives are in danger! Let's go! [*He takes to his heels, runs a few yards across the stage and comes back to the* ARCHITECT, *who has not moved.*] Let's go! [*He takes flight again, but runs round and round the* ARCHITECT, *who takes out a cigarette and lights it. A shot is heard.*] He's shooting!

ARCHITECT: Don't be afraid. You're in no danger while you're with me.

BÉRENGER: What about that shot? Oh, no... no... You don't make me feel safer! [*He moves restlessly about and starts shaking.*]

ARCHITECT: It's only a game... Yes... Just now, it's only a game, to tease you! I'm the City Architect, a municipal civil servant, he doesn't attack the Civil Service. When I've retired, it'll be different, but for the moment...

BÉRENGER: Let's go. Get away from here. I can't wait to leave your beautiful district...

ARCHITECT: There you are, you see, you *have* changed your mind!

BÉRENGER: You mustn't hold it against me!

ARCHITECT: I don't care. I haven't been asked to detail volunteers and compel them to live here by choice. No one's obliged to live dangerously if he doesn't want that sort of life!... When the district's completely depopulated, they'll pull it down.

BÉRENGER: [*still hurrying round and round the* ARCHITECT] Depopulated?

ARCHITECT: People will decide to leave it in the end... or they'll all be killed. Oh, it'll take a bit of time...

BÉRENGER: Let's be off, quick! [*He goes round and round, faster and faster, with his head well down.*] The rich aren't always happy either, nor are the people who live in the residential districts... or the radiant ones... There are no radiant ones!... It's even worse than the other districts, in ours, the busy crowded ones!... Oh, Monsieur, I feel so upset about it. I feel shattered, stunned... My tiredness has come on again... There's no point in living! What's the good of it all, what's the good if it's only to bring us to this? Stop it, you must stop it, Superintendent.

ARCHITECT: Easy to say.

BÉRENGER: I suppose you *are* the police superintendent of the district too?

ARCHITECT: As a matter of fact, that is also one of my duties. It always is for special architects like me.

BÉRENGER: You're really hoping to arrest him before you retire?

ARCHITECT: [*coldly annoyed*] Naturally, we're doing all we can!... Look out, not that way, you'll get lost, you're always going round in circles, going back in your own tracks.

BÉRENGER: [*pointing quite close to him*] Ooh! Is that still the same pool?

ARCHITECT: One's enough for him.

BÉRENGER: Are those the same bodies as just now?

ARCHITECT: Three a day is a fair average, what more do you want?

BÉRENGER: Show me the way!... Let's go!...

ARCHITECT: [*taking him by the arm and guiding him*] This way.

BÉRENGER: And the day started so well! I shall always see those people drowned, I shall always have that picture in my mind.

ARCHITECT: That's what comes of being so emotional!

BÉRENGER: Never mind, it's better to know it all, better to know it all!...

[*The lighting changes. Now it is grey, and there are faint sounds of the street and the trams.*]

ARCHITECT: Here we are! We're not in the radiant city any more, we've gone through the gates. [*He lets go of* BÉRENGER'*s arm.*] We're on the outer boulevard. You see, over there? There's your tram. That's the stop.

BÉRENGER: Where?

ARCHITECT: There, where those people are waiting. It's the terminus. The tram starts off in the opposite direction and takes you straight to the other end of the town, takes you home!

[*You can just see, in perspective, some streets beneath a rainy sky, a few outlines and vague red lights. The designer should see that* very gradually *everything becomes more real. The change should be brought about by the lighting and with a very small number of props: shop-signs, and advertisements should slowly appear one after the other, but not more than three or four in all.*]

BÉRENGER: I'm frozen.

ARCHITECT: You *are.* You're shivering.

BÉRENGER: It's the shock.

ARCHITECT: It's the cold, too. [*He stretches out his hand to feel the raindrops.*] It's raining. Half sleet, half snow.

[BÉRENGER *nearly slips over.*]

Be careful, it's slippery, the pavement's wet. [*He holds him up.*]

BÉRENGER: Thank you.

ARCHITECT: Put your overcoat on or you'll catch cold.

BÉRENGER: Thank you. [*He puts his overcoat on and feverishly ties his scarf round his neck.*] Brr. Goodbye, Monsieur Superintendent!

ARCHITECT: You're not going straight back home! No one's expecting you... You've plenty of time to have a drink. Do you good. Go on, let yourself go, it's time for that drink before dinner. There's a bistro over there, near the tram-stop, just by the cemetery. They sell wreaths too.

BÉRENGER: You seem to be in a good mood again. I'm not.

ARCHITECT: I was never in a bad one.

BÉRENGER: In spite of...

ARCHITECT: [*interrupting him, as the sign of the bistro lights up*] Have to look life in the face, you know! [*He lays his hand on the handle of an imaginary door, beneath the sign of the bistro.*] Let's go in.

BÉRENGER: I don't feel much like it...

ARCHITECT: Go on in.

BÉRENGER: After you, Monsieur Superintendent.

ARCHITECT: No please, after you.

[*He pushes him. Noise of the bistro door. They come into the shop : this may be the same corner of the stage where the imaginary greenhouse and then the* ARCHITECT'*s imaginary office was before. They go and sit down on two chairs by the little table. They are doubtless next to the big windows of the shop. In the event of the table and chairs having been removed previously, a folding table can be brought on by the* OWNER OF THE BISTRO *when he appears. Two folding chairs could also be picked up from the floor of the stage by* BÉRENGER *and the* ARCHITECT].

Sit down, sit down. [*They sit down.*] You *do* look cheerful! Don't take it to heart so! If we thought about all the misfortunes of mankind we could never go on living. And we must live! All the time there are children with their throats cut, old men starving, mournful widows, orphan girls, people dying, justice miscarrying, houses collapsing on the tenants... mountains crumbling away... massacres, and floods, and dogs run over... That's how journalists earn their daily bread. Everything has it's bright side. In the end it's the bright side you've got to bear in mind.

BÉRENGER: Yes, Monsieur Superintendent, yes... but having been so close and seen with my own eyes... I can't remain indifferent. *You* may have got used to it, you with your two professions.

ARCHITECT: [*slapping* BÉRENGER *on the shoulder*] You're too impressionable, I've told you before. Got to face facts. Come on now, pull yourself together, where's your will-power! [*He slaps him on the shoulder again.* BÉRENGER *nearly falls off the chair.*] You seem fit enough, whatever you say, although you look so sorry for yourself. You're healthy in mind and body!

BÉRENGER: I don't say I'm not. What I'm suffering from doesn't show, it's theoretical, spiritual.

ARCHITECT: I see.

BÉRENGER: You're being sarcastic.

ARCHITECT: I wouldn't dream of it. I've seen quite a few cases like yours among my patients.

BÉRENGER: Yes, of course, you're a doctor too.

ARCHITECT: When I've a minute to spare, I do a little general medicine, I took over from a psychoanalyst and was assistant to a surgeon in my youth, I've also studied sociology... Come on now, let's try and cheer you up. [*Clapping his hands.*] Monsieur!

BÉRENGER: I'm not as versatile as you.

[*From the wings on the left can be heard the voice of a* CLOCHARD.]

CLOCHARD: [*off*] When I left the Merchant Navy
   I got spliced to young Octavie!

VOICE OF OWNER: [*loud voice*] Be right with you, Monsieur Superintendent! [*Change of tone; still in the wings to the* CLOCHARD:]
Get out of here, go and get drunk somewhere else!

CLOCHARD: [*off. Thick voice*] What's the point? I'm drunk already!

[*The drunken* CLOCHARD *appears from the left, brutally pushed on stage by the* OWNER, *a dark fat character with great hairy arms.*]
I got drunk at your place, paid for it, shouldn't have given me the stuff!

OWNER: I told you to get out! [*To* ARCHITECT:] Glad to see you, Monsieur Superintendent.

ARCHITECT: [*to* BÉRENGER] You see... We aren't in the beautiful district any more, people's manners aren't so good to start with.

CLOCHARD: [*still being pushed by the* OWNER] What you up to?

BÉRENGER: [*to* ARCHITECT] So I see!

OWNER: [*to* CLOCHARD] Off you go... Look, the Superintendent's over there!

CLOCHARD: Not doing anyone any harm! [*While still being pushed he stumbles and falls full length, but picks himself up without protest.*]

ARCHITECT: [*to* OWNER] Two Beaujolais.

OWNER: Right, sir. I've got some of the real stuff for you. [*To the* CLOCHARD, *who is getting up :*] Get out and close the door behind you, don't let me catch you again. [*He goes off left.*]

ARCHITECT: [*to* BÉRENGER] Still feeling depressed?

BÉRENGER: [*with a helpless gesture to the empty air*] What do you expect!

[*The* OWNER *appears with two glasses of wine, while the* CLOCHARD *closes the door in mime and leaves the shop.*]

OWNER: Your Beaujolais, Monsieur Superintendent!

CLOCHARD: [*going off right, still staggering and singing*]:
When I left the Merchant Navy
I got spliced to young Octavie!

OWNER: [*to* ARCHITECT] You want a snack, Monsieur Superintendent?

ARCHITECT: Give us a couple of sandwiches.

OWNER: I've got a first-class rabbit pâté, pure pork!

[BÉRENGER *shows signs of wanting to pay.*]

ARCHITECT: [*laying his hand on* BÉRENGER'S *arm, to stop him*] No, no, not you! This is on me! [*To* OWNER:] This is on me!

OWNER: Right, Monsieur Superintendent! [*He goes off left. The* ARCHITECT *takes a sip of the wine.* BÉRENGER *does not touch his.*]

BÉRENGER: [*after a short pause*] If only you had a description of him.

ARCHITECT: But we have. At least we know how he looks to his victims. Pictures of him have been stuck on all the walls. We've done our best.

BÉRENGER: How did you get them?

ARCHITECT: They were found on the bodies of the drowned. Some of the people have been brought back to life for a moment and they even provided other information. We know how he sets about it too. So does everyone in the district.

BÉRENGER: But why aren't they more careful? They only have to avoid him.

ARCHITECT: It's not so simple. I tell you, every evening there are always two or three who fall into the trap. But *he* never gets caught.

BÉRENGER: It's beyond me.

[*The* ARCHITECT *takes another sip of wine. The* OWNER *brings the two sandwiches and goes out.*]

I'm amazed... but you, Monsieur Superintendent, seem almost amused by the whole business.

ARCHITECT: I can't help it. After all, it is quite interesting. You see, it's there... Look through the window. [*He pretends to be pulling an imaginary curtain aside; or perhaps a real curtain could have appeared; he points to the left:*] You see... it's there, at the tram-stop, he strikes. When the people get off to go home, they walk to the gates, because they're not allowed to use their private cars outside the radiant city, and that's when he comes to meet them, disguised as a beggar. He starts whining, as they all do, asks for alms and tries to rouse their pity. The usual thing: just out of hospital, no work, looking for a job, nowhere to spend the night. That's not what does the trick, that's only a start. He's feeling his way, he chooses a likely prey, gets into converstation, hangs on and won't be shaken off. He offers to sell a few small articles he takes from his basket, artificial flowers, birds, old-style nightcaps, maps... postcards... American cigarettes, obscene little drawings, all sorts of objects. Generally his offerings are refused, his client hurries on, no time to spare. Still haggling, they both arrive at the pool you already know. Then, suddenly, the big moment arrives; he suggests showing the Colonel's photo. This is irresistible.

As it's getting rather dark, the client leans forward to get a better view. But now it's too late. A close scrutiny of the picture is a disturbing experience. Taking advantage of this he gives a push and the victim falls in the pool and is drowned. The blow is struck, all he has to do now is to look for fresh prey.

BÉRENGER: What's so extraordinary is that people know and still let themselves be taken in.

ARCHITECT: That's the trick, you know. He's never been caught in the act.

BÉRENGER: Incredible! Incredible!

ARCHITECT: And yet it's true! [*He bites into his sandwich.*] You're not drinking? Or eating?

[*Noise of a tram arriving at the stop.* BÉRENGER *instinctively raises his head quickly and goes to pull the curtain aside to look through the window in the direction of the tram-stop.*]

That's the tram arriving.

BÉRENGER: Groups of people are getting out!

ARCHITECT: Of course. The people who live in the district. Going home.

BÉRENGER: I can't see any beggars.

ARCHITECT: You won't. He'll not show himself. He knows we're here.

BÉRENGER: [*turning his back to the window and coming back to the* ARCHITECT, *who also has his back to the window, to sit down again*] Perhaps it would be a good idea if you had a plainclothes inspector permanently on duty at this spot.

ARCHITECT: You want to teach me how to do my job? Technically, it's not possible. Our inspectors are overworked, they've got other things to do. Besides, *they'd* want to see the Colonel's photo too. There have been five of them drowned already like that. Ah... If we could prove his identity, we'd know where to find him!

[*Suddenly a cry is heard, and the heavy sound of a body falling into water.*]

BÉRENGER: [*jumping to his feet*] Did you hear that?

ARCHITECT: [*still seated, biting his sandwich*] He's struck again. You see how easy it is to stop him. As soon as your back's turned, a second's inattention, and there you are... One second, that's all he needs.

BÉRENGER: It's terrible, terrible!

[*Muttering voices are heard, alarmed voices coming from the wings, the sound of footsteps, and a police car's screaming brakes.*] [*Wringing his hands:*] Do something, do something... Intervene, move!...

ARCHITECT: [*calmly, still sitting, sandwich in hand, after another sip*] It's far too late now. Once again, he's taken us unawares...

BÉRENGER: Perhaps it's just a big stone he's thrown in the water... to tease us!

ARCHITECT: That *would* surprise me. And the cry?

[*The* OWNER *comes in from the left.*]

Now we'll know everything, anyway. Here comes our informer.

OWNER: It's the girl, the blonde one...

BÉRENGER: Dany? Mademoiselle Dany? It can't be!

ARCHITECT: It is. Why not? She's my secretary, my ex-secretary. And I gave her fair warning not to leave my staff. She was safe there.

BÉRENGER: Oh God, God, God!

ARCHITECT: She was in the Civil Service! He doesn't attack the Service! But no, she wanted her 'liberty'! That'll teach her. She's found it now, her liberty. I was expecting this...

BÉRENGER: Oh God, oh God! Poor girl... She didn't have time to say Yes to me!

ARCHITECT: [*continuing*] I was even sure it would happen! Unless she'd gone right out of the district as soon as she left the Service.

BÉRENGER: Mademoiselle Dany! Mademoiselle Dany! Mademoiselle Dany! [*Lamentation*]

ARCHITECT: [*continuing*] Ah! People are so determined to have

their own way, and above all the victims are so determined
to revisit the scene of the crime! That's how they get caught!

BÉRENGER: [*almost sobbing*] Ooh! Monsieur Superintendent.
Monsieur Superintendent, it's Mademoiselle Dany, Mademoiselle Dany! [*He crumples up on his chair, in a state of collapse.*]

ARCHITECT: [*to* OWNER] Make the usual report, routine, you
know. [*He takes his telephone from his pocket:*] Hullo?...
Hullo?... Another one... It's a young woman... Dany...
the one who worked with us... No one caught in the act...
Just suspicions... the same ones... yes!... One moment!
[*He lays the telephone on the table.*]

BÉRENGER: [*suddenly jumps to his feet*] We can't, we mustn't let
things go on like this! It's got to stop! It's got to stop!

ARCHITECT: Control yourself. We've all got to die. Let the investigation take its usual course!

BÉRENGER: [*runs off, slamming the imaginary shop-door with a bang,
which is however heard*] It can't go on! We must *do* something!
We must, we must, we must! [*He goes off right.*]

OWNER: Au revoir, Monsieur! [*To* ARCHITECT:] He might say
goodbye!

ARCHITECT: [*still seated, he watches him go, like the* OWNER, *who is
standing with his arms folded or his hands on his hips; then, as soon
as* BÉRENGER *has gone, the* ARCHITECT *tosses off the rest of his wine
and pointing to* BÉRENGER'*s full glass says to the* OWNER] Drink it!
Eat the sandwich too!

[*The* OWNER *sits down in* BÉRENGER'*s place. On the telephone:*]
Hullo! No evidence! Close the case! Crime unsolved! [*He
puts the telephone back in his pocket.*]

OWNER: [*drinking*] Santé! [*He bites into the sandwich.*]

CURTAIN

ACT TWO

BÉRENGER'*s room. Dark and low-ceilinged, but lighter in the*

centre opposite the window. Near this long low window a chest.
To the right of it a gloomy recess; in this dark patch an armchair,
French Regency style, rather knocked about, in which, as the
curtain rises, ÉDOUARD *is sitting, silently. At the beginning of the*
Act he is not visible, nor is the armchair, because of the darkness
that reigns in BÉRENGER'S *ground-floor room.*
In the centre, in the brightest part, a large table in front of the
window, with notebooks and papers, a book, an inkstand and
a fancy penholder like a goose-quill.
A red worn-out armchair with one arm missing is a few feet to the
left of the table. In the left hand wall, more shadowy corners.
In the rest of the room you can make out in the half-light the
shapes of old pieces of furniture: an old writing-desk and a chest
of drawers with a threadbare tapestry on the wall above it; there
is also a chair and another red armchair. Next to the window, on
the right, a small table, a footstool and some shelves with a few
books. On the top an old gramophone.
At the front of the stage on the left is the door that gives on the
landing. Hanging from the ceiling an old chandelier: on the floor a
faded old carpet. On the right hand wall a mirror in a baroque
frame, which shines so little at the beginning of the act that it is
difficult to tell what the object is. Beneath the mirror an old
chimney-piece.
The curtains are not drawn, and through the window you can see
the street, the windows of the ground floor opposite and a part of
the front of a grocer's shop.
The decor of Act II is very much constructed, heavy, realistic and
ugly; it contrasts strongly with the lack of decor and the simple
lighting effects of Act I.
When the curtain rises the window lights the middle of the stage
and the central table with a pale yellowish light. The walls of the
house opposite are a dirty grey colour. Outside the weather is dull;
it is half snowing, half drizzling.
Sitting in the armchair in the darkest corner of BÉRENGER'S *room,*
to the right of the window, ÉDOUARD *is neither seen nor heard at*

the start of the Act. He will be seen later, after BÉRENGER's
*arrival: thin, very pale, feverish-looking, dressed in black, with a
mourning band round his right arm, a black felt hat, black overcoat, black shoes, white shirt with starched collar and black tie.
Now and again, but only after* BÉRENGER's *arrival,* ÉDOUARD
*will cough or clear his throat; from time to time he spits into a great
white handkerchief with a black border, which he fastidiously
returns to his pocket.*

A few moments before the rise of the curtain the VOICE OF THE
CONCIERGE *is already heard coming from the left, that is from the
landing in the block of flats.*

CONCIERGE: [*singing*] When it's cold it's not hot,
>   When it's hot, it's because it's cold!
Oh dear, you can sweep as much as you like, it's dirty all day
long, what with their snow and their coal dust.

[*Noise of a broom knocking against the door, then the* CONCIERGE
is heard singing again:]

>   When it's cold it's not hot,
>   When it's hot it's because it's cold,
>   When it's cold, it can't be hot!
>   When it's hot, how can it be cold?
>   What *is* it then when it's cold?
>   Cold as cold, and that's your lot!

[*During the song of the* CONCIERGE *there are sounds of ham-
mering from the floor above, a radio blaring and trucks and
motorcycles approaching and dying away; at one point too the
shouts of children in the schoolyard during recreation: all this must
be slightly distorted, caricatured, so the cries of the schoolchildren
sound like dogs yapping; the idea is to make the uproar sound
worse, but in a way that is partly unpleasant and partly comic.*]

MAN'S VOICE: [*preceded by the noise of footsteps on the stairs and the
barking of a dog*] Good morning, Madame la Concierge.

VOICE OF CONCIERGE: Good morning, Monsieur Lelard! You're
late leaving this morning!

MAN's VOICE: I've had some work to do at home. I've been asleep. Feel better now. Going to post my letters.

VOICE OF CONCIERGE: You've a funny sort of job! Always working with papers! Writing all those letters, you must have to think all the time.

MAN's VOICE: It's not writing them that makes me think, but sending them off.

VOICE OF CONCIERGE: Yes, you've got to know who to send them to! Can't send them to *anyone*! Mustn't send them all to the same person, eh?

MAN's VOICE: Still, got to earn your living by the sweat of your brow, as the prophet says.

VOICE OF CONCIERGE: There's too much education these days, that's where things go wrong. Take sweeping, even that's not as easy as it used to be.

MAN's VOICE: Still, got to earn your living anyway, to pay your income tax.

VOICE OF CONCIERGE: Minister in Parliament, that's the best job. They don't *pay* taxes, they *collect* them.

MAN's VOICE: Even poor chaps like them have to earn their living, just like anyone else.

VOICE OF CONCIERGE: Yes, the rich are probably as poor as us, if there's any left these days.

MAN's VOICE: Ah yes, that's life.

VOICE OF CONCIERGE: Ah yes, afraid so!

MAN's VOICE: Ah yes, Madame.

VOICE OF CONCIERGE: Ah yes, Monsieur. It's a dog's life, and we all end up in the same place, a hole in the ground. That's where my husband is, forty years ago he died, and it's just like yesterday. [*A dog barks at the entrance.*] Shut up, Treasure. [*She must have clouted the dog with her broom, for you can hear his plaintive yelps. A door bangs.*] Go back in. [*To the* MAN *presumably:*] Oh well, goodbye Monsieur Lelard. Careful now, it's slippery outside, the pavements are all wet. Stinking weather!

MAN'S VOICE: I'll say it is. We were talking about life, Madame, we've got to be philosophical, you know!

VOICE OF CONCIERGE: Don't you talk to me about philosophers! I once got it into my head to be all stoical and go in for meditation. They never taught me anything, even that Marcus Aurelius. Doesn't really do any good. We know as much as he does. We all have to find our own way out. If there was one, but there isn't.

MAN'S VOICE: Ah yes!...

VOICE OF CONCIERGE: And do without feelings too, how are we meant to find room for them? They don't enter into our account of things. How would feelings help *me* sweep my staircase?

MAN'S VOICE: I haven't read the philosophers.

VOICE OF CONCIERGE: You haven't missed much. That's what comes of being educated like you. Philosophy's no good, except to put in a test-tube. May turn it a pretty colour, if you're lucky!

MAN'S VOICE: You shouldn't say that.

VOICE OF CONCIERGE: Philosophers! They're no good, except for a concierge like me.

MAN'S VOICE: You shouldn't say that, Madame, they're good for everyone.

VOICE OF CONCIERGE: I know what I'm talking about. You, you only read *good* books. I read the *philosophers*, because I've no money, the twopenny halfpenny philosophers. You, even if you've no money either, at least you can go to a library. You've got books to *choose* from... and what's the good of it, I ask you, you ought to know.

MAN'S VOICE: Philosophy, I say, is good for learning a philosophy of life!

VOICE OF CONCIERGE: I know all about the philosophy of life.

MAN'S VOICE: Good for you, Madame!

[*The broom knocks against the bottom of the door of* BÉRENGER'S *room.*]

VOICE OF CONCIERGE: Oh dear, oh dear, what a dirty house this is! It's the slush!

MAN'S VOICE: Plenty of that about. Oh well, I'm off this time, time's pressing on. Au revoir, Madame, keep smiling.

VOICE OF CONCIERGE: Thanks, Monsieur Lelard! [*The entrance door is banged violently.*] Oh, that's clever of him, silly fool will smash the door next, and *I'll* have to pay for it!

MAN'S VOICE: [*politely*] Did you say something, Madame?

VOICE OF CONCIERGE: [*more politely still, sweetly*] It's nothing, Monsieur Lelard, just chatting to myself, learning to talk! Makes the time go quicker!

[*The broom knocks against the bottom of the door of* BÉRENGER'S *room.*]

MAN'S VOICE: I quite thought you'd called me. Sorry.

VOICE OF CONCIERGE: Oh well, we all make mistakes, you know, Monsieur! Can't help it! No harm done. [*The front door is slammed violently again.*] He's gone this time. Tell him the same thing over and over again, he doesn't listen, him and his doors. Anybody'd think he was deaf! Likes to pretend he is, but he can hear all right! [*She sings:*]
     When it's cold, it's not hot.

[*Yapping of the dog, more muffled.*] Shut up, Treasure! Ah, call that a dog! You wait, I'll knock hell out of you! [*You can hear the door of the* CONCIERGE'S *room opening. The dog yelps. The same door bangs again.*]

ANOTHER MAN'S VOICE: [*after the sound of footsteps: slightly foreign accent*] Good morning, Madame la Concierge! Mademoiselle Colombine, she live here?

VOICE OF CONCIERGE: Can't say I know the name! There aren't any foreigners in the house. Only French people.

SECOND MAN: [*at the same time the upstairs radio is turned up very loud*] But they told me she live on fifth floor this block.

VOICE OF CONCIERGE: [*shouting to make herself heard*] Can't say I know the name, I tell you!

SECOND MAN'S VOICE: Please, Madame? [*Coming from the street on *the right, the lumbering sound of a truck, which suddenly brakes a few seconds later.*]

VOICE OF CONCIERGE: [*still shouting*] I tell you I don't know the name!

SECOND MAN'S VOICE: This Number Thirteen, Twelfth Street?

VOICE OF CONCIERGE: [*as before*] What Street?

SECOND MAN'S VOICE: [*louder*] This Number Thirteen...

VOICE OF CONCIERGE: [*yelling*] Don't shout so loud. I can hear you. Of course it's Number Thirteen, Twelfth Street. Can't you read? It's written up outside.

SECOND MAN'S VOICE: Then it must be here Mademoiselle Colombine lives!

TRUCK DRIVER VOICE: [*in the street*] Goddam learn to drive!

VOICE OF CONCIERGE: I know better than you.

CAR DRIVER'S VOICE: [*in the street*] Don't you goddam me!

VOICE OF CONCIERGE: Oh, I see, Mademoiselle Colombine, perhaps you mean Monsieur Lecher's concubine?

TRUCK DRIVER'S VOICE: [*in the street*] Bastard! Pimp!

SECOND MAN'S VOICE: Yes, that's it! Latcher!

VOICE OF CONCIERGE: Latcher, Lecher, it's all the same!

CAR DRIVER: [*in the street*] Can't you be polite, damn you?

VOICE OF CONCIERGE: So it's the redhead you're after! If she's the one, *she* lives here, I told you she did! You want to say what you mean! Take the elevator!

TRUCK DRIVER: [*in the street*] Son of a bitch!

CAR DRIVER: [*in the street*] Son of a bitch, yourself. [*Combined noises of the elevator going up, the radio, vehicles starting up again in the street, and then the splutter of a motorbike; for a split second you can see the motorcyclist through the window, passing in the street.*]

VOICE OF CONCIERGE: [*loudly*] Don't forget to shut the elevator door after you! [*To herself:*] They always forget, especially foreigners! [*She sings:*]

Of course you never get on, if you stay in the same places,
But do you really get on, if you're always changing places?

[*The door of the* CONCIERGE'*s flat is heard banging; she has gone in:
the dog yaps, her voice is more muffled:*] Yes, come on, my little
Treasure! Who hasn't had his lump of sugar? Here it is, here's
your sugar for you! [*Yapping*] Take that! [*The dog howls. In
the street two people can be seen through the window, coming on
from the left. Or possibly you just hear them talking, without seeing
them. Two* OLD MEN, *both decrepit, who hobble along painfully,
taking small steps and leaning on their sticks.*]

1ST O.M.: Terrible weather.

2ND O.M.: Terrible weather.

1ST O.M.: What you say?

2ND O.M.: Terrible weather. What *you* say?

1ST O.M.: I said: terrible weather.

2ND O.M.: Hang on to my arm, you might slip over.

1ST O.M.: Hang on to my arm, you might slip over.

2ND O.M.: I used to know some surprising people, very surprising.

CLOCHARD: [*appearing from the right on the pavement opposite: he is
singing*] When I left the Merchant Navy. [*He looks up at the
windows; some coins could be thrown down.*]

1ST O.M.: What did they do, these surprising people?

2ND O.M.: They surprised everyone!

CLOCHARD: I got spliced to young Octavie!

1ST O.M.: And where did these surprising people surprise?
[*The* CLOCHARD *does as before.*]

2ND O.M.: They surprised in society circles... everywhere they
surprised!

1ST O.M.: When did you know them, these surprising people?

CLOCHARD: [*as before*] When I left the Merchant Navy...
[*Still looking up at the windows of the upper floors, he makes off
left and disappears.*]

2ND O.M.: In the old days, the old days...

1ST O.M.: Do you still see them sometimes?

GROCER: [*coming out of the shop opposite, looking furious and gazing
up at a first-floor window*] Hey Madame!

2ND O.M.: Ah, my dear chap, there aren't any more nowadays, there aren't any more people who surprise... [*He is seen disappearing on the right, and you can hear:*] All that's gone. I only know two of them today... two surprising people...

GROCER: Hey Madame! Who do you take me for?

2ND O.M.: ...only two. One of them's retired and the other's deceased. [*The* IST OLD MAN *disappears too.*]

GROCER: [*as before*] I mean... who do you take me for?

VOICE OF CLOCHARD: [*singing*] The Captain of the tanker.

GROCER: [*as before*] Who do you take me for? I'm a shopkeeper, Madame, not a ragman! [*He goes furiously back to his shop.*]

VOICE OF CLOCHARD: [*moving away*]

Sent for me and said
If you want to get spliced to young Octavie
You'd better leave the Merchant Navy...

VOICE OF IST O.M.: [*moving away*] If there were any, you wouldn't notice. Surprising people don't surprise any more.

[*From the right the noise of recreation, which has already been heard quietly, redoubles in intensity. A schoolbell rings.*]

SCHOOLMASTER VOICE: Back to class! Back to class!

VOICE FROM THE STREET: We've fifty-eight delivery boys...

SCHOOLMASTER VOICE: Silence! [*Stamping of feet, shouting, noise of desks, etc. from the right.*] Silence! Silence!

VOICE FROM THE STREET: We've fifty-eight delivery boys!

[*The children in the school are silent.*]

SCHOOLMASTER VOICE: History lesson: the people's representatives came to the gates of the palace of Queen Marie Antoinette. And they shouted...

VOICE FROM THE STREET: We've fifty-eight delivery boys!

SCHOOLMASTER VOICE: They shouted: we haven't any more cake, Your Majesty, give us cake. There isn't any left, replied the Queen.

VOICE FROM THE STREET: We've fifty-eight delivery boys!

SCHOOLMASTER VOICE: There isn't any left, why don't you eat bread? Then the people grew angry and cut off the Queen's head. When the Queen saw that she'd lost her head, she was so upset she had a stroke. She couldn't get over it, whatever the doctors did. They weren't up to much at the time.

VOICE FROM THE STREET: We've fifty-eight delivery boys!

GRUFF VOICE: [*in the street*] We were seven thousand feet up, when suddenly I saw the wing of our plane coming off.

ANOTHER VOICE: [*thin and piping*] You don't say!

GRUFF VOICE: All right, I said to myself, we've still got one left. The passengers all piled up on one side of the plane to keep an even keel and it went flying on with one wing.

PIPING VOICE: Were you frightened?

GRUFF VOICE: You wait... suddenly the second wing fell off, and then the engines... and the propellers... and we were seven thousand feet up!

PIPING VOICE: Phew!

GRUFF VOICE: This time I thought we'd had it... [*The voice fades:*] Really had it, no way out... Well, do you know what saved us? Give you three guesses...

VOICE FROM THE STREET: Our fifty-eight delivery boys waste too much time urinating. Five times a day, on average, they interrupt their deliveries to satisfy a personal need. The time is not deducted from their wages. They take advantage of this, so they've got to be disciplined; they can make water in turn once a month for four and a half hours without interruption. That will save all the coming and going, which sends up our costs. After all, *camels* store up water.

1ST VOICE FROM BELOW: I went to catch my train, find my compartment and sit down in my reserved seat. The train was about to leave. Just at that minute in comes a gentlemen with the same seat and the same number as me. Out of politeness I gave my seat up and went and stood in the corridor. He hardly said thank you. I stood for two hours. In the end the train stopped at a station and the man got off. I went and sat down again, as the seat was mine in the first place. Again the train pulled out. An hour later it stopped at another station. And the

same man gets in again and wants his seat back! Legally had
he any right to it? It was my seat as well as his, but he claimed
second occupant's rights. We went to law about it. The judge
said the man was entitled to extra privileges, because he was a
blue-blooded critic*, and it was only modesty made him conceal his identity.

ANOTHER VOICE FROM BELOW: Who was the gentleman?

1ST VOICE: A national hero. Harold Hastings de Hobson.*

2ND VOICE: How did he manage to catch the same train again?

1ST VOICE: He took a short cutting.

VOICE FROM THE STREET: [*closer*] We've fifty-eight delivery boys.
    [*The two* OLD MEN *reappear in the street from the opposite
    direction, that is from the left.*]

1ST O.M.: I was invited to the wedding reception, of course...
    I wasn't very satisfied because all I like is *coq au vin*...

2ND O.M.: They didn't serve any *coq au vin*?

1ST O.M.: They *did*. But they didn't tell me it was *coq au vin*, so
    it didn't taste right.

2ND O.M.: Was it really *coq au vin*?

1ST O.M.: It WAS *coq au vin*, but as I didn't know, the whole
    meal was a farce.

2ND O.M.: I wish I'd been invited instead of you. I *like* my
    dishes *farcis*. [*They go off.*]

VOICE FROM THE STREET: We've fifty-eight delivery boys!

VOICE FROM RIGHT: We must seriously raise the question of our
    finances.

VOICE FROM ABOVE: Has the problem been considered by the
    delegation of deputy delegates?

VOICE FROM LEFT: We must seriously raise the question of *their*
    finances.

VOICE FROM ABOVE: We must seriously raise the question of the

---

* There is a pun here in the original on the name of the French writer and dra-
matic critic, Morvan Lebesque. Harold Hobson is a natural choice in England for
his well known admiration of French drama. American readers might like to pun
on the name of an American critic. Tr.

finances of our delivery boys.

ANOTHER VOICE FROM LEFT: No, the problem's been solved by the delegate of the deputy delegation.

VOICE FROM RIGHT: After all, production is production! The whole basis of the problem must be re-examined.

VOICE FROM LEFT: With our overseers and our underseers, our visionaries and our viewfinders, we shall form an organizational basis, a common funds committee.

VOICE FROM ABOVE: The seers and the underseers will form development committees for companies of contractors who will form special communities...

VOICE FROM RIGHT: There's the basic organizational principle and the organizational aspect of the superstructure.

VOICE FROM LEFT: What about our fifty-eight delivery boys?

VOICE FROM ABOVE: After work, we must organize leisure.

VOICE FROM BELOW: Concentrated leisure.

VOICE FROM LEFT: We must force the pace of leisure.

[*For some seconds thick fog darkens the stage: for a while the sounds from outside are muffled, all you can hear are vague snatches of dialogue.*]

VOICE OF CONCIERGE: [*after a banging of doors in the entrance*] Oh, when the fog's mixed with the factory smoke, you can't hear a word! [*Strident whistle from a factory hooter.*] Thank God for the hooters!

[*The fog has lifted, and on the other side of the street, you can see the* CLOCHARD *singing:*]

CLOCHARD: The second in command
          Sent for me and told me
          To marry my Octavie
          To marry my Octavie

[*The street sounds fade a little to facilitate the following scene.*]
          And I'd be as good a slavey
          As I'd once been in the Navy!

[*In the entrance a door is heard banging, while the* CLOCHARD, *still singing, looks up at the windows to catch the coins as they*

the glass it looks even worse.]

CONCIERGE: Monsieur Bérenger! I say, Monsieur Bérenger!

[*At the same time the* POSTMAN *is heard knocking at the door.*]

POSTMAN'S VOICE: Monsieur Bérenger! Telegram, Monsieur
Bérenger!

CONCIERGE: Monsieur Bérenger, there's a telegram for you...
fine state of affairs! [*Pause*] Where on earth can he be? He's
never at home! [*She raps on the window again, while the* POST-
MAN'S *knocking continues.*] Some people go for walks, got
nothing better to do, and we work our fingers to the bone!...
He's not there! [*She disappears: she must be near the entrance as
you can see her arm brandishing the broom out of one corner of the
window.*]

POSTMAN'S VOICE: If he's not in, he's not in. And you said he
never went out!

VOICE OF CONCIERGE: I didn't! Give me the telegram, I'll give it
to him! [*She disappears completely.*] I'm the one cleans his
windows!

POSTMAN'S VOICE: I'm not allowed to give it to you. I can't.

VOICE OF CONCIERGE: That's that, then, keep it.

POSTMAN'S VOICE: I'll give it you anyway. Here it is.

CONCIERGE: Now I've got to keep a look-out for him! Oh dear!
[*Pause. The noises have suddenly ceased, after the dying fall of
one last factory siren. Perhaps too the* CONCIERGE *has been heard
for one last time abusing her dog, which yelps as usual. A few
moments' silence. Then, passing along the street close to the window,* BÉRENGER *can be seen coming home. He has his overcoat on
and is clutching his hat in his right hand; he is swinging his arm
vigorously. He is walking with his head down. Once he has gone
past the window his steps are heard in the entrance. Then his key
turns in the lock.*]

VOICE OF CONCIERGE: [*very polite*] Why, it's you, Monsieur
Bérenger! Had a nice walk? You need some fresh air! Good
idea!

VOICE OF BÉRENGER: Good morning, Madame.

VOICE OF CONCIERGE: If you've been for a walk, you must have gone out. Didn't hear you go. Why didn't you tell me, I hadn't got a key to do your room. How could I know? *I* was ready. Telegram came for you.

[*Pause.* BÉRENGER *has stopped opening the door to read the telegram.*]

I hope it wasn't urgent? I read it, you see. It's the old clothes man. Wants you, urgently. Nothing to worry about.

[*The key is again heard grating in the lock. The door of* BÉRENGER'*s room opens quietly. The* CONCIERGE *is heard angrily muttering words that are indistinguishable, then she bangs the door of her flat and the dog squeals. The figure of* BÉRENGER *can be picked out in the dim room. He advances slowly towards the centre of the stage. The silence is complete. He turns the electric light switch and the stage lights up.* ÉDOUARD *is seen in his corner, with his hat on his head, wearing his overcoat, his briefcase at his feet, clearing his throat. Surprised, first by the coughing, then almost at the same time by the sight of* ÉDOUARD *himself,* BÉRENGER *gives a jump.*]

BÉRENGER: Oh, what are you doing here?

ÉDOUARD: [*in a thin, rather high-pitched voice, almost childlike, as he gets up coughing, picking up his briefcase, which he keeps in his hand*] Your place isn't very warm. [*He spits into his handkerchief. To do this he has laid his briefcase down again and taken his right hand out of his pocket; this arm is slightly withered and visibly shorter than the other. Then, carefully and methodically, he folds his handkerchief again, puts it back in his pocket and picks up his briefcase.*]

BÉRENGER: You startled me... I wasn't expecting you, what are you doing here?

ÉDOUARD: Waiting for you. [*Putting his deformed hand back in his pocket.*] How are you, Bérenger?

BÉRENGER: How did you get in?

ÉDOUARD: Through the door, of course. I opened it.

BÉRENGER: How? I had the keys with me!

ÉDOUARD: [*taking some keys from his pocket and showing them to* BÉRENGER] So did I! [*He puts the keys back in his pocket.*]

BÉRENGER: How did you get those keys? [*He lays his hat on the table.*]

ÉDOUARD: But... you let me have them for a while yourself, so I could come to your flat when I liked, and wait for you if you were out.

BÉRENGER: [*trying to remember*] *I* gave you those keys?... When?... I don't remember at all...

ÉDOUARD: You gave them to me all the same. How else could I have got them?

BÉRENGER: Édouard, it's amazing. Still, if you say...

ÉDOUARD: I promise you did... I'm sorry, Bérenger, I'll give them back if you don't want me to have them.

BÉRENGER: Oh... no, no... keep them, Édouard, keep them now you've got them. I'm sorry, I've a bad memory. I don't remember giving them to you.

ÉDOUARD: Well, you did... you remember, it was last year, I think. One Sunday when...

BÉRENGER: [*interrupting him*] The concierge didn't tell me you were waiting.

ÉDOUARD: I don't suppose she saw me, it's my fault, I didn't know I had to ask *her* if I could come to your flat. I thought you told me it wasn't necessary. But if you don't want me here...

BÉRENGER: That's not what I mean. I'm always pleased to see you.

ÉDOUARD: I don't want to be in the way.

BÉRENGER: You know it's not that at all.

ÉDOUARD: Thanks.

BÉRENGER: It's losing my memory that upsets me... [*To himself:*] Still, the concierge oughtn't to have left the flats this morning!... [*To* ÉDOUARD:] What's wrong with you? You're trembling.

ÉDOUARD: Yes, I am. I don't feel very well. I'm cold.

BÉRENGER: [*taking the sound hand in his, while* ÉDOUARD *stuffs the*

other in his pocket] You've still got a temperature. Coughing
and shivering. You're very pale and your eyes look feverish.

ÉDOUARD: My lungs... they're not improving... after all the
time I've had trouble with them...

BÉRENGER: And this building's so badly heated... [*Without taking
his overcoat off he goes and sinks morosely into an armchair near the
table, while* ÉDOUARD *remains standing.*] Do sit down, Édouard.

ÉDOUARD: Thank you, thanks very much. [*He sits down again on
the chest, cautiously setting his briefcase down near him, within
reach; he always seems to be keeping an eye on it. A moment's
silence. Then, noticing how gloomy* BÉRENGER *is looking and how
he is sighing:*] You seem so sad, you look worn out and
anxious...

BÉRENGER: [*to himself*] If that was all...

ÉDOUARD: *You're* not ill too, are you?... What's wrong? Has
something happened to you?

BÉRENGER: No, no... nothing at all. I'm like that... I'm not
cheerful by nature! Brrr... I'm cold too! [*He rubs his hands.*]

ÉDOUARD: I'm sure something's happened to you. You're more
nervous than usual, you're quite jumpy! Tell me about it, if
I'm not being indiscreet, it may help.

BÉRENGER: [*getting up and taking a few excited paces in the room*]
I've got good reason.

ÉDOUARD: What's wrong?

BÉRENGER: Oh, nothing, nothing and everything... everything...

ÉDOUARD: I should like a cup of tea, if I may...

BÉRENGER: [*suddenly adopting the serious tones of a tragic pronouncement*] My dear Édouard, I am shattered, in despair, inconsol-
able!

ÉDOUARD: [*without changing the tone of his voice*] Shattered by
what, in despair about what?

BÉRENGER: My fiancée has been murdered.

ÉDOUARD: I beg your pardon?

BÉRENGER: My fiancée has been murdered, do you hear?

ÉDOUARD: Your fiancée? Since when have you been engaged? You never told me you were thinking of getting married. Congratulations. My condolences too. Who was she?

BÉRENGER: To be honest... She wasn't exactly my fiancée... just a girl, a young girl who might have been.

ÉDOUARD: Ah yes?

BÉRENGER: A girl who was as beautiful as she was sweet and tender, pure as an angel. It's terrible. Too terrible.

ÉDOUARD: How long had you known her?

BÉRENGER: Always, perhaps. Since this morning anyway.

ÉDOUARD: Quite recently.

BÉRENGER: She was snatched from me... snatched away!... I... [*Gesture of the hand.*]

ÉDOUARD: It must be very hard... please, have you any tea?

BÉRENGER: I'm sorry, I wasn't thinking... With this tragedy... which has ruined my life! Yes, I've got some.

ÉDOUARD: I understand.

BÉRENGER: You couldn't understand.

ÉDOUARD: Oh yes I do.

BÉRENGER: I can't offer you tea... It's gone mouldy. I'd forgotten.

ÉDOUARD: Well, a glass of rum, please... I'm quite numb with cold...

[BÉRENGER *produces a bottle of rum, fills a small glass for* ÉDOUARD *and offers it to him while he says:*]

BÉRENGER: No one will ever take her place. My life is over. It's a wound that will never heal.

ÉDOUARD: You really have been wounded, poor old thing! [*Taking the glass of rum.*] Thanks! [*Still in a tone of indifference:*] Poor old thing!

BÉRENGER: And if that was all, if there was nothing but the murder of that unfortunate girl. Do you know the things that happen in the world, awful things, in our town, terrible things, you can't imagine... quite near here... comparatively close... morally speaking it's actually here! [*He strikes his*

breast. ÉDOUARD *has swallowed his rum, chokes and coughs.*]
Aren't you feeling well?

ÉDOUARD: It's nothing. It's so strong. [*He goes on coughing.*] I
must have swallowed it the wrong way.

BÉRENGER: [*gently hitting* ÉDOUARD *on the back to stop him coughing
and with the other hand taking his glass from him*] I thought I'd
found everything again, got it all back. [*To* ÉDOUARD:]
Stretch your head up and look at the ceiling. It'll stop. [*He goes
on:*] All I'd lost and all I hadn't lost, all that had been mine and
all that had never been mine...

ÉDOUARD: [*to* BÉRENGER, *who is still hitting him on the back*] Thank
you... that's enough... you're hurting... stop it, please.

BÉRENGER: [*going to place the little glass on the table while* ÉDOUARD
spits into his handkerchief] I thought the spring had returned for
ever... that I'd found the unfindable again, the dream, the key,
life... all that we've lost while we've gone on living.

ÉDOUARD: [*clearing his throat*] Yes. Of course.

BÉRENGER: All our muddled aspirations, all the things we
vaguely yearn for, from the depths of our being, without even
realizing... Oh, I thought I'd found everything... It was unexplored territory, magically beautiful.

ÉDOUARD: The girl was unexplored?...

BÉRENGER: No. The place. The girl, if you like, too!

ÉDOUARD: You're always searching for something out of the
way. Always aiming at something out of reach.

BÉRENGER: But I tell you it wasn't. This girl...

ÉDOUARD: The answer is that it *is,* and so is *she* now. Your pro-
blems are so complicated, so impractical. You've always been
dissatisfied, always refused to resign yourself.

BÉRENGER: That's because I'm suffocating... The air I have to
breathe is not the kind that's made for me.

ÉDOUARD: [*clearing his throat*] Think yourself lucky you don't
suffer from ill-health, you're not a sick man or an invalid.

BÉRENGER: [*without paying attention to what* ÉDOUARD *is saying*]
No. No. I've seen it, I thought I'd got somewhere... some-

where like a different universe. Yes, only beauty can make the spring flowers bloom eternally... everlasting flowers... but I'm sorry to say it was only a light that lied!... Once again everything fell into chaos... in a flash, in a flash! The same collapse, again and again... [*All this is said in a declamatory tone half way between sincerity and parody.*]

ÉDOUARD: You think only of yourself.

BÉRENGER: [*with slight irritation*] That's not true! Not true. I don't just think of myself. It's not for myself... not only for myself that I'm suffering right now, that I refuse to accept things! There comes a time when they're too horrible, and you can't...

ÉDOUARD: But that's the way of the world. Think of me, I'm a sick man... I've come to terms...

BÉRENGER: [*interrupting him*] It weighs on you, it weighs on you terribly, especially when you think you've seen... when you've thought you could hope... Oh!... then you can't go on... I'm tired... she's dead and they're dead and they'll all be killed... no one can stop it.

ÉDOUARD: But how did she die, this fiancée who perhaps wasn't? And who else is going to be killed, apart from the ones who usually get killed? What in fact are you talking about? Is it your dreams that are being killed? Generalities don't mean a thing.

BÉRENGER: I'm not talking through my hat...

EDOUARD: I'm sorry. I just can't understand you. I don't...

BÉRENGER: You're always wrapped up in your own little world. You never know anything. Where have you been living?

ÉDOUARD: Tell me about it then, give me some details.

BÉRENGER: It's absolutely incredible. There is in our town, though you're not aware of it, one beautiful district.

ÉDOUARD: Well?

BÉRENGER: Yes, there's one beautiful district. I've found it, I've just come from there. It's called the radiant city.

ÉDOUARD: Well, well!

BÉRENGER: In spite of it's name it's not a model neighbourhood, a happy or a perfect one. A criminal, an insatiable murderer, has turned it into hell.

ÉDOUARD: [coughing] I'm sorry, I can't help coughing!

BÉRENGER: You heard what I said?

ÉDOUARD: Perfectly: a murderer's turned it into hell.

BÉRENGER: He terrorizes and kills everyone. The district's getting deserted. It'll soon cease to exist.

ÉDOUARD: Oh yes, of course. I know! It must be that beggar who shows people the Colonel's photo and while they're looking at it throws them in the water! It's a trick to catch a fool. I thought you meant something else. If that's all it is...

BÉRENGER: [surprised] You knew? Knew all about it?

ÉDOUARD: Of course, I've known for a long time. I thought you were going to tell me something fresh, that there was another beautiful district.

BÉRENGER: Why did you never tell me anything about it?

ÉDOUARD: I didn't think there was any point. The whole town knows the story. I'm surprised even, you didn't know about it before, it's old news. Who doesn't know?... There didn't seem any need to tell you.

BÉRENGER: What? You mean everyone knows?

ÉDOUARD: That's what I said. You see, even I knew. It's a known fact, accepted and filed away. Even the schoolchildren know.

BÉRENGER: Even the schoolchildren?... Are you sure?

ÉDOUARD: Of course I am. [He clears his throat.]

BÉRENGER: How could children at school have found out?...

ÉDOUARD: Must have heard their parents talking... or grandparents... the schoolmaster too when he teaches them to read and write... Would you give me a little more rum?... Or perhaps not, it's so bad for me... I'd better go without. [Taking up his explanation again:] It's a pity, I agree.

BÉRENGER: A great pity! A terrible pity...

ÉDOUARD: What can we do about it?

BÉRENGER: Now it's my turn to say how very surprised I am to see you taking the matter so calmly... I always thought you were a sensitive, humane man.

ÉDOUARD: Perhaps I am.

BÉRENGER: But it's atrocious. Atrocious.

ÉDOUARD: I agree, I don't deny it.

BÉRENGER: Your indifference makes me sick! And I don't mind saying it to your face.

ÉDOUARD: Well you know... I...

BÉRENGER: [louder] Your indifference makes me sick!

ÉDOUARD: Don't forget... this is all new to you...

BÉRENGER: That's no excuse. You disappoint me, Édouard, frankly you disappoint me...

[ÉDOUARD has a violent bout of coughing; he spits into his hand-kerchief. BÉRENGER rushes up to ÉDOUARD, who nearly collapses.] You're really ill.

ÉDOUARD: A glass of water.

BÉRENGER: At once. I'll go and fetch one. [Supporting him.] Lie down here... on the couch...

ÉDOUARD: [between coughs] My briefcase... [BÉRENGER bends down to pick up ÉDOUARD's briefcase. In spite of his state of collapse, ÉDOUARD springs away from BÉRENGER to get hold of it himself.] No... let me... [He takes the briefcase from BÉRENGER's hand, then, still weak and supported by BÉRENGER, he reaches the couch, still clinging to the briefcase, and lies down with BÉRENGER's help, the briefcase at his side.]

BÉRENGER: You're soaked in perspiration...

ÉDOUARD: And frozen stiff as well, oh... this cough... it's awful...

BÉRENGER: You mustn't catch cold. Would you like a blanket?

ÉDOUARD: [shivering] Don't worry. It's nothing... it'll pass...

BÉRENGER: Settle down and rest.

ÉDOUARD: A glass of water.

BÉRENGER: At once... I'll fetch one.

[He hurries out to fetch a glass of water; you can hear the water running at the tap. Meanwhile ÉDOUARD raises himself on one

*elbow and stops coughing; with one anxious hand he checks the
lock of his enormous black briefcase, and then, somewhat relieved,
lies back again still coughing but not so loudly.* ÉDOUARD *must
not give the impression he is trying to deceive* BÉRENGER: *he is
really ill and he has other worries, his briefcase for example. He
wipes his brow.* BÉRENGER *returns with the glass of water.*]
Feel better?

ÉDOUARD: Thanks... [*He takes a sip of the water and* BÉRENGER
takes the glass from him.] I'm sorry, it's stupid of me. I'm all
right now.

BÉRENGER: I'm the one to say I'm sorry. I should have realized...
When you're ill yourself, when you're really a sick man, like
you, it's hard to get carried away by something else... I've not
been fair to you. After all, these terrible crimes in the radiant
city might be the cause of your illness. It must have affected
you, consciously or otherwise. Yes, I'm sure it's that that's
eating you away. I confess it's wrong to pass judgment too
lightly. You can't know people's hearts...

ÉDOUARD: [*getting up*] I'm freezing here...

BÉRENGER: Don't get up. I'll go and fetch a blanket.

ÉDOUARD: I'd rather we went for a little walk, for the fresh air.
I waited for you too long in this cold. I'm sure it's warmer
outside.

BÉRENGER: I'm so tired emotionally, so depressed. I'd rather
have gone to bed... Still, if that's what you really want, I
don't mind coming with you for a while!

ÉDOUARD: That's very charitable of you!

[ÉDOUARD *puts his black-ribboned felt hat on again, buttons his
dark overcoat and dusts it down, while* BÉRENGER *also puts his hat
on.* ÉDOUARD *picks up his heavy, bulging black briefcase.*
BÉRENGER *walks in front of him, turning his back to* ÉDOUARD,
*who, as he passes the table, lifts the briefcase over it. As he does so,
the briefcase opens and a part of the contents spill over the table:
at first, large photographs.*]
My briefcase!

BÉRENGER: [*turning round at the noise*] What the... ah!

[*They both make a quick movement to the briefcase at the same time.*]

ÉDOUARD: Leave it to me.

BÉRENGER: No, wait, I'll help you... [*He sees the photos.*] But... but... what have you got there?

[*He picks up one of the photos. ÉDOUARD tries, but without appearing too alarmed, to take it back from him, to hide the other photos falling from his briefcase with his hands, and push them back. BÉRENGER, who has held on to the photo, looks at it in spite of ÉDOUARD's opposition.*]

What is it?

ÉDOUARD: I expect it's a photo... some photos...

BÉRENGER: [*still holding the photo and inspecting it*] It's an army man, with a moustache and pips... A Colonel with his decorations, the Military Cross... [*He picks up other photos.*] More photos! And always the same face.

ÉDOUARD: [*also looking*] Yes... it is... it's a Colonel. [*He seems to be trying to lay his hands on the photos; meanwhile a lot of others keep on pouring over the table.*]

BÉRENGER: [*with authority*] Let me see! [*He dives into the briefcase, pulls out more photos and looks at one:*] Quite a nice face. With the kind of expression that makes you feel sorry for him. [*He takes out more photos. ÉDOUARD mops his brow.*] What *is* all this? Why, it's the photo, the famous photo of the Colonel! You had it in there... you never told me!

ÉDOUARD: I'm not always looking inside my briefcase!

BÉRENGER: But it *is* your briefcase all right, you're never without it.

ÉDOUARD: That's no reason...

BÉRENGER: Oh well... We'll take the opportunity, while we're at it, of having another look!

[BÉRENGER *sticks his hands into the huge black briefcase.* ÉDOUARD *does the same with his own too-white hand, whose twisted fingers are now very clearly visible.*]

More photos of the Colonel... and more... and more...
[*To* ÉDOUARD, *who is now taking things out of the briefcase too,
and looking astonished:*] What are these?

ÉDOUARD: You can see, they're artificial flowers.

BÉRENGER: There are masses of them!... And these... Look,
dirty pictures... [*He inspects them while* ÉDOUARD *goes and
looks over his shoulder:*] Nasty!

ÉDOUARD: Excuse me! [*He takes a step away.*]

BÉRENGER: [*discarding the obscene photos and continuing his inventory*]
Some sweets... money-boxes... [*They both take from the
briefcase a heterogeneous collection of articles.*]... children's
watches!... What are they doing here?

ÉDOUARD: [*stammering*] I... I don't know... I tell you...

BÉRENGER: What do you make of it?

ÉDOUARD: Nothing. What *can* you make of it?

BÉRENGER: [*still taking from the briefcase, which is like a conjurer's
bottomless bag, an amazing quantity of all types of objects, which
cover the whole surface of the table and even fall on the floor*]...
pins... and more pins... pen-holders... and these... and
these... what's that?

[*Much should be made of this scene: some of the objects can fly
away on their own, others can be thrown by* BÉRENGER *to the four
corners of the stage.*]

ÉDOUARD: That?... I don't know... I don't know at all... I
know nothing about it.

BÉRENGER: [*showing him a box*] What on earth's this?

ÉDOUARD: [*taking it in his hand*] Looks to me like a box, isn't it?

BÉRENGER: It is. A cardboard box. What's inside?

ÉDOUARD: I don't know. I don't know. I couldn't tell you.

BÉRENGER: Open it, go on, open it.

ÉDOUARD: [*almost indifferently*] If you like... [*He opens the box.*]
Nothing there! Oh yes, another box... [*He takes the small
box out.*]

BÉRENGER: And that box?

ÉDOUARD: See for yourself.

BÉRENGER: [*taking a third box from the second box*] Another box.
[*He looks into the third box.*] Inside there's another box. [*He
takes it out.*] And another inside that... [*He looks into the fourth
box.*] And another box inside that... and so on, ad infinitum!
Let's look again...

ÉDOUARD: Oh, if you want... But it'll stop us going for a
walk...

BÉRENGER: [*taking boxes out*] Box... after box... after box...
after box... after box...!

ÉDOUARD: Nothing but boxes...

BÉRENGER: [*taking a handful of cigarettes from the briefcase*] Cigarettes!

ÉDOUARD: Those belong to me! [*He starts collecting them, then
stops.*] Take one if you like...

BÉRENGER: Thanks, I don't smoke.

[ÉDOUARD *puts a handful of cigarettes in his pocket, while others
scatter over the table and fall on the floor.* BÉRENGER *stares at*
ÉDOUARD:]

These things belong to that monster! You had them in here!

ÉDOUARD: I didn't know, I didn't know about it! [*He goes to take
the briefcase back.*]

BÉRENGER: No, no. Empty it all! Go on!

ÉDOUARD: It makes me tired. You can do it yourself, but I don't
see what use it is. [*He passes him the gaping briefcase.*]

BÉRENGER: [*taking another box out*] It's only another box.

ÉDOUARD: I told you.

BÉRENGER: [*looking inside the empty briefcase*] There's nothing else.

ÉDOUARD: Can I put the things back? [*He begins picking up the
objects and putting them back in the briefcase, higgledy-piggledy.*]

BÉRENGER: The monster's things! Those are the monster's
things. It's extraordinary...

ÉDOUARD: [*as before*] Er... yes... there's no denying it... It's
true.

BÉRENGER: How do they come to be in your briefcase?

ÉDOUARD: Really... I... What do you expect me to say?...

You can't always explain everything... May I put them back?

BÉRENGER: I suppose so, yes, why not... What good could they be to us? [*He begins helping* ÉDOUARD *to fill the briefcase with the things he has taken out; then suddenly, as he is about to put back the last box, the one he did not examine, it opens and scatters over the table all kinds of documents as well as several dozen visiting cards. All this is in the style of a conjuring trick.*] Look, visiting cards.

ÉDOUARD: Yes. Visiting cards. So they are, how amazing... well I never!

BÉRENGER: [*inspecting the visiting cards*] That must be his name...

ÉDOUARD: Whose name?

BÉRENGER: The criminal's name, of course, the criminal's name!

ÉDOUARD: You think so?

BÉRENGER: It seems obvious to me.

ÉDOUARD: Really, why?

BÉRENGER: You can see for yourself, can't you! All the visiting cards have the same name. Look and read! [*He offers* ÉDOUARD *a few of the cards.*]

ÉDOUARD: [*reading the name written on the cards*] You're right... the same name... the same name on them all... It's quite true!

BÉRENGER: Ah... but... my dear Édouard, this is getting more and more peculiar, yes, [*Looking at him:*] more and more peculiar!

ÉDOUARD: You don't think...

BÉRENGER: [*taking the objects he mentions from the box*] And here's his address...

[ÉDOUARD *gently clears his throat, appearing slightly worried.*] And his identity card... a photo of him!... It's him all right... His own photo clipped to the Colonel's. [*With growing excitement:*] An address book... with the names and addresses... of all his victims!... We'll catch him, Édouard, we'll catch him!

ÉDOUARD: [*suddenly producing a neat little box; he could take it from his pocket or from one of his sleeves, like a conjuror, a folding box perhaps, which he flicks into shape as he shows it*] There's this too...

BÉRENGER: [*excited*] Quick, show me! [*He opens the little box and takes out more documents, which he lays out on the table.*] A note-book... [*He turns the pages:*] 'January 13th; today I shall kill... January 14th, yesterday evening I pushed an old woman with goldrimmed spectacles into the lake...' It's his private diary! [*He eagerly turns the pages, while* ÉDOUARD *appears very un-easy.*] 'January 23rd, nothing to kill today. January 25th, nothing to get my teeth into today either...'

ÉDOUARD: [*timidly*] Aren't we being indiscreet?

BÉRENGER: [*continuing*] 'January 26th, yesterday evening, just when I'd given up hope and was getting bored stiff, I managed to persuade two people to look at the Colonel's photo near the pool... February, tomorrow I think I'll be able to persuade a young blonde girl I've been after for some time to look at the photo...' Ah, that must be Dany, my poor fiancée...

ÉDOUARD: Seems quite likely.

BÉRENGER: [*still turning the pages*] Why look, Édouard, look, it's incredible...

ÉDOUARD: [*reading over* BÉRENGER'*s shoulder*] Criminology. Does that mean something?

BÉRENGER: It means it's an essay on crime... Now we've got his profession of faith, his credo... Here it is, you see. Have a look...

ÉDOUARD: [*as before: reading*] A detailed confession.

BÉRENGER: We've got him, the devil!

ÉDOUARD: [*as before: reading*] Future projects. Plan of campaign.

BÉRENGER: Dany, dear Dany, you'll be revenged. [*To* ÉDOUARD:] That's all the proof you need. We can have him arrested. Do you realize?

ÉDOUARD: [*stammering*] I didn't know... I didn't know...

BÉRENGER: So many human lives you could have saved.

ÉDOUARD: [*as before*] Yes... I see now. I feel awful about it. I didn't know. I never know what I've got in my briefcase, I never look inside.

BÉRENGER: Carelessness like that is unforgivable.

ÉDOUARD: It's true, forgive me, I'm so sorry.

BÉRENGER: After all, you don't mean to say these things got here all by themselves! You must have found them or been given them.

ÉDOUARD: [*coughing, mopping his brow and staggering*] I'm asham-ed... I can't explain... I don't understand... I...

BÉRENGER: Don't blush. I'm really sorry for you, old chap. Don't you realize you're partly responsible for Dany's murder... and for so many others?

EDOUARD: I'm sorry... I didn't know.

BÉRENGER: Let's see what's to be done now. [*Heavy sigh.*] I'm afraid it's no good regretting the past. Feeling sorry won't help.

ÉDOUARD: You're right, you're right, you're right. [*Then, making an effort of memory:*] Ah yes, I remember now. It's funny, well, no, I suppose it isn't funny. The criminal sent me his private diary, his notes and index cards a very long time ago, asking me to publish them in a literary journal. That was before the murders were committed.

BÉRENGER: And yet he notes down what he's just done... In detail... It's like a log-book.

ÉDOUARD: No, no. Just then, they were only projects... imaginary projects. I'd forgotten the whole affair. I don't think he really intended to carry out all those crimes. His imagination carried him away. It's only later he must have thought of putting his plans into operation. *I* took them all for idle dreams of no importance...

BÉRENGER: [*raising his arms to Heaven*] You're so *innocent!*

ÉDOUARD: [*continuing*] Something like a murder story, poetry or literature...

BÉRENGER: Literature can lead anywhere. Didn't you know that?

ÉDOUARD: We can't stop writers writing, or poets dreaming.

BÉRENGER: We ought to.

ÉDOUARD: I'm sorry I didn't give it more thought and see the connection between these documents and what's been happening...

[*While talking,* ÉDOUARD *and* BÉRENGER *start making an attempt to collect and restore to the briefcase the various objects scattered over the table, the floor and the other pieces of furniture.*]

BÉRENGER: [*putting things back in the briefcase*] And yet the connection is simply between the intention and the act, no more no less, it's clear as daylight...

ÉDOUARD: [*taking a big envelope from his pocket*] There's still this!

BÉRENGER: What is it? [*They open the envelope:*] Ah, it's a map, a plan... Those crosses on it, what do they mean?

ÉDOUARD: I think... why yes... they're the places where the murderer's meant to be...

BÉRENGER: [*inspecting the map, which is spread right out on the table*] And this? Nine fifteen, thirteen twenty-seven, fifteen forty-five, nineteen three...

ÉDOUARD: Probably his timetable. Fixed in advance. Place by place, hour by hour, minute by minute.

BÉRENGER: ... Twenty-three hours, nine minutes, two seconds...

ÉDOUARD: Second by second. He doesn't waste time. [*He says this with a mixture of admiration and indifference.*]

BÉRENGER: Let's not waste ours either. It's easy. We notify the police. Then they just have to pick him up. But we must hurry, the offices of the Prefecture close before nightfall. Then there's no one there. Between now and tomorrow he might alter his plan. Let's go quickly and see the Architect, the Superintendent.

ÉDOUARD: You're becoming quite a man of action. *I*...

BÉRENGER: [*continuing*] We'll show him the proof!

ÉDOUARD: [*rather weakly*] I'll come if you like.

BÉRENGER: [*excited*] Let's go, then. Not a moment to lose! We'll finish putting all this away.

[*They pile the objects as best they can into the huge briefcase, into their pockets and the lining of their hats.*]

Mustn't forget any of the documents... quick.

ÉDOUARD: [*still more weakly*] Yes, all right.

BÉRENGER: [*who has finished filling the briefcase, although there could still be several visiting cards and other objects on the floor and the table*] Quick, don't go to sleep, quick, quick... We need all the evidence... Now then, close it properly... lock it...

[ÉDOUARD, *who is rather harassed, tries in vain to lock the briefcase with a small key; he is interrupted by a fit of coughing.*]

Double lock it!... This is no time for coughing!

[ÉDOUARD *goes on trying and struggles not to cough*].

BÉRENGER: Oh God, how clumsy you are, you've no strength in your fingers. Put some life into it, come on!... Get a move on. Oh, give it to me! [*He takes the briefcase and the key from* ÉDOUARD.]

ÉDOUARD: I'm sorry, I'm not very good with my hands...

BÉRENGER: It's *your* briefcase and you don't even know how to close it... Let me have the key, can't you.

[*He snatches the key quite roughly from* ÉDOUARD, *who had taken it back from him.*]

ÉDOUARD: Take it then, here you are, there.

BÉRENGER: [*fastening the briefcase*] How do you think you can close it without a key? That's it. Keep it...

ÉDOUARD: Thank you.

BÉRENGER: Put it in your pocket or you'll lose it.

[ÉDOUARD *obeys.*]

That's the way. Let's go... [*He makes for the door, reluctantly followed by* ÉDOUARD, *and turns round to say:*] Don't leave the light on, switch it off, please.

[ÉDOUARD *turns back and goes to switch off. To do this he sets the briefcase down near the chair: he will leave it behind.*]

Come on... Come on... Hurry up... Hurry... [*They both go out quickly. You can hear the door opening and slammed shut, then their footsteps in the entrance. While the noises of the town become audible again, you can see the two in the street. In their haste they bump into the* CONCIERGE, *who can be seen in front of the window.* BÉRENGER *is pulling* ÉDOUARD *along by the hand.*]

CONCIERGE: [*who has just been knocked into, while* BÉRENGER *and* ÉDOUARD *disappear*] Of all the...! [*She goes on muttering, incomprehensibly.*]

CURTAIN

ACT THREE

A wide avenue in an outlying part of the town. At the back of the stage the view is masked by a raised pavement, a few yards wide, with a railing along the edge. Steps, also with a railing, leading up from street to pavement in full view of the audience. This short flight of stone steps should be like those in some of the old streets of Paris, such as the Rue Jean de Beauvais.

Later, at the back, there is a setting sun, large and red, but without brilliance: the light does not come from there.

So at the back of the stage it is as though there were a kind of wall, four and a half or six feet high, according to the height of the stage. In the second half of the act this wall will have to open to reveal a long street in perspective with some buildings in the distance: the buildings of the Prefecture.

To the right of the stage, in the foreground, a small bench.

Before the curtain rises you can hear shouts of 'Long live Mother Peep's geese! Long live Mother Peep's geese!'

The curtain goes up.

On the raised part of the stage, near the railing, is MOTHER PEEP, *a fat soul resembling the* CONCIERGE *of Act II. She is addressing a crowd which is out of sight: all you can see are two or three flags, with the device of a goose in the middle. The white goose stands out against the green background of the flags.*

PEEP: [*also carrying a green flag with a goose in the middle*] People, listen to me. I'm Mother Peep and I keep the public geese! I've a long experience of politics. Trust me with the chariot of state, drawn by my geese, so I can legislate. Vote for *me*. Give *me* your confidence. Me and my geese are asking for power. [*Shouts from the crowd, the flags are waved: 'Long live Mother Peep! Long live Mother Peep's geese!'* BÉRENGER *comes in from the right, followed by* ÉDOUARD, *who is out of breath.* BÉRENGER *drags him after him, pulling him by the sleeve. In this way they cross the stage from right to left and from left to right. During the dialogue between* ÉDOUARD *and* BÉRENGER, MOTHER PEEP *cannot be heard speaking, but she will be seen gesticulating and opening her mouth wide. The acclamation of the hidden crowd forms no more than a quiet background of sound.* MOTHER PEEP'*s words and the sound of voices can of course be heard between the speeches of* ÉDOUARD *and* BÉRENGER.]

BÉRENGER: Come along, hurry up, do hurry up. Just one more effort. It's down there, right at the end. [*He points.*] Down there, the Prefecture buildings, we must arrive in time, before the offices close, in half an hour it'll be too late. The Architect, I mean the Superintendent, will have gone, and I've told you why we can't wait for tomorrow. Between now and then the killer might make off... or find some fresh victims! He must know I'm on his track.

ÉDOUARD: [*breathless but polite*] Wait a minute, please, you've made me run too fast.

PEEP: Fellow citizens, citizenesses...

BÉRENGER: Come on, come on.

ÉDOUARD: Let me have a rest... I can't keep going.

BÉRENGER: We haven't got time.

PEEP: Fellow citizens, citizenesses...

ÉDOUARD: I can't go on. [*He sits down on the bench.*]

BÉRENGER: All right, then. For one second, not more. [*He remains standing, near the bench.*] I wonder what all that crowd's for.

ÉDOUARD: Election meeting.

PEEP: Vote for us! Vote for us!

BÉRENGER: Looks like my concierge.

ÉDOUARD: You're seeing things. She's a politician, Mother Peep, a keeper of geese. A striking personality.

BÉRENGER: The name sounds familiar, but I've no time to listen.

ÉDOUARD: [to BÉRENGER] Sit down for a moment, you're tired.

PEEP: People, you are mystified. You shall be demystified.

BÉRENGER: [to ÉDOUARD] I haven't time to feel tired.

VOICE FROM THE CROWD: Down with mystification! Long live Mother Peep's geese!

ÉDOUARD: [to BÉRENGER] I'm sorry. Just a second. You said a second.

PEEP: I've raised a whole flock of demystifiers for you. They'll demystify you. But to demystify, you must first mystify. We need a new mystification.

BÉRENGER: We haven't time, we haven't time!

VOICE FROM THE CROWD: Up with the mystification of the demystifiers!

BÉRENGER: We haven't a moment to lose! [He sits down all the same, consulting his watch:] Time's getting on.

VOICE FROM THE CROWD: Up with the new mystification!

BÉRENGER: [to ÉDOUARD] Let's go.

ÉDOUARD: [to BÉRENGER] Don't worry. You know perfectly well the time's the same as it was just now.

PEEP: I promise you I'll change everything. And changing everything means changing nothing. You can change the names, but the things remain the same. The old mystifications haven't stood up to psychological and sociological analysis. The new one will be foolproof and cause nothing but misunderstanding. We'll bring the lie to perfection.

BÉRENGER: [to ÉDOUARD] Let's go!

ÉDOUARD: If you like.

BÉRENGER: [noticing that ÉDOUARD, who is painfully rising to his feet, no longer has his briefcase] Where's your briefcase?

ÉDOUARD: My briefcase? What briefcase? Ah yes, my briefcase. It must be on the bench. [He looks on the bench.] No. It's not on the bench.

BÉRENGER: It's extraordinary! You always have it with you!

ÉDOUARD: Perhaps it's *under* the bench.

PEEP: We're going to disalienate mankind.

BÉRENGER: [*to* ÉDOUARD] Look for it, why don't you look for it? [*They start looking for the briefcase under the bench, then on the floor of the stage.*]

PEEP: [*to crowd*] To disalienate mankind, we must alienate each individual man... and there'll be soup kitchens for all!

VOICE FROM THE CROWD: Soup kitchens for all and Mother Peep's geese!

BÉRENGER: [*to* ÉDOUARD] We must find it, hurry! Where could you have left it?

PEEP: [*to crowd, while* BÉRENGER *and* ÉDOUARD, *look for the briefcase, the former frantically, the latter apathetically*] We won't persecute, but we'll punish, and deal out justice. We won't colonize, we'll occupy the countries we liberate. We won't exploit men, we'll make them productive. We'll call compulsory work voluntary. War shall change its name to peace and everything will be altered, thanks to me and my geese.

BÉRENGER: [*still searching*] It's incredible, unbelievable, where can it have got to? I hope it hasn't been stolen. That would be a catastrophe, a catastrophe!

VOICE FROM THE CROWD: Long live Mother Peep's geese! Long live soup for the people!

PEEP: When tyranny is restored we'll call it discipline and liberty. The misfortune of one is the happiness of all.

BÉRENGER: [*to* ÉDOUARD] You don't realize, it's a disaster, we can't do a thing without proof, without the documents. They won't believe us.

ÉDOUARD: [*to* BÉRENGER, *nonchalantly*] Don't worry, we'll find it again. Let's look for it quietly. The great thing is to keep calm. [*They start searching again.*]

PEEP: [*to the crowd*] Our political methods will be more than scientific. They'll be para-scientific. Our reason will be founded on anger. And there'll be soup kitchens for all.

VOICE FROM THE CROWD: Long live Mother Peep! Long live the geese! Long live the geese!

VOICE FROM THE CROWD: And we'll be disalienated, thanks to Mother Peep.

PEEP: Objectivity is subjective in the para-scientific age.

BÉRENGER: [*wringing his hands, to* ÉDOUARD] It's one of the criminal's tricks.

ÉDOUARD: [*to* BÉRENGER] It's interesting, what Mother Peep says!

VOICE FROM THE CROWD: Long live Mother Peep!

BÉRENGER: [*to* ÉDOUARD] I tell you it's one of the criminal's tricks!

ÉDOUARD: [*to* BÉRENGER] You think so?

[*From the left a man appears in top hat and tails, dead drunk, holding a briefcase.*]

MAN: I am... [*Hiccup*]... I am for... [*Hiccup*]... the re-habilitation of the hero.

BÉRENGER: [*noticing the man*] There it is! He's got it! [*He makes for the* MAN.]

ÉDOUARD: Long live Mother Peep!

BÉRENGER: Where did you find that briefcase? Give it back!

MAN: Don't you favour the rehabilitation of the hero?

PEEP: [*to the crowd*] As for the intellectuals...

BÉRENGER: [*trying to pull the briefcase away from the* MAN] Thief!... Let go of that briefcase!

PEEP: [*to the crowd*]We'll make them do the goose-step! Long live the geese!

MAN: [*between two hiccups, clinging on to the briefcase*] I didn't steal it. It's *my* briefcase.

VOICE FROM THE CROWD: Long live the geese!

BÉRENGER: [*to* MAN] Where did you get it from? Where did you buy it?

MAN: [*hiccuping while being shaken by* BÉRENGER, *to* ÉDOUARD] Are you sure it's your briefcase?

ÉDOUARD: I think so... Looks like it.

BÉRENGER: [*to* MAN] Give it back to me, then!

MAN: I'm for the hero!

BÉRENGER: [*to* ÉDOUARD] Help me! [BÉRENGER *tackles the* MAN.]

ÉDOUARD: Yes, of course. [*He goes up to the* MAN, *but lets* BÉ-
RENGER *tackle him on his own. He is looking at* MOTHER PEEP.]

PEEP: While they're demystifying the mystifications demystified
long ago, the intellectuals will give us a rest and leave *our*
mystifications alone.

VOICE FROM THE CROWD: Long live Mother Peep!

MAN: I tell you it's mine!

PEEP: They'll be stupid, that means intelligent. Cowardly, that
means brave. Clear-sighted, that means blind.

ÉDOUARD & VOICE FROM THE CROWD: Long live Mother Peep!

BÉRENGER: [*to* ÉDOUARD] This is no time to stand and gape.
Leave Mother Peep alone.

ÉDOUARD: [*to* MAN, *coolly*] Give him the briefcase or else tell him
where you bought it.

MAN: [*hiccup*] We need a hero!

BÉRENGER: [*to* MAN, *having at last managed to get hold of the briefcase*] What's inside?

MAN: I don't know. Papers.

BÉRENGER: [*opening the briefcase*] At last! Drunken sot.

ÉDOUARD: What do you mean by a hero?

PEEP: We'll march backwards and be in the forefront of history.

MAN: [*while* BÉRENGER *digs into the briefcase, and* ÉDOUARD *has a
look over his shoulder, absentmindedly*] A hero? A man who dares
to think against history and react against his times. [*Loudly*]
Down with Mother Peep!

BÉRENGER: [*to* MAN] You're blind drunk!

MAN: A hero fights his own age and creates a different one.

BÉRENGER: [*taking bottles of wine out of the* MAN's *briefcase*]
Bottles of wine!

MAN: Half empty! That's not a crime!

PEEP: ... for history has reason on its side...

MAN: [*pushed by* BÉRENGER, *he staggers and falls on his behind,
exclaiming*] ... when reason's lost its balance...

BÉRENGER: And are you reasonable to get drunk like this? [*To* ÉDOUARD:] Where the devil *is* your briefcase, then?

MAN: Didn't I tell you it was mine? Down with Mother Peep!

ÉDOUARD: [*still indifferent and without moving*] How do I know? You can see I'm looking for it.

VOICE FROM THE CROWD: Up Mother Peep! Up Mother Peep's geese! She changes everything by changing nothing.

BÉRENGER: [*to* ÉDOUARD] I shan't forgive you for this!

MAN: [*stumbling to his feet*] Down with Mother Peep!

ÉDOUARD: [*to* BÉRENGER, *snivelling*] Oh, don't go on at me! I'm not well.

BÉRENGER: [*to* ÉDOUARD] I can't help it, I'm sorry! Think of the state *I'm* in!

> [*At this moment a little* OLD MAN, *with a pointed white beard, who looks shy and is poorly dressed, comes in from the right, holding in one hand an umbrella and in the other a huge black briefcase, identical with the one* ÉDOUARD *had in Act II.*]

MAN: [*pointing to the* OLD MAN] There's your briefcase! That must be the one!

> [BÉRENGER *makes a dive at the* OLD MAN.]

PEEP: If an ideology doesn't apply to real life, we'll say it does and it'll all be perfect. The intellectuals will back us up. They'll find us anti-myths to set against the old ones. We'll replace the myths...

BÉRENGER: [*to* OLD MAN] I beg pardon, Monsieur.

PEEP: ... by slogans... and the latest platitudes!...

OLD MAN: [*raising his hat*] I beg pardon, Monsieur, can you tell me where the Danube is?

MAN: [*to* OLD MAN] Are you for the hero?

BÉRENGER: [*to* OLD MAN] Your briefcase looks just like my friend's. [*Pointing to him:*] Monsieur Édouard.

ÉDOUARD: [*to* OLD MAN] How do you do?

VOICE FROM THE CROWD: Up Mother Peep!

OLD MAN: [*to* ÉDOUARD] Danube Street, please?

BÉRENGER: Never mind about Danube Street.

OLD MAN: Not Danube *Street*. The Danube.

MAN: But this is Paris.

OLD MAN: [*to* MAN] I know. I *am* a Parisian.

BÉRENGER: [*to* OLD MAN] It's about the briefcase!

MAN: [*to* OLD MAN] He wants to see what you've got in your briefcase.

OLD MAN: That's nobody's business. I don't even ask myself. I'm not so inquisitive.

BÉRENGER: Of your own free will or by force you're going to show us...

[BÉRENGER, *the* MAN *and even* ÉDOUARD *try to take the brief-case from the* OLD MAN, *who fights back, protesting.*]

OLD MAN: [*struggling*] I won't let you!

PEEP: No more profiteers. It's me and my geese...

[*They are all round the* OLD MAN, *harrying him and trying to take the briefcase from him: the* MAN *manages to get it away from him first, then the* OLD MAN *snatches it back and* ÉDOUARD *lays hands on it, only to lose it again to the* OLD MAN: *they also get hold of the* MAN's *briefcase again, realize their mistake when they see the bottles and give it him back, etc.*]

BÉRENGER: [*to* ÉDOUARD] Idiot!

[*He gets hold of the briefcase, the* OLD MAN *takes it back again and the* MAN *takes it from him.*]

MAN: [*offering it to* ÉDOUARD] Here it is!

[*The* OLD MAN *snatches it and tries to run away, the others catch him, etc. Meanwhile* MOTHER PEEP *is continuing her speech:*]

PEEP ... me and my geese who'll dole out public property. Fair shares for all. I'll keep the lion's share for myself and my geese...

VOICE FROM THE CROWD: Up the geese!

PEEP: ... to give my geese more strength to draw the carts of state.

VOICE FROM THE CROWD: The lion's share for the geese! The lion's share for the geese!

MAN: [*shouting to* MOTHER PEEP] And we'll be free to criticize?

PEEP: Let's all do the goose-step!

VOICE FROM THE CROWD: The goose-step, the goose-step!

MAN: Free to criticize?

PEEP: [*turning to the* MAN] Everyone will be free to say if the goose-step's not well done!

[*A kind of rhythmic marching is heard and the crowd shouting:* 'The goose-step, the goose-step!' *Meanwhile the* OLD MAN *has managed to escape with his briefcase. He goes off left followed by* BÉRENGER. ÉDOUARD, *who has made as if to follow* BÉRENGER *and the* OLD MAN, *turns back and goes to lie down on the bench, coughing. The* MAN *goes up to him.*]

MAN: [*to* ÉDOUARD] Aren't you well? Have a swig! [*He tries to offer him a half-empty bottle of wine.*]

ÉDOUARD: [*refusing*] No thank you.

MAN: Yes, yes. It'll do you good. Cheer you up.

ÉDOUARD: I don't want to be cheered up.

[*The* MAN *makes the protesting* ÉDOUARD *drink; wine is spilt on the ground; the bottle too can fall and break. The* MAN *goes on making* ÉDOUARD *drink, while he speaks to* MOTHER PEEP:]

MAN: [*very drunk*] Science and art have done far more to change thinking than politics have. The real revolution is taking place in the scientists' laboratories and in the artists' studios. Einstein, Oppenheimer, Breton, Kandinsky, Picasso, Pavlov, they're the ones who are really responsible. They're extending our field of knowledge, renewing our vision of the world, transforming us. Soon the means of production will give everyone a chance to live. The problem of economics will settle itself. Revolutions are a barbarous weapon, myths and grudges that go off in your face. [*He takes another bottle of wine from his briefcase and has a good swig.*] Penicillin and the fight against dypsomania are worth more than politics and a change of government.

PEEP: [*to* MAN] Bastard! Drunkard! Enemy of the people! Enemy of history! [*To the crowd:*] I denounce this man: the drunkard, the enemy of history.

VOICE FROM THE CROWD: Down with history's enemy! Let's kill

the enemy of history!

ÉDOUARD: [*painfully getting up*] We are all going to die. That's the only alienation that counts!

BÉRENGER: [*comes in holding the* OLD MAN's *briefcase*] There's nothing in the briefcase.

OLD MAN: [*following* BÉRENGER] Give it back to me, give it back!

MAN: I'm a hero! I'm a hero! [*He staggers quickly to the back of the stage and climbs up the stairs to* MOTHER PEEP.] I don't think like other people! I'm going to tell them!

BÉRENGER: [*to* OLD MAN] It's not Édouard's briefcase, here it is, I'm sorry.

ÉDOUARD: Don't go. It's heroism to think against your times, but madness to say so.

BÉRENGER: It's not *your* briefcase. So where the devil *is* yours?

[*Meanwhile the* MAN *has reached the top of the steps, next to* MOTHER PEEP.]

PEEP: [*producing a huge briefcase, which has not been noticed up to now, and brandishing it*] Let's have a free discussion! [*She hits the* MAN *over the head with her briefcase.*] Rally round, my geese! Here's pasture for you!

[MOTHER PEEP *and the* MAN *fall struggling on the raised pavement. During the following scene either* MOTHER PEEP's *head or the* MAN's *or both at once will become visible, in the midst of a frightful hubbub of voices crying: 'Up Mother Peep! Down with the drunk!' Then, at the end of the following dialogue* MOTHER PEEP's *head reappears alone, for the last time: it is hideous. Before disappearing, she says: 'My geese have liquidated him. But only physically.' Punch and Judy style.*]

ÉDOUARD: The wise man says nothing. [*To* OLD MAN:] Doesn't he, Monsieur?

BÉRENGER: [*wringing his hands*] But where is it? We must have it.

OLD MAN: Where are the banks of the Danube? You can tell me *now*.

[*He straightens his clothes, shuts his briefcase and takes back his umbrella.* MOTHER PEEP's *briefcase has opened as she hit the* MAN *and rectangular cardboard boxes have fallen from it to the ground.*]

BÉRENGER: There's your briefcase, Édouard! It's Mother Peep's. [*He notices the boxes.*] And there are the documents.

ÉDOUARD: You think so?

OLD MAN: [*to* ÉDOUARD] Damn it, he's got a mania for running after briefcases! What's he looking for?

[BÉRENGER *bends down, picks up the boxes and then comes back to the front of the stage to* ÉDOUARD *and the* OLD MAN, *looking disappointed.*]

ÉDOUARD: It's my briefcase he wants to find!

BÉRENGER: [*showing the boxes*] It's not the documents! It's only the goose game!

OLD MAN: I haven't played that for a long time.

BÉRENGER: [*to* ÉDOUARD] It's no concern of yours! It's the brief-case we're after... the briefcase with the documents. [*To the* OLD MAN:] The evidence, to arrest the criminal!

OLD MAN: So that's it, you should have said so before.

[*It is at this moment that* MOTHER PEEP's *head appears for the last time to make the remark already mentioned. Immediately after-wards the noise of the engine of a truck is heard, which drowns the voices of the crowd and the three characters on the stage, who go on talking and gesticulating without a word being heard. A* POLICE SERGEANT *appears, who should be unusually tall: with a white stick he taps the invisible people on the other side of the wall over the head.*]

POLICEMAN: [*only visible from head to waist, wielding the stick in one hand and blowing his whistle with the other*] Come along now, move on there. [*The crowd cries: 'The Police, the Police. Up the Police.' The* POLICEMAN *continues moving them on in the same way, so that the noise of the crowd gradually dies and fades right away. A huge military truck coming from the left blocks half the upper part of the stage.*]

ÉDOUARD: [*indifferently*] Look, an army truck!

BÉRENGER: [*to* ÉDOUARD] Never mind about that.

[*Another military truck coming from the opposite side blocks the*

other half of the upper part of the stage, just leaving enough room
for the POLICEMAN *in between the two trucks.*]

OLD MAN: [*to* BÉRENGER] You should have said you were looking for your friend's briefcase with the documents. I know
where it is.

POLICEMAN: [*above, blowing his whistle, between the trucks*] Move
along there, move along.

OLD MAN: [*to* BÉRENGER] Your friend must have left it at home,
in your hurry to leave.

BÉRENGER: [*to* OLD MAN] How did you know?

ÉDOUARD: He's right, I should have thought! Were you watching us?

OLD MAN: Not at all. It's a simple deduction.

BÉRENGER: [*to* ÉDOUARD] Idiot!

ÉDOUARD: I'm sorry... We were in such a hurry!

[*A young* SOLDIER *gets out of the military truck, holding a bunch*
of red carnations. He uses it as a fan. He goes and sits on the top of
the wall, the flowers in his hand, his legs dangling over the edge.]

BÉRENGER: [*to* ÉDOUARD] Go and fetch it, go and fetch it at once!
You're impossible! I'll go and warn the Superintendent, so
he'll wait for us. Hurry and join me as soon as you can. The
Prefecture's right at the end. In an affair like this I don't like
being alone on the road. It's not pleasant. You understand?

ÉDOUARD: Of course I do, I understand. [*To* OLD MAN:] Thank
you, Monsieur.

OLD MAN: [*to* BÉRENGER] Could you tell me now where the
Danube Embankment is?

BÉRENGER: [*to* ÉDOUARD, *who hasn't moved*] Well, hurry up!
Don't stand there! Come back quick.

ÉDOUARD: All right.

BÉRENGER: [*to* OLD MAN] I don't know, Monsieur, I'm sorry.

ÉDOUARD: [*making off very slowly to the right, where he disappears,*
saying nonchalantly] All right, then, I'll hurry. I'll hurry. Won't
be long. Won't be long.

BÉRENGER: [*to* OLD MAN] You must ask, ask a policeman!

[*On his way out* ÉDOUARD *nearly knocks into a* 2ND POLICE-MAN, *who appears blowing his whistle and waving his white stick about too : he should be immensely tall, perhaps he could walk on stilts.*]

ÉDOUARD: [*dodging the* POLICEMAN, *who doesn't look at him*] Oh, sorry! [*He disappears.*]

BÉRENGER: [*to* OLD MAN] There's one. You can find out.

OLD MAN: He's very busy. Do you think I dare?

BÉRENGER: Yes, of course, He's all right.

[BÉRENGER *goes to the back of the stage after crying one last time after* ÉDOUARD: '*Hurry up!*' *The* OLD MAN *very shyly and hesitantly approaches the* 2ND POLICEMAN.]

OLD MAN: [*timidly, to the* 2ND POLICEMAN] I beg your pardon! I beg your pardon!

BÉRENGER: [*he has gone right to the back of the stage and has one foot on the first step of the stairs*] I must hurry!

1ST POL.: [*between two blasts, pointing his white stick down at* BÉRENGER *to make him move away*] Move on, move on there.

BÉRENGER: It's terrible. What a traffic jam! I'll never, never get there. [*Addressing first one, then the other* POLICEMAN:] It's a good thing we've got you here to keep the traffic moving. You've no idea what bad luck this hold-up is for me!

OLD MAN: [*to* 2ND POLICEMAN] Excuse me, please, Monsieur. [*Before addressing the* POLICEMAN *the* OLD MAN *has respectfully removed his hat and made a low bow ; the* POLICEMAN *takes no notice, he is getting excited, making signals which are answered by the* POLICEMAN *the other side of the wall with his white stick, while he too energetically blows his whistle.* BÉRENGER *goes frantically from one to the other.*]

BÉRENGER: [*to* 1ST POLICEMAN] Oh, hurry up, I've got to get by. I've a very important mission. It's humanitarian.

1ST POL.: [*who goes on blowing and signing* BÉRENGER *on with his stick*] Move along!

OLD MAN: [*to* 2ND POLICEMAN] Monsieur... [*To* BÉRENGER:] He won't answer. He's too busy.

BÉRENGER: Oh, these trucks are here for good. [*He looks at his watch:*] Luckily, it's still the same time. [*To* OLD MAN:] Ask him, go on and ask him, he won't bite you.

OLD MAN: [*to* 2ND POLICEMAN, *still blowing his whistle*] Please, Monsieur.

2ND POL.: [*to the* 1ST] Get them to go back! [*Sound of the engines of the still stationary trucks.*] Make them go forward! [*Same sound.*]

SOLDIER: [*to* BÉRENGER] If I knew the city I'd tell him the way. But I'm not a native.

BÉRENGER: [*to* OLD MAN] The policeman's bound to give you satisfaction. That's his privilege. Speak louder.

[*The* SOLDIER *goes on fanning himself with his bunch of red flowers.*]

OLD MAN: [*to* 2ND POLICEMAN] I'm sorry, Monsieur, listen, Monsieur.

2ND POL. What?

OLD MAN: Monsieur, I'd like to ask you a simple question.

2ND POL.: [*sharply*] One minute! [*To* SOLDIER:] You, why have you left your truck, eh?

SOLDIER: I... I... but it's stopped!

BÉRENGER: [*aside*] Good Heavens, that Policeman's got the Superintendent's voice! Could it be him? [*He goes to have a closer look:*] No. He wasn't so tall.

2ND POL.: [*to* OLD MAN *again, while the other* POLICEMAN *is still controlling the traffic*] What's that you wanted, you there?

BÉRENGER: [*aside*] No, it's not him. His voice wasn't quite as hard as that.

OLD MAN: [*to* 2ND POLICEMAN] The Danube Embankment, please, Monsieur l'Agent, I'm sorry.

2ND POL.: [*his reply is aimed at the* OLD MAN *as well as the* 1ST POLICEMAN *and the invisible drivers of the two trucks; it precipitates a scene of general chaos, which should be comic, involving everyone; even the two trucks move*] To the left! To the right! Straight on! Straight back! Forward!

[*The* 1ST POLICEMAN, *the upper part of whom only is seen above,*
moves his head and white stick in obedience to his words:
BÉRENGER *makes parallel gestures, still standing on the same spot:*
the SOLDIER *does the same with his bunch of flowers. The* OLD
MAN *steps to the left, then to the right, then straight on, straight*
back and forward.]

BÉRENGER: [*aside*] All the police have the same voice.

OLD MAN: [*returning to the* 2ND POLICEMAN] Excuse me, Monsieur, excuse me, I'm rather hard of hearing. I didn't quite
understand which way you told me to go... for the Danube
Embankment, please...

2ND POL.: [*to* OLD MAN] You trying to take a rise out of me? Oh
no, there are *times*...

BÉRENGER: [*aside*] The Superintendent was much more pleasant...

2ND POL.: [*to* OLD MAN] Come on... Clear off... deaf or daft
... bugger off! [*Blasts on the whistle from the* 2ND POLICEMAN,
who starts dashing about and knocks into the OLD MAN, *who drops*
his walking stick.]

SOLDIER: [*on the steps*] Your stick, Monsieur.

OLD MAN: [*picking up his stick, to the* 2ND POLICEMAN] Don't
lose your temper, Monsieur l'Agent, don't lose your temper!
[*He is very frightened.*]

2ND POL.: [*still directing the traffic jam*] Left...

BÉRENGER: [*to* OLD MAN, *while the trucks move a little at the back of*
the stage, threatening for a moment to crush the 1ST POLICEMAN]
That policeman's behaviour is disgraceful!

1ST POL.: Look out, half-wits!

BÉRENGER: [*to* OLD MAN]... after all, he has a duty to be polite
to the public.

1ST POL.: [*to the supposed drivers of the two trucks*] Left!

2ND POL.: [*as above*] Right!

BÉRENGER: [*to* OLD MAN] ... It must be part of their regulations!
... [*To the* SOLDIER:] Mustn't it?

1ST POL.: [*as before*] Right!

SOLDIER: [*like a child*] I don't know... [*Fanning himself with his flowers.*] *I've* got my flowers.

BÉRENGER: [*aside*] When I see his boss, the Architect, I'll tell him about it.

2ND POL.: [*as before*] Straight on!

OLD MAN: It doesn't matter, Monsieur l'Agent, I'm sorry... [*He goes out left.*]

2ND POL.: [*as before*] To the left, left!

BÉRENGER: [*while the* 2ND POLICEMAN *is saying faster and faster and more and more mechanically:* 'Straight on, left, right, straight on, forwards, backwards, etc....' *and the* IST POLICEMAN *repeats his orders in the same way, turning his head from right to left etc. like a puppet*] I think, Soldier, we're too polite, far too nervous with the police. We've got them into bad habits, it's our fault!

SOLDIER: [*offering the bunch of flowers to* BÉRENGER, *who has come close to him and climbed up one or two steps*] See how good they smell!

BÉRENGER: No thank you, I don't.

SOLDIER: Can't you see they're carnations?

BÉRENGER: Yes, but that's not the point. I've simply got to keep going. This hold-up's a disaster!

2ND POL.: [*to* BÉRENGER, *then he goes towards the young* SOLDIER, *when* BÉRENGER *moves away from him*] Move on.

BÉRENGER: [*moving away from the* POLICEMAN *who has just addressed this order to him*] You don't like these trucks either, Monsieur l'Agent. I can see that in your face. And how right you are!

2ND POL.: [*to* IST POLICEMAN] Go on blowing your whistle for a minute.

[*The* IST POLICEMAN *goes on as before.*]

IST POL.: All right! Carry on!

BÉRENGER: [*to* 2ND POLICEMAN] The traffic's getting impossible. Especially when there are things... things that can't wait...

2ND POL.: [*to the* SOLDIER, *pointing at the bunch of red carnations the latter is still holding and fanning himself with*] Haven't you got anything better to do than play with that?

SOLDIER: [*politely*] I'm not doing any harm, Monsieur l'Agent, that's not stopping the trucks from moving.

2ND POL.: It puts a spoke in the wheels, wise guy! [*He slaps the* SOLDIER *across the face: the* SOLDIER *says nothing. The* POLICEMAN *is so tall that he does not need to climb the steps to reach the* SOLDIER.]

BÉRENGER: [*aside, in the centre of the stage, indignantly*] Oh!

2ND POL.: [*snatching the flowers from the* SOLDIER *and hurling them into the wings*] Lunatic! Aren't you ashamed of yourself? Get back in that truck with your mates.

SOLDIER: All right, Monsieur l'Agent.

2ND POL.: [*to* SOLDIER] Look alive there, stupid bastard!

BÉRENGER: [*in the same position*] Going much too far!

SOLDIER: [*climbing back into the truck with the help of the* IST POLICEMAN's *fist and the* 2ND POLICEMAN's *stick*] Yes, all right, I will! [*He disappears into the truck.*]

BÉRENGER: [*in the same position*] Much too far!

2ND POL.: [*to the other invisible soldiers who are supposed to be in the trucks and who could perhaps be represented by puppets or simply be painted sitting on painted benches in the trucks*] You're blocking the road! We're fed up with your damned trucks!

BÉRENGER: [*aside, in same position*] In my view a country's done for if the police lays its hand... and its fingers on the Army.

2ND POL.: [*turning to* BÉRENGER] What's the matter with you? It's none of your business if...

BÉRENGER: But I didn't say anything, Monsieur l'Agent, not a thing...

2ND POL.: It's easy to guess what's going on in the minds of people of your type!

BÉRENGER: How do you know what I...

2ND POL.: Never you mind! You try and put your wrong thinking right.

BÉRENGER: [*stammering*] But it's not that, Monsieur, not that at all, you're mistaken, I'm sorry, I'd not... I'd never... on the contrary, I'd even...

2ND POL.: What are you up to here anyway? Where are your identification papers?

BÉRENGER: [*looking in his pockets*] Oh well, if that's what you want, Monsieur l'Agent... You've a right to see them...

2ND POL.: [*who is now in the centre of the stage, close to* BÉRENGER, *who naturally looks very small beside him*] Come on, quicker than that. I've no time to waste!

1ST POL.: [*still above, between the two trucks*] Hey! You leaving me on my own to unscramble this traffic? [*He blows his whistle.*]

2ND POL.: [*shouting to the* 1ST] Just a minute, I'm busy. [*To* BÉRENGER:] Quicker than that. Well, aren't they coming, those papers?

BÉRENGER: [*who has found his papers*] Here they are, Monsieur l'Agent.

2ND POL.: [*examining the papers, then returning them to* BÉRENGER] Well... All in order!

[*The* 1ST POLICEMAN *blows his whistle and waves his white stick. The truck engines are heard.*]

1ST POL.: [*to* 2ND] Doesn't matter. We'll get him yet, next time.

BÉRENGER: [*to* 2ND POLICEMAN, *taking his papers back*] Thanks very much, Monsieur l'Agent.

2ND POL.: You're welcome...

BÉRENGER: [*to* 2ND POLICEMAN, *who is about to move off*] Now you know who I am and all about my case, perhaps I can ask for your help and advice.

2ND POL.: I don't know about your case.

BÉRENGER: Yes, you do, Monsieur l'Agent. You must have realized I'm looking for the killer. What else could I be doing round here?

2ND POL.: Stopping me from controlling the traffic, for example.

BÉRENGER: [*without hearing the last remark*] We can lay hands on him, I've all the evidence... I mean, Édouard has, he's bringing it along in his briefcase... Theoretically I've got it... meanwhile I'm off to the Prefecture, and it's still a long way... Can you send someone with me?

2ND POL.: Hear that? He's got a nerve!

1ST POL.: [*interrupting his mime, to the* 2ND] Is he one of us? He an informer?

2ND POL.: [*to* 1ST] He's not even that! Who does he think he is! [*He blows his whistle for the traffic.*]

BÉRENGER: Listen to me, please, this is really serious. You've seen for yourself. I'm a respectable man.

2ND POL.: [*to* BÉRENGER] What's it all got to do with you, eh?

BÉRENGER: [*drawing himself up*] I beg your pardon, but I *am* a citizen, it matters to me, it concerns us all, we're all responsible for the crimes that... You see, I'm a really serious citizen.

2ND POL.: [*to* 1ST] Hear that? Likes to hear himself talk.

BÉRENGER: I'm asking you once more, Monsieur l'Agent! [*To the* 1ST:] I'm asking you, too!

1ST POL.: [*still busy with the traffic*] That's enough, now.

BÉRENGER: [*continuing, to* 2ND POLICEMAN] ... you, too: can you send someone with me to the Prefecture? I'm a friend of the Superintendent's, of the Architect's.

2ND POL.: That's not my department. I suppose even you can see I'm in 'traffic control'.

BÉRENGER: [*plucking up more courage*] I'm a friend of the Superintendent's...

2ND POL.: [*bending down to* BÉRENGER *and almost shouting in his ear*] I'm-in-traffic-control!

BÉRENGER: [*recoiling slightly*] Yes, I see, but... all the same... in the public interest... public safety, you know!

2ND POL.: Public safety? *We* look after that. When we've the time. Traffic comes first!

1ST POL.: What *is* this character? Reporter?

BÉRENGER: No, Messieurs, no, I'm *not* a reporter... Just a citizen, that's all...

1ST POL.: [*between two blasts on the whistle*] Has he got a camera?

BÉRENGER: No, Messieurs, I haven't, search me... [*He turns out his pockets.*] ... I'm *not* a reporter...

2ND POL.: [*to* BÉRENGER] Lucky you hadn't got it on you or I'd have smashed your face in!

BÉRENGER: I don't mind your threats. Public safety's more important than I am. He killed Dany too.

2ND POL.: Who's this Dany?

BÉRENGER: He killed her.

1ST POL.: [*between two blasts, signals and shouts of: Right! Left!*] It's his tart...

BÉRENGER: No, Monsieur, she's my fiancée. Or was to be.

2ND POL.: [*to* 1ST] That's it all right. He wants revenge on account of his tart!

BÉRENGER: The criminal must pay for his crime!

1ST POL.: Phew! They can talk themselves silly, some of them!

2ND POL.: [*louder, turning to* BÉRENGER *again*] It's not my racket, get it? I don't give a good goddam for your story. If you're one of the boss's pals, go and see him and leave me in goddam peace.

BÉRENGER: [*trying to argue*] Monsieur l'Agent... I... I...

2ND POL.: [*as before, while the* 1ST POLICEMAN *laughs sardonically*] I keep the peace, so leave *me* in peace! You know the way... [*He points to the back of the stage, blocked by the trucks.*] So bugger off, the road's clear!

BÉRENGER: Right, Monsieur l'Agent, right, Monsieur l'Agent!

2ND POL.: [*to* 1ST, *ironically*] Let the gentleman through!

[*As though by magic the trucks move back; the whole set at the back of the stage is movable, and so comes apart*]

Let the gentleman through!

[*The* 1ST POLICEMAN *has disappeared with the back wall and the trucks; now, at the back of the stage, you can see a very long street or avenue with the Prefecture buildings in the far distance against the setting sun. A miniature tram crosses the stage far away.*]

Let the gentleman through!

1ST POL.: [*whose face appears over the roof of one of the houses in the street that has just appeared*] Come on, get moving! [*He gestures to him to start moving and disappears.*]

BÉRENGER: That's just what I'm doing...

2ND POL.: [*to* BÉRENGER] I hate you!

[*It is the* 2ND POLICEMAN's *turn to make a sudden disappearance: the stage has got slightly darker.* BÉRENGER *is now alone.*]

BÉRENGER: [*calling after the* 2ND POLICEMAN, *who has just disappeared*] I've more right to say that than you have! Just now I haven't got time... But you haven't heard the last of me! [*He shouts after the vanished* POLICEMAN:] You-haven't-heard-the-last-of-me!!

[*The* ECHO *answers: last-of-me...*

BÉRENGER *is now quite alone on the stage. The miniature tram is no longer visible at the back. It is up to the producer, the designer and the electrician to bring out* BÉRENGER's *utter loneliness, the emptiness around him and the deserted avenue somewhere between town and country. A part of the mobile set could disappear completely to increase the area of the stage.* BÉRENGER *should appear to be walking for a long time in the ensuing scene; if there is no revolving stage he can make the steps without advancing. It might in fact be possible to have the walls back again to give the impression of a long, narrow passage, so that* BÉRENGER *seems to be walking into some ambush; the light does not change; it is twilight, with a red sun glowing at the back of the stage. Whether the stage is broad and open or reduced by flats to represent a long, narrow street, there is a still, timeless half-light.*

While he is walking, BÉRENGER *will grow more and more anxious; at the start, he sets off, or appears to, at a fast pace; then he takes to turning round more and more frequently until his walk has become hesitant; he looks to right and left, and then behind him again, so that in the end he appears to be on the point of flight, ready to turn back; but he controls himself with difficulty and after a great effort decides to go forward again; if the set is movable and can be changed without having to lower the curtain or the lights,* BÉRENGER *might just as well walk from one end of the stage to the other, and then come back, etc.*

Finally, he will advance cautiously, glancing all round him; and yet, *at the end of the Act when the last character in the play makes his appearance—or is first heard, or heard and seen at the same time—*BÉRENGER *will be taken by surprise: so this character should appear just when* BÉRENGER *is looking the other way. The appearance of this character must, however, be prepared for by* BÉRENGER *himself:* BÉRENGER'*s mounting anguish should make the audience aware that the character is getting nearer and nearer.*]

BÉRENGER: [*starting to walk, or appearing to, and at the same time turning his head in the direction of the* POLICEMEN *towards the wings on the right, and shaking his fist at them*] I can't do everything at once. Now for the murderer. It'll be your turn next. [*He walks in silence for a second or two, stepping it out.*] Outrageous attitude! I don't believe in reporting people, but I'll talk to the Chief Superintendent about it, you bet I will! [*He walks in silence.*] I hope I'm not too late! [*The noise of the wind: a dead leaf flutters down and* BÉRENGER *turns up his overcoat collar.*] And now, on top of everything else, the wind's got up. And the light's going. Will Édouard be able to catch me up in time? Will he catch me up in time? He's so slow! [*He walks on in silence while the set changes.*] Everything will have to be changed. First we must start by reforming the police force... All they're good for is teaching you manners, but when you really *need* them... when you want them to protect you... they couldn't care less... they let you down... [*He looks round:*] They and their trucks, they're a long way off already... Better hurry. [*He sets off again.*] I *must* get there before it's dark. It can't be too safe on the road. Still a long way... Not getting any nearer... I'm not making any progress. It's as though I wasn't moving at all. [*Silence*] There's no end to this avenue and its tramlines. [*Silence*] ... There's the boundary anyway, the start of the Outer Boulevards... [*He walks in silence.*] I'm shivering. Because of the cold wind. You'd think I was frightened, but I'm not. I'm used to being alone... [*He walks in silence.*] I've always been alone... And yet I love the human race, but at a distance. What's that matter, when I'm interested in the fate of mankind? Fact is, I *am doing* something... [*He smiles.*] Doing... acting... acting, not play-acting, doing! Well, really I'm even running risks, you might say, for mankind... and for Dany too. Risks? The Civil Service will protect me. Dear Dany, those policemen defiled your memory. I'll make them pay. [*He looks behind him, ahead, then behind again; he stops.*] I'm half way there. Not quite. Nearly... [*He sets off again at a not very determined pace; while he walks he glances behind him:*] Édouard! That you, Édouard? [*The Echo answers: ouard... ouard...*] No... it's not Édouard... Once he's arrested, bound hand and foot, out of harm's way, the spring will come back for ever, and every city will be radiant... I shall have my reward. That's not what I'm after. To have done my duty, that's enough... So long as it's not too late, so long as it's not too late. [*Sound of the wind or the cry of an animal.* BÉRENGER *stops.*] Supposing I went back... to look for Édouard? We could go to the Prefecture tomorrow. Yes, I'll go tomorrow, with Édouard... [*He turns in his tracks and takes a step on the road back.*] No. Édouard's sure to catch me up in a moment or two. [*To himself:*] Think of Dany. I must have revenge for Dany. I must stop the rot. Yes, yes, I know I can. Besides, I've gone too far now, it's darker that way than the way I'm going. The road to the Prefecture is still the safest. [*He shouts again:*] Édouard! Édouard!

ECHO: É-dou-ard... ou...ard...

BÉRENGER: Can't see now whether he's coming or not. Perhaps he's quite near. Go on again. [*Setting off again with great caution.*] Doesn't seem like it, but I've covered some ground... Oh yes I have, no doubt about it... You wouldn't think so, but I *am* advancing... advancing... Ploughed fields on my right, and this deserted street... No risk of a traffic jam now anyway, you can keep going. [*He laughs. The echo vaguely repeats the laugh.* BÉRENGER, *scared, looks round:*] What's that?... It's the echo... [*He resumes his walking.*] No one there, stupid ... Over there, who's that? There, behind that tree! [*He rushes behind a leafless tree, which could be part of the moving scene.*] Why, no, it's nobody... [*The leaf of an old newspaper falls from the tree.*] Aah!... Afraid of a newspaper now. What a fool I am! [*He bursts out laughing. The echo repeats:... fool... I... am... and distorts the laugh.*] I must get further... I must go on! Advancing under cover of the Civil Service... advancing... I must... I must... [*Halt*] No, no. It's not worth it, in any case I'll arrive too late. Not my fault, it's the fault of the... fault of the... of the traffic, the hold-up made me late ... And above all it's Édouard's fault ... he forgets everything, every blessed thing... Perhaps the murderer will strike again tonight... [*With a start:*] I've simply got to stop him. I must go. I'm going. [*Another two or three paces in the direction of the supposed Prefecture:*] Come to think of it, it's all the same really, as it's too late. Another victim here or there, what's it matter in the state we're in... We'll go tomorrow, go tomorrow, Édouard and I, and much simpler that way, the offices will be closed this evening, perhaps they are already... What good would it do to... [*He shouts off right into the wings:*] Édouard! Édouard!

ECHO: É...ard...e...ard...

BÉRENGER: He won't come now. No point in thinking he will. It's too late. [*He looks at his watch:*] My watch has stopped... Never mind, there's no harm putting it off... I'll go tomorrow, with Édouard!... The Superintendent will arrest him tomorrow. [*He turns round.*] Where am I? I hope I can find my way home? It's in this direction! [*He turns round again quickly and suddenly sees the* KILLER *quite close to him.*] Ah!...

[*The set has of course stopped changing. In fact there is practically no scenery. All there is is a wall and a bench. The empty waste of a plain and a slight glow on the horizon. The two characters are picked out in a pale light, while the rest is in semi-darkness. Derisive laugh from the* KILLER: *he is very small and puny, ill-shaven, with a torn hat on his head and a shabby old gaberdine; he has only one eye, which shines with a steely glitter, and a set expression on his still face; his toes are peeping out of the holes in his old shoes. When the* KILLER *appears, laughing derisively, he should be standing on the bench or perhaps somewhere on the wall: he calmly jumps down and approaches* BÉRENGER, *chuckling unpleasantly, and it is at this moment that one notices how small he is. Or possibly there is no Killer at all.* BÉRENGER *could be talking to himself, alone in the half-light.*]

It's him, it's the killer! [*To the* KILLER:] So it's you, then!

[*The* KILLER *chuckles softly:* BÉRENGER *glances round, anxiously.*]

Nothing but the dark plain all around... You needn't tell me, I can see that as well as you.

[*He looks towards the distant Prefecture. Soft chuckle from the* KILLER.]

The Prefecture's too far away? That's what you just meant? I know.

[*Chuckle from the* KILLER.]

Or was that me talking?

[*Chuckle from the* KILLER.]

You're laughing at me! I'll call the police and have you arrested.

[*Chuckle from the* KILLER.]

It's no good, you mean, they wouldn't hear me?

[*The* KILLER *gets down from the bench or the wall and approaches* BÉRENGER, *horribly detached and vaguely chuckling, both hands in his pockets. Aside:*] Those dirty cops left me alone with him on purpose. They wanted to make me believe it was just a private feud.

[*To the* KILLER, *almost shouting:*] Why? Just tell me why?

[*The* KILLER *chuckles and gives a slight shrug of the shoulders: he is quite close to* BÉRENGER, *who should appear not only bigger but also stronger than the almost dwarf-like* KILLER. BÉRENGER *has a burst of nervous laughter.*]

Oh, you really are rather puny, aren't you? Too puny to be a criminal! I'm not afraid of you! Look at me, look how much

stronger I am. I could knock you down, knock you flying with
a flick of my fingers. I could put you in my pocket. Do you
realize?

[*Same chuckle from the* KILLER.]

I'm-not-afraid-of-you!

[*Chuckle from the* KILLER.]

I could squash you like a worm. But I won't. I want to understand. You're going to answer my questions. After all, you are
a human being. You've got reasons, perhaps. You must explain,
or else I don't know what... You're going to tell me why...
Answer me!

[*The* KILLER *chuckles and gives a slight shrug of the shoulders.*
BÉRENGER *should be pathetic and naive, rather ridiculous; his
behaviour should seem sincere and grotesque at the same time, both
pathetic and absurd. He speaks with an eloquence that should
underline the tragically worthless and outdated commonplaces he is
advancing.*]

Anyone who does what you do does it perhaps because...
Listen... You've stopped me from being happy, and stopped a
great many more... In that shining district of the town,
which would surely have cast its radiance over the whole
world... a new light radiating from France! If you've any
feeling left for your country... it would have shone on you,
would have moved you too, as well as countless others, would
have made you happy in yourself... a question of waiting, it
was only a matter of patience... *im*patience, that's what
spoils everything... yes, you would have been happy,
happiness would have come even to you, and it would have
spread, perhaps you didn't know, perhaps you didn't believe
it... You were wrong... Well, it's your own happiness
you've destroyed as well as mine and that of all the others...

[*Slight chuckle from the* KILLER.]

I suppose you don't believe in happiness. You think happiness
is impossible in this world? You want to destroy the world
because you think it's doomed. Don't you? That's it, isn't it?

Answer me!

[*Chuckle from the* KILLER.]

I suppose you never thought for a single moment that you'd
got it wrong. You were sure you were right. It's just your
stupid pride. Before you finally make up your mind about this,
at least let other people experiment for themselves. They're
trying to realize a practical and technical ideal of happiness,
here and now, on this earth of ours; and they'll succeed,
perhaps, how can *you* tell? If they don't, then you can think
again...

[*Chuckle from the* KILLER.]

You're a pessimist?

[*Chuckle from the* KILLER.]

You're a nihilist?

[*Chuckle from the* KILLER.]

An anarchist?

[*Chuckle from the* KILLER.]

Perhaps you don't like happiness? Perhaps happiness is different
for you? Tell me your ideas about life. What's your philosophy? Your motives? Your aims? Answer me!

[*Chuckle from the* KILLER.]

Listen to me: you've hurt me personally in the worst possible
way, destroying everything... all right, forget that... I'll not
talk about myself. But you killed Dany! What had Dany done
to you? She was a wonderful creature, with a few faults of
course, I suppose she was rather hot-tempered, liked her own
way, but she had a kind heart, and beauty like that is an excuse
for anything! If you killed every girl who liked her own way
just because she liked her own way, or the neighbours because
they make a noise and keep you awake, or someone for holding different opinions from you, it would be ridiculous,
wouldn't it? Yet that's what you do! Don't you? Don't you?

[*Chuckle from the* KILLER.]

We won't talk about Dany any more. She was my fiancée, and
you might believe it's all just a personal matter. But tell me

this... what had that Officer in the Engineers done to you, that Staff Officer?

[*Chuckle from the* KILLER.]

All right, I know... I understand, there are some people who hate a uniform. Rightly or wrongly they see it as the symbol of an abuse of power, of tyranny, and of war, which destroys civilizations. Right: we won't raise the question, it might take us too far, but that woman...

[*Chuckle from the* KILLER.]

...you know the one I mean, that young redhead, what had *she* done to you? What had you got against *her?* Answer me!

[*Chuckle from the* KILLER.]

We'll suppose you hate women, then: perhaps they betrayed you, didn't love you, because you're not, let's face it, you're not much to look at... it's not fair, I agree, but there's more than just the sexual side to life, there are some religious people who've given that up for all time... you can find satisfaction of a different kind in life and overcome that feeling of resentment...

[*Chuckle from the* KILLER.]

But the child, that child, what had he done to you? Children can't be guilty of anything, can they? You know the one I mean: the little fellow you pushed into the pool with the woman and the officer, poor little chap... our hopes are in the children, no one should touch a child; everyone agrees about that.

[*Chuckle from the* KILLER.]

Perhaps you think the human race is rotten in itself. Answer me!! You want to punish the human race even in a child, the least impure of all... We could debate the problem, if you like publicly, defend and oppose the motion, what do you say?

[*Chuckle from the* KILLER, *who shrugs his shoulders.*]

Perhaps you kill all these people out of kindness! To save them from suffering! For you, life is just suffering! Perhaps you want to cure people of the haunting fear of death? You think like

others before you, that man is and always will be the sick
animal, in spite of all social, technical or scientific progress, and
I suppose you want to carry out a sort of universal mercy-
killing? Well you're mistaken, you're wrong. Answer me!

[*Chuckle from the* KILLER.]

Anyway, if life's of little value, if it's too short, the suffering of
mankind will be short too: whether men suffer thirty or forty
years, ten years more or less, what's it matter to you? Let people
suffer if that's what they want. Let them suffer as long as they're
willing to suffer... Besides, time goes by, a few years hardly
count, they'll have a whole eternity of *not* suffering. Let them
die in their own time and it will all be over quite soon. Everything will flicker out and finish on its own. Don't hurry things
up, there's no point.

[*Chuckle from the* KILLER.]

Why, you're putting yourself in an absurd position, if you
think you're doing mankind a service by destroying it, you're
wrong, that's stupid! Aren't you afraid of ridicule? Eh?
Answer me that!

[*Chuckle from the* KILLER: *loud, nervous laugh from* BÉRENGER.
Then, after watching the KILLER *for a while* :]

I see this doesn't interest you. I haven't laid my finger on the
real problem, on the spot that really hurts. Tell me: do you
hate mankind? Do you hate mankind?

[*Chuckle from the* KILLER.]

But why? Answer me!

[*Chuckle from the* KILLER.]

If that *is* the case, don't vent your spleen on men, that's no
good, it only makes you suffer yourself, it hurts to hate, better
despise them, yes, I'll allow you to despise them, isolate yourself from them, go and live in the mountains, become a
shepherd, why not, and you'll live among sheep and dogs.

[*Chuckle from the* KILLER.]

You don't like animals either? You don't love anything that's
alive? Not even the plants?... What about stones and stars,

the sun and the blue sky?

[*Chuckle and shrug of the shoulders from the* KILLER.]

No. No, I'm being silly. One can't hate everything. Do you
believe society's rotten, that it can't be improved, that revo-
lutionaries are fools? Or do you believe the existence of the
universe is a mistake?

[*The* KILLER *shrugs his shoulders.*]

Why can't you answer me, answer me! Oh! Argument's impossible with you! Listen, you'll make me angry, I warn you!
No... no... I mustn't lose my self-control. I *must* understand
you. Don't look at me like that with your glittering eye. I'm
going to talk frankly. Just now I meant to have my revenge,
for myself and the others. I wanted to have you arrested, sent
to the guillotine. Vengeance is stupid. Punishment's not the
answer. I was furious with you. I was after your blood... as
soon as I saw you... not *immediately*, not that very moment,
no, but a few seconds later, I... it sounds silly, you won't
believe me, and yet I must tell you... yes... you're a human
being, we're the same species, we've got to understand each
other, it's our duty, a few seconds later, I loved you, or almost... because we're brothers, and if I hate *you*, I can't help
hating *myself*...

[*Chuckle from the* KILLER.]

Don't laugh: it exists, fellow feeling, the brotherhood of man,
I know it does, don't sneer...

[*Chuckle and shrug of the shoulders from the* KILLER.]

... ah... but you're a... you're nothing but a... now listen
to this. *We're* the strongest, *I'm* stronger physically than you
are, you're a helpless feeble little runt! What's more, I've the
law on my side... the police!

[*Chuckle from the* KILLER.]

Justice, the whole force of law and order!

[*Chuckle from the* KILLER.]

I mustn't, I *mustn't* get carried away... I'm sorry...

[*Chuckle from the* KILLER: BÉRENGER *mops his brow.*]

You've got more self-control than I have... but I'll calm down, I'll calm down... no need to be afraid... You don't *seem* very frightened... I mean, don't hold it against me... but you're not even scared, are you?... No, it's not that, that's not what I mean... Ah yes, yes... perhaps you don't realize. [*Very loud:*] Christ died on the Cross for *you*, it was for *you* he suffered, he *loves* you ... And you really need to be loved, though you think you don't!

[*Chuckle from the* KILLER.]

I swear to you that the blessed saints are pouring out tears for you, torrents and oceans of tears. You're soaked in their tears from head to foot, it's impossible for you not to feel a little wet!

[*Chuckle from the* KILLER.]

Stop sneering like that. You don't believe me, you don't believe me!... If Christ's not enough for you, I give you my solemn word I'll have an army of saviours climbing new Calvaries just for you, and have them crucified for love of you!... They must exist and I'll find them! Will that do?

[*Chuckle from the* KILLER.]

Do you want the whole world to destroy itself to give you a moment of happiness, to make you smile just once? That's possible too! I'm ready myself to embrace you, to be one of your comforters; I'll dress your wounds, because you *are* wounded, aren't you? You've suffered, haven't you? You're still suffering? I'll take pity on you, you know that now. Would you like me to wash your feet? Then perhaps you'd like some new shoes? You loathe sloppy sentimentality. Yes, I can see it's no good trying to touch your feelings. You don't want to be trapped by tenderness! You're afraid it'll make a fool of you. You've a temperament that's diametrically opposed to mine. All men are brothers, of course, they're like each other, but they're not always alike. And they've one thing in common. There must be one thing in common, a common language... What is it? What is it?

[*Chuckle from the* KILLER.]

Ah, I know now, I know... You see, I'm right not to give up
hope for you. We can speak the language of reason. It's the
language that suits you best. You're a scientific man, aren't you,
a man of the modern era, I've guessed it now, haven't I, a
cerebral man? You deny love, you doubt charity, it doesn't
enter into your calculations, and you think charity's a cheat,
don't you, don't you?

[*Chuckle from the* KILLER.]

I'm not blaming you. I don't despise you for that. After all,
it's a point of view, a possible point of view, but between ourselves, listen here: what do you get out of all this? What good
does it do *you*? Kill people if you like, but in your mind...
leave them alive in the flesh.

[*Shrug of the shoulders and chuckle from the* KILLER.]

Oh, yes, in your opinion that would be a comic contradiction.
Idealism you'd call it, you're for a practical philosophy, you're
a man of action. Why not? But where's the action leading
you? What's the final object? Have you asked yourself the
question of ultimate ends?

[*A more accentuated chuckle and shrug of the shoulders from the*
KILLER.]

It's an action that's utterly sterile in fact, it wears you out. It
only brings trouble... Even if the police shut their eyes to it,
which is what usually happens, what's the good of all the
effort, the fatigue, the complicated preparations and exhausting
nights on the watch... people's contempt for you? Perhaps
you don't mind. You earn their fear, it's true, that's something.
All right, but what do you do with it? It's not a form of
capital. You don't even exploit it. Answer me!

[*Chuckle from the* KILLER.]

You're poor now, aren't you? Do you want some money? I
can find you work, a decent job... No. You're not poor?
Rich then?... Aaah, I see, neither rich nor poor!

[*Chuckle from the* KILLER.]

I see, you don't want to work: well, you shan't then. I'll look after you, or as I'm poor myself, I'd better say I'll arrange for me and my friends to club together, I'll talk to the Architect about it. And you'll lead a quiet life. We'll go to the cafés and the bars, and I'll introduce you to girls who aren't too difficult... Crime doesn't pay. So stop being a criminal and we'll pay you. It's only common sense.

[*Chuckle from the* KILLER.]

You agree? Answer, answer, can't you? You understand the language!... Listen I'm going to make you a painful confession. Often, I have my doubts about everything too. But don't tell anyone. I doubt the point of living, the meaning of life, doubt my own values and every kind of rational argument. I no longer know what to hang on to, perhaps there's no more truth or charity. But if that's the case, be philosophical; if all is vanity, if charity is vanity, crime's just vanity too... When you know everything's dust and ashes, you'd be a fool if you set any store by crime, for that would be setting store by life... That would mean you were taking things seriously... and then you'd be in complete contradiction with yourself. [*Gives nervous laugh :*] Eh? It's obvious. It's only logic, I caught you there. And then you'd be in a bad way, you'd be feeble-minded, a poor specimen. Logically we'd have the right to make fun of you! Do you want us to make fun of you? Of course you don't. You must have your pride, respect your own intelligence. There's nothing worse than being stupid. It's much more compromising than being a criminal, even madness has a halo round it. But to be stupid? To be ignorant? Who can accept that?

[*Chuckle from the* KILLER.]

Everyone will point at you and laugh!

[*Chuckle from the* KILLER: BÉRENGER *is obviously more and more baffled.*]

There's the idiot going by, there's the idiot! Ha! Ha! Ha!

[*Chuckle from the* KILLER.]

He kills people, gives himself all that trouble—Ha! Ha! Ha!—

and doesn't get anything out of it, it's all for nothing... Ha!
Ha! Do you want to hear that said, be taken for an idiot, an
idealist, a crank who 'believes' in something, who 'believes' in
crime, the simpleton! Ha! Ha! Ha!

[*Chuckle from the* KILLER.]

... Who believes in crime for its own sake! Ha! Ha! [*His
laugh suddenly freezes.*] Answer me! That's what they'll say,
yes... if there's anyone left to say it... [*Wrings his hands,
clasps them, kneels down and begs the* KILLER:] I don't know what
else I can say to you. We must have done something to hurt
you.

[*Chuckle from the* KILLER.]

Perhaps there's no wrong on our side.

[*Chuckle from the* KILLER.]

I don't know. It may be my fault, it may be yours. It may not
be yours or mine. It may not be anyone's fault. What you're
doing may be wrong or it may be right, or it may be neither
right nor wrong. I don't know how to tell. It's possible that
the survival of the human species is of no importance, so what
does it matter if it disappears... perhaps the whole universe is
no good and you're right to want to blast it all, or at least
nibble at it, creature by creature, piece by piece... or perhaps
that's wrong. I don't know any more, I just don't know. You
may be mistaken, perhaps mistakes don't really exist, perhaps
it's we who are mistaken to want to exist... say what you
believe, can't you? *I* can't, *I* can't.

[*Chuckle from the* KILLER.]

Some think just *being* is a mistake, an aberration.

[*Chuckle from the* KILLER.]

Perhaps your pretended motives are only a mask for the real
cause you unconsciously hide from yourself. Who knows.
Let's sweep all these reasons away and forget the trouble you've
already caused...

[*Chuckle from the* KILLER.]

Agreed? You kill without reason in that case, and I beg you, without reason I implore you, yes, please *stop*... There's no reason why you should, naturally, but please stop, just because there's *no reason* to kill or not to kill. You're killing people for nothing, save them for nothing. Leave people alone to live their stupid lives, leave them all alone, even the policemen... Promise me you'll stop for at least a month... *please* do as I ask, for a week, for forty-eight hours, to give us a chance to breathe... You will do that, won't you?...

[*The* KILLER *chuckles softly; very slowly he takes from his pocket a knife with a large shining blade and plays with it.*]

You filthy dirty moronic imbecile! You're ugly as a monkey! Fierce as a tiger, stupid as a mule...

[*Slight chuckle from the* KILLER.]

I'm on my knees, yes... but it's not to beg for mercy...

[*Slight chuckle from the* KILLER.]

It's to take better aim... I'm going to finish you, and then I'll stamp on you and squash you to pulp, you stinking rotten carcass of a hyena! [*Takes two pistols from his pockets and aims them at the* KILLER, *who doesn't move a muscle.*] I'll kill you, you're going to pay for it, I'll shoot and shoot, and then I'll hang you, I'll chop you into a thousand pieces, I'll throw your ashes into Hell with the excrement you came from, you vomit of Satan's mangy cur, criminal cretin...

[*The* KILLER *goes on playing with the blade of his knife; slight chuckle and shrug of the shoulders, but he does not move.*]

Don't look at me like that, I'm not afraid of you, you shame creation.

[BÉRENGER *aims without firing at the* KILLER, *who is two paces away, standing still, chuckling unpleasantly and quietly raising his knife.*]

Oh... how weak my strength is against your cold determination, your ruthlessness! And what good are bullets even, against the resistance of an infinitely stubborn will! [*With a start:*] But I'll get you, I'll get you...

[*Then, still in front of the* KILLER, *whose knife is raised and who is chuckling and quite motionless,* BÉRENGER *slowly lowers his two old-fashioned pistols, lays them on the ground, bends his head and then, on his knees with his head down and his arms hanging at his side, he stammers:*]

Oh God! There's nothing we can do. What can we do... What can we do...

[*While the* KILLER *draws nearer, still chuckling, but very very softly.*]

CURTAIN

London, August 1957

MACBETT

PERFORMANCE NOTICE

Macbett was first performed on January 27, 1972 at the Théâtre de la Rive Gauche in Paris.

The English language premiere was performed by the Yale Repertory Theatre in New Haven, Connecticut on March 16, 1973. It was directed by William Peters, John McAndrew and Alvin Epstein; music composed by Gregory Sandow; sound by Carol M. Waaser; scenery design by Enno Poersch; lighting design by Ian Rodney Calderon; costume design by Maura Beth Smolover; and with the following cast:

MACBETT	Alvin Epstein
DUNCAN	Eugene Troobnick
LADY DUNCAN LADY MACBETT FIRST WITCH	Carmen de Lavallade
SECOND WITCH LADY IN WAITING	Deborah Mayo
MAID	Amandina Lihamba
GLAMISS	John McAndrew
CANDOR	William Peters
BANCO MONK MACOL	Stephen Joyce
BISHOP	Michael Gross

PERFORMANCE NOTICE

SOLDIERS, GENERALS
BUTTERFLY HUNTER
GUESTS, CROWD,
LEMONADE SELLER,
ETC.

Josepha G. Grifasi
Michael Gross
Amandina Lihamba
John McCaffrey
Paul Schierhorn
Michael Quigley

A field.

GLAMISS *and* CANDOR. GLAMISS *enters from left as* CANDOR *enters from right.*

They come on without acknowledging each other and stand center stage, facing the audience.

Pause.

GLAMISS (*turning toward* CANDOR) Good morning, Baron Candor.

CANDOR (*turning toward* GLAMISS) Good morning, Baron Glamiss.

GLAMISS Listen, Candor.

CANDOR Listen, Glamiss.

GLAMISS This can't go on.

CANDOR This can't go on.

GLAMISS and CANDOR are angry. Their anger and derision become more and more emphatic. One can hardly make out what they're saying. The text serves only as a basis for their mounting anger.

3

GLAMISS (*derisively*) Our sovereign . . .

CANDOR (*ditto*) Duncan. The beloved Archduke Duncan.

GLAMISS Yes, beloved. Well beloved.

CANDOR Too well beloved.

GLAMISS Down with Duncan.

CANDOR Down with Duncan.

GLAMISS He hunts on my land.

CANDOR For the benefit of the State.

GLAMISS So he says . . .

CANDOR He *is* the State.

GLAMISS I give him ten thousand chickens a year and their eggs.

CANDOR So do I.

GLAMISS It may be all right for others . . .

CANDOR But not for me!

GLAMISS Me neither.

CANDOR If they're prepared to take it, that's their business . . .

GLAMISS He's drafting my men into his army.

CANDOR The National army.

GLAMISS Sucking me dry.

CANDOR Sucking us dry.

GLAMISS Taking my men. My army. Turning my own men against me.

CANDOR And me.

GLAMISS Never seen anything like it.

CANDOR My ancestors would turn over in their grave . . .

GLAMISS So would mine!

CANDOR And there's all his cronies and parasites.

GLAMISS Who fat themselves on the sweat of our brow.

4

CANDOR   The fat of our chickens.

GLAMISS   Of our sheep.

CANDOR   Of our pigs.

GLAMISS   Swine.

CANDOR   Of our bread.

GLAMISS   Ten thousand chickens, ten thousand horses, ten thousand recruits. What does he do with them? He can't eat them all. The rest just goes bad.

CANDOR   And a thousand young girls.

GLAMISS   We know what he does with them.

CANDOR   Why should we owe him? It's he who owes us.

GLAMISS   More than he can pay.

CANDOR   Not to mention the rest.

GLAMISS   Down with Duncan.

CANDOR   Down with Duncan.

GLAMISS   He's no better than we are.

CANDOR   Worse, if anything.

GLAMISS   Much worse.

CANDOR   Much much worse.

GLAMISS   Just thinking about it makes my blood boil.

CANDOR   It really gets me worked up.

GLAMISS   My honor.

CANDOR   My glory.

GLAMISS   Our ancestral rights.

CANDOR   My property.

GLAMISS   My land.

CANDOR   Our right to happiness.

GLAMISS   He doesn't give two hoots.

CANDOR   He doesn't give one!

GLAMISS   We're not nobodies.

CANDOR   Far from it.

GLAMISS   We stand for something.

CANDOR   We're not just "things."

GLAMISS   We're nobody's fool—least of all Duncan's. Ha, beloved sovereign!

CANDOR   He won't lead me up the garden path or sell me down the river.

GLAMISS   Sell me up the river or lead me down the garden path.

CANDOR   Even in my dreams.

GLAMISS   Even in my dreams he haunts me like a living nightmare.

CANDOR   We must get rid of him.

GLAMISS   We must get rid of him—lock, stock, and barrel.

CANDOR   Lock, stock, and barrel.

GLAMISS   We want freedom.

CANDOR   The right to make more and more money. Self-rule!

GLAMISS   Liberty.

CANDOR   Running our own affairs!

GLAMISS   And his!

CANDOR   *And* his!

GLAMISS   We'll split it between us.

CANDOR   Half and half.

GLAMISS   Half and half.

CANDOR   He's a lousy administrator.

GLAMISS   He's unfair!

CANDOR   We'll establish justice.

GLAMISS   We'll reign in his stead.

CANDOR   We'll take his place.

CANDOR *and* GLAMISS *walk toward each other.*
They look stage right, where BANCO *enters.*

MACBETT

CANDOR   Hail Banco, gallant general.

GLAMISS   Hail Banco, great captain.

BANCO   Hail Glamiss. Hail Candor.

GLAMISS (*aside to* CANDOR)   Not a word about you-know-what. He's loyal to Duncan.

CANDOR (*to* BANCO)   We were just going for a little stroll.

GLAMISS (*to* BANCO)   Very warm for this time of year.

CANDOR (*to* BANCO)   Would you like to sit down for a moment?

BANCO   No thanks. I'm taking my morning constitutional.

GLAMISS   Ah yes. Very good for your health.

CANDOR   We admire your courage, you know.

BANCO   I do my best for King and Country.

GLAMISS (*to* BANCO)   Quite right, too.

CANDOR   You're doing a grand job.

BANCO   Now gentlemen, if you'll excuse me. (*He goes out left.*)

CANDOR   Farewell, Banco.

GLAMISS   Farewell, Banco. (*To* CANDOR) We can't count on him.

CANDOR (*half drawing his sword*)   He's got his back turned. We could kill him now if you like. (*He tiptoes several paces toward* BANCO.)

GLAMISS   Not yet. The time isn't ripe. Our army is unprepared. We need more time. It will be soon enough.

CANDOR *sheathes his sword.* MACBETT *enters stage right.*

CANDOR (*to* GLAMISS)   Here's another of the Grand Duke's loyal subjects.

GLAMISS Hail Macbett.

CANDOR Hail Macbett, faithful and virtuous gentleman.

MACBETT Hail Baron Candor. Hail Baron Glamiss.

GLAMISS Hail Macbett, great general. (*Aside to* CAN-
DOR) He mustn't suspect anything. Act natural.

CANDOR Glamiss and I are great admirers of your
fidelity, your loyalty toward our beloved sovereign,
the Archduke Duncan.

MACBETT Why shouldn't I be faithful and loyal? After
all, I took the oath of allegiance.

GLAMISS No, that's not what we meant. On the contrary, you're quite right. Congratulations.

CANDOR His gratitude no doubt is very satisfying.

MACBETT (*with a broad smile*) The generosity of King
Duncan is legendary. He always has the good of the
people at heart.

GLAMISS (*winking at* CANDOR) Quite right, too.

CANDOR We're sure he does.

MACBETT Duncan is generosity incarnate. He gives
away all he possesses.

GLAMISS (*to* MACBETT) You must have done quite
well by him.

MACBETT He's also brave.

CANDOR Great exploits testify to his courage.

GLAMISS It's common knowledge.

MACBETT He's everything they say he is. Our sovereign is good, he's loyal, and his wife, our queen, the
Archduchess, is every bit as good as she is beautiful.
She is charitable. She helps the poor. She tends the
sick.

CANDOR How could we not admire such a man?—A
perfect man. A perfect ruler.

GLAMISS How could we not be loyal in the face of such loyalty? How could we not be generous amidst such generosity?

MACBETT (*almost suiting the action to the word*) I'd fight to the death against anyone who said the contrary.

CANDOR We're convinced, absolutely convinced, that Duncan is the most virtuous ruler the world has ever known.

GLAMISS He is virtue itself.

MACBETT I do my best to follow his example. I try to be as courageous, virtuous, loyal, and good as he is.

GLAMISS That's not easy.

CANDOR Because he's a very good man indeed.

GLAMISS And Lady Duncan is very beautiful.

MACBETT I do my best to resemble him. Farewell, gentlemen. (*He goes off left.*)

GLAMISS He almost convinced me, for a minute.

CANDOR He's a believer. A . . . .

GLAMISS He's incorruptible.

CANDOR A dangerous character. He and Banco are the commanders-in-chief of the Archduke's army.

GLAMISS You're not trying to back out, are you?

CANDOR No—certainly not. I don't think so.

GLAMISS (*hand on his sword*) Just don't try it, that's all.

CANDOR No, I won't. I really won't. Yes, yes, of course you can count on me. Of course, of course! Of course!

GLAMISS Right. Let's get a move on then—polish our weapons, gather our men, prepare our armies. We shall attack at dawn. Tomorrow evening Duncan will be beaten and we shall share the throne.

CANDOR You do believe Duncan's a tyrant, don't you?

GLAMISS   A tyrant, a usurper, a despot, a dictator, a miscreant, an ogre, an ass, a goose—and worse. The proof is, he's in power. If I didn't believe it, why should I want to depose him? My motives are thoroughly honorable.

CANDOR   I suppose you're right.

GLAMISS   Let's swear to trust each other completely.

> CANDOR *and* GLAMISS *draw their swords and salute each other.*

GLAMISS   I trust you and I swear on my sword to be absolutely loyal.

CANDOR   I trust you and I swear on my sword to be absolutely loyal.

> *They sheathe their swords and go out quickly,* GLAMISS *to the left,* CANDOR *to the right.*

Pause. The stage is empty. Great play should be made here with the lighting on the cyclorama and with sound effects, which eventually becomes a sort of musique concrète.

Shots are fired. Flashes. We should see the ripple of gunfire. A conflagration in the sky on the backcloth.

Equally a very bright light could come from above which would be reflected off the stage. Storm and lightning.

The sky clears. A beautiful red sky on the backcloth. A tragic sky. At the same time as the horizon clears, and turns red, the sounds of machine-gun fire become more and more infrequent and fade into the distance.

Shouts, death rattles, the groans of the wounded are heard—then more shots. A wounded man screams shrilly.

The clouds clear. A large deserted plain. The wounded man stops screaming. After two or three seconds' silence a woman's shrill scream is heard.

This should go on for a long time before the characters in the next scene appear. The lighting and the sound effects should have nothing naturalistic about them— especially toward the end. The contributions of the lighting designer and sound technicians are of crucial importance here.

Toward the end of the sound track, a SOLDIER *fences his way across the stage from left to right—flourishes, lunges, salutes, corps a corps, feints, direct attacks, all sorts of parries.* All this happens quickly.

The noises stop for a while before beginning again. Silence. The flourishes, etc., happen quickly. There should be nothing balletic about them.

A woman, disheveled and weeping, runs across the stage from left to right.

The LEMONADE SELLER *enters stage right.*

LEMONADE SELLER Lemonade. Cool and refreshing. Soldiers and civilians, buy my lovely lemonade. Roll up, roll up. Who wants to wet his whistle? There's a truce on. Better make the most of it. Lemonade, lemonade. Cure the wounded, lemonade to keep you from getting frightened. Lemonade for soldiers. One franc a bottle, four for three francs. It's also good for scratches, cuts, and bruises.

> TWO SOLDIERS *come on from left. One is carrying the other on his back.*

LEMONADE SELLER (*to the* FIRST SOLDIER)   Wounded?
SOLDIER   No. Dead.
LEMONADE SELLER   Sword?
SOLDIER   No.
LEMONADE SELLER   Bayonet?
SOLDIER   No.
LEMONADE SELLER   Pistol shot?
SOLDIER   Heart attack.

> *The* TWO SOLDIERS *go out right.*

LEMONADE SELLER   Lemonade. Cool and refreshing. Lemonade, for soldiers. Good for the heart. Good for the shakes. The willies. The heebeejeebees.

> ANOTHER SOLDIER *enters right.*

LEMONADE SELLER   Refreshing drinks.
SECOND SOLDIER   What are you selling?
LEMONADE SELLER   Lemonade. It heals wounds.
SECOND SOLDIER   I'm not wounded.
LEMONADE SELLER   Keeps you from getting scared.
SECOND SOLDIER   I'm never scared.
LEMONADE SELLER   One franc a bottle. It's good for the heart as well.
SECOND SOLDIER (*tapping his breastplate*)   I've got seven under here.
LEMONADE SELLER   Good for scratches, too.

SECOND SOLDIER   Scratches? I've certainly got a few of
those. We fought long and hard. With this. (*He shows
his club.*) And this. (*He shows his sword.*) But especially with this. (*He shows his dagger.*) You shove
it in his belly . . . in his guts. That's the part I like
best. Look, there's still some blood on it. I use it to
cut my bread and cheese with.

LEMONADE SELLER   I can see well enough from here.

SECOND SOLDIER   Scared, are you?

LEMONADE SELLER (*terrified*)   Lemonade, lemonade.
Good for stiff necks, colds, gout, measles, smallpox.

SECOND SOLDIER   I killed as many of 'em as I could.
Mashed 'em up something horrible. They yelled and
the blood spurted. What a do! It ain't always as larky
as that. Give me a drink.

LEMONADE SELLER   It's on the house, general.

SECOND SOLDIER   I'm not a general.

LEMONADE SELLER   Major.

SECOND SOLDIER   I'm not a major.

LEMONADE SELLER   You soon will be, though. (*Gives
him a drink.*)

SECOND SOLDIER (*after several gulps*)   Revolting. Cat's
piss. What a nerve. It's daylight robbery.

LEMONADE SELLER   You can have your money back.

SECOND SOLDIER   You're shaking. You're scared. It
doesn't stop you getting the shakes, does it? (*He
draws his dagger.*)

LEMONADE SELLER   Don't do that—please.

   A bugle call.

SECOND SOLDIER (*sheathing his dagger and going off
left*)   Lucky for you I haven't got time. But just you
wait. I'll get to you again.

LEMONADE SELLER (*alone, trembling*) Whew, he really scared me. I hope the other side wins and cuts him up into little pieces—minced meat and mashed potatoes. Bastard. Swine. Shithead. (*Change.*) Lemonade, lemonade. Cool and refreshing. Three francs for four.

He goes out right slowly at first, then gradually getting quicker as the SOLDIER, *with his sword and dagger, re-appears stage left.*

> *The* SOLDIER *catches the* LEMONADE SELLER *just as he's going off into the wings. All we can see, in profile or from behind, is that the* SOLDIER *strikes the* LEMONADE SELLER, *and we hear him cry out. The* SOLDIER *disappears as well.*
>
> *The noise of shooting, screams, etc. begins again, but softer now, further away. The sky flares up again, etc.*
>
> MACBETT *enters upstage. He is exhausted. He sits down on a milestone. In his hand is a naked sword. He looks at it.*

MACBETT The blade of my sword is all red with blood. I've killed dozens and dozens of them with my bare hands. Twelve dozen officers and men who never did me any harm. I've had hundreds and hundreds of others executed by firing squad. Thousands of others were roasted alive when I set fire to the forests where they'd run for safety. Tens of thousands of men, women, and children suffocated to death in cellars, buried under the rubble of their houses which I'd blown up. Hundreds of thousands were drowned in the Channel in desperate attempts to escape. Millions died of fear or committed suicide. Ten million others died of anger, apoplexy, or a broken heart. There's not enough ground to bury them all. The bloated bodies of the dead have sucked up all the water from the lakes in which they throw themselves. There's no more water. Not even enough vultures to do the job. There are still some survivors, can you imagine? They're still fighting. We must make an end of it. If you cut their heads off, the blood spurts from their throats in fountains. Gallons of blood. My soldiers drown in it. Battalions, brigades, divisions, army corps with their commanders, brigadiers first, then in descending order of rank, lieutenant-generals, major-generals and field màrshals. The severed heads of our enemies spit in our face and mock us. Arms shorn from their trunks go on brandishing their swords and firing pistols. Amputated feet kick us up the backside. They were all traitors, of course. Enemies of the people—and of our beloved sovereign, the Archduke Duncan, whom God preserve. They wanted to overthrow him. With the help of foreign soldiers. I was right, I think. In the heat of battle, you often lay about you indiscriminately. I hope I didn't kill any of our friends by mistake. We were fighting shoulder to shoulder. I hope I didn't tread on their toes. Yes, we're in the right. I've come to rest awhile on this stone. I'm feeling a little queasy. I've left Banco in sole command of the army. I'll go and relieve him in a bit. It's strange— in spite of all this exertion, I haven't got much of an appetite. (*He pulls a large handkerchief out of his pocket and mops his brow and the rest of his face.*) I thrashed about a bit too hard. My wrist aches. Luckily it's nothing serious. It's been quite a pleasant day, really. Feeling quite bucked. (*He shouts to his orderly, stage right.*) Go and clean my sword in the river and bring me something to drink.

The ORDERLY *enters and goes out with the sword. He comes back immediately, without having completely left the stage.*

ORDERLY   One clean sword and a jug of wine.

MACBETT *takes the sword.*

MACBETT   Good as new.

He sheathes the sword and drinks from the jug of wine, while the ORDERLY *goes out left.*

No. No regrets. They were traitors after all. I obeyed my sovereign's orders. I did my duty. (*Putting the jug down.*) It's good, this wine. I'm quite rested now. Well, back to the grind. (*He looks upstage.*) Here's Banco. Hey. How's it going?

BANCO *or his* VOICE   They're just about retreating. Take over from me, will you? I'm going to take a bit of a breather. I'll join you in a bit.

MACBETT   We mustn't let Glamiss escape. I'll go and surround them. Quickly.

MACBETT *goes off upstage.* MACBETT *and* BANCO *resemble each other. Same costume, same beard.*

BANCO *enters right. He is exhausted. He sits down on a boundary stone. In his hand is a naked sword. He looks at it.*

BANCO   The blade of my sword is all red with blood.
I've killed dozens and dozens of them with my own
hand. Twelve dozen officers and men who never did
me any harm. I've had hundreds and hundreds of
others executed by the firing squad. Thousands of
others were roasted alive when I set fire to the forests
where they'd run for safety. Tens of thousands of
men, women and children suffocated to death in cellars, buried under the rubble of their houses which
I'd blown up. Hundreds of thousands were drowned
in the Channel in desperate attempts to escape. Millions died of fear or committed suicide. Ten million
others died of anger, apoplexy or a broken heart.
There's not enough ground to bury them all. The
bloated bodies of the dead have sucked up all the
water from the lakes in which they threw themselves.
There's no more water. Not even enough vultures to
do the job. There are still some survivors, can you
imagine? They're still fighting. We must make an
end of it. If you cut their heads off, the blood spurts
from their throats in fountains. Gallons of blood. My
soldiers drown in it. Battalions, brigades, divisions,
army corps with their commanders, brigadiers first,
then in descending order of rank, lieutenant-generals, major-generals and field marshals. The severed heads of our enemies spit in our face and
mock us. Arms shorn from their trunks go on waving
swords or firing pistols. Amputated feet kick us up
the backside. They were traitors, of course. Enemies
of the people—and of our beloved sovereign, the
Archduke Duncan, whom God preserve. They wanted
to overthrow him. With the help of foreign soldiers.
I was right, I think. In the heat of battle, you often

lay about you indiscriminately. I hope I didn't kill any of our friends by mistake. We were fighting shoulder to shoulder. I hope I didn't tread on their toes. Yes, we're in the right. I've come to rest awhile on this stone. I'm feeling a little queasy. I've left Macbett in sole command of the army. I'll go and relieve him in a bit. It's strange—in spite of all this exertion I haven't got much of an appetite. (*He pulls a large handkerchief out of his pocket and mops his brow and the rest of his face.*) I thrashed about a bit too hard. My wrist aches. Luckily it's nothing serious. It's been quite a pleasant day, really. Feeling quite bucked. (*He shouts to his orderly, stage right.*) Go and clean my sword in the river and bring me something to drink.

The ORDERLY *enters and goes out with the sword. He comes back immediately, without having completely left the stage.*

ORDERLY   One clean sword and a jug of wine.

BANCO *takes the sword.*

BANCO   Good as new.

He sheathes the sword and drinks from the jug of wine, while the ORDERLY *goes out left.*

No. No regrets. They were traitors after all. I obeyed my sovereign's orders. I did my duty. (*Putting the jug down.*) It's good, this wine. I'm quite rested now. Well, back to the grind. (*He looks upstage.*) Here's Macbett. Hey. How's it going?

MACBETT

MACBETT *or his* VOICE   They're just about retreating.
Come and join me and we'll finish them off.
BANCO   We mustn't let Glamiss escape. We'll surround
them. I'll be right with you. (BANCO *goes out upstage.*)

*The sounds of battle well up again. The conflagration
in the sky is brighter now.*

Pounding brutal music.

*A woman crosses the stage from left to right. She is
quite unconcerned and has a basket over her arm as if
she were going shopping.*

*The sound dies away again until it is little more than
a background murmur.*

*The stage is empty for a few moments, then ridiculously
lavish fanfares drown out the noise of battle.*

An OFFICER *in Duncan's army comes on quickly from
the left and stops stage center. He is carrying a sort of
armchair or portable throne.*

OFFICER   Our lord, the Archduke Duncan and the
Archduchess.

LADY DUNCAN *and the* ARCHDUKE *come on left.*
LADY DUNCAN *is in front of the* ARCHDUKE. *She is
wearing a crown and a long green dress with a
flower on it. She is the only character in the play
who dresses with a certain flair.* DUNCAN *mounts
the throne. The two others stand on either side of
him.*

19

OFFICER Come on, my lord. It's all right. The battle
has moved on. We're out of range here. Not even a
sniper about. Don't be afraid. There are even people
strolling about.

DUNCAN Has Candor been defeated. If so, have they
executed him? Have they killed Glamiss as I ordered?

OFFICER I hope so. You should have looked a bit more
closely. The horizon is all red. It looks as if they're
still at it, but a long way off now. We must wait till
it's over. Be patient, my lord.

DUNCAN What if Macbett and Banco have been
routed?

LADY DUNCAN You take the field yourself.

DUNCAN If they've been beaten, where can I hide?
The king of Malta is my enemy. So is the emperor of
Cuba. *And* the prince of the Balearic Isles. And the
kings of France and Ireland, and what's more, I've
got lots of enemies at the English court. Where can
I hide?

OFFICER It's all right, my lord. You just leave it to
Macbett and Banco. They're good generals—brave,
energetic, skilled strategists. They've proved their
worth time and again.

DUNCAN I don't seem to have much choice. In any
case I'm going to take one or two precautions. Saddle
my best horse, the one who doesn't kick, and get my
launch ready, the most stable vessel on the seven
seas, the one with all the lifeboats. If only I could
give orders to the moon—make it full, and order the
stars to come out. For I really should travel by night.
That's the safest thing. Safety first, I always say. I
better bring a little money along, just in case. But

where shall we go? Canada perhaps, or the United States.

OFFICER   Just wait a little while. Don't lose heart.

A WOUNDED SOLDIER *staggers on.*

DUNCAN   What's that drunk doing here?

OFFICER   He's not drunk. He's wounded.

DUNCAN   If you come from the battle, give me a report. Who's won?

SOLDIER   Does it matter?

OFFICER   Who's won? Was there a winner? You're in the presence of your king.

DUNCAN   I am your sovereign—the Archduke Duncan.

SOLDIER   Oh, I'm sorry, sir. I'm a bit wounded. I've been stabbed and shot. (*He staggers.*)

DUNCAN   It's no good pretending to faint. Answer me! Was it them or us?

SOLDIER   I'm not sure. It all got a bit too much for me. To tell you the truth, I left early. Before the end.

DUNCAN   You should have stayed.

OFFICER   Then he wouldn't be here to answer your questions.

DUNCAN   He left "before the end" as if it was a boring play.

SOLDIER   I fell down. Passed out. Came round again. Got up as best I could and, as best I could, dragged myself here.

DUNCAN (*to the* SOLDIER)   Are you sure you're one of ours?

SOLDIER   Who do you mean, "ours"?

OFFICER   The Archduke's and the Archduchess's, of course. They're standing right here in front of you.

SOLDIER   I didn't see you on the battlefield, my lord.

DUNCAN (*to the* SOLDIER)   What were your generals' names?

SOLDIER   I don't know. I was just coming out of the pub and a sergeant on horseback lassoed me. My mates were lucky. They got away. I tried to resist, but they hit me over the head, tied me up and carried me off. They gave me a sword. Oh, I seem to have dropped it somewhere. And a pistol. (*He puts the pistol to his head and pulls the trigger.*) Out of ammunition. Must have fired it all. There were a load of us out there on the field and they made us shout "Long live Glamiss and Candor."

DUNCAN   Traitor, you're one of our enemies.

OFFICER   I shouldn't cut his head off if I were you, my lord. Not if you want to hear the rest.

SOLDIER   And then they shot at us, and we shot at them.

DUNCAN   Who's "they"?

SOLDIER   And then they took us prisoner. And then they told me if you want to keep a head on your shoulders, you'd better join us. They told us to shout "Down with Candor, down with Glamiss." And then we shot at them and they shot at us. I was hit several times, wounded in the thigh, and then I guess I fell down. Then I woke up and the battle was still going on a long way away. There was nothing but heaps of dying men all around me. So, as I said I started walking; and my right leg is hurting, and my left leg is hurting, and I'm losing blood from the wound in my thigh. And then I got here . . . That's all I've got to say—except that I'm still bleeding. (*Gets up painfully. Totters.*)

DUNCAN   This idiot's made me none the wiser.

SOLDIER   That's all I've got to say. I don't know any more.

DUNCAN (*to* LADY DUNCAN)   He's a deserter.

LADY DUNCAN *draws her dagger. Her arm is poised to stab the* SOLDIER.

SOLDIER   Oh, don't bother yourself ma'am. (*He gestures off right.*) I'll just crawl over to that tree there and kick off. You can save yourself the trouble. (*He goes staggering off, left.*)

LADY DUNCAN   At least he's polite. Unusual for a soldier.

From the right, the noise of a body falling.

DUNCAN (*to the* OFFICER)   Stay here and defend me. I may need you. (*To* LADY DUNCAN) Quickly, take one of the horses, trot up to the front, then come back and tell me what's going on. Don't get too near though. I'll look through my telescope.

LADY DUNCAN *goes out right. While* DUNCAN *is looking through his telescope, we can see* LADY DUNCAN *upstage on her horse. Then* DUNCAN *folds up his telescope.*

Meanwhile, the OFFICER *has been standing with his sword drawn, looking menacingly in all directions.* DUNCAN *goes out right followed by the* OFFICER *carrying the armchair.*

23

Scene: near the battlefield.

Shouts of "Victory! Victory! Victory! . . ." coming from downstage left and right.

The word "victory" is repeated, modulated, orchestrated until the end of the following scene.

Sound of a horse galloping closer and closer is heard from the wings right. An ORDERLY *hurries on left.*

ORDERLY (*shading his eyes*) Is that a horse? I think it's coming nearer. Yes. It's coming toward us at full tilt.

BANCO (*comes on from left and shades his eyes*) I wonder what the rider wants, galloping so fast on that magnificent stallion. It must be a messenger.

ORDERLY It's not a man. It's a woman.

> *Sound of neighing. The hoof beats stop.* LADY DUNCAN *appears, a riding crop in her hand.*

BANCO It's her Highness, the Archduchess, the Archduchess. I humbly greet your highness. (*He bows, then kneels to kiss the Archduchess's hand.*) What is your Highness doing so near the battlefield? We're proud and happy that your Highness takes such an interest in our silly squabbles. As for our own life, we hold it at a pin's fee, but we are worried about your Highness's safety.

LADY DUNCAN Duncan has sent me for news. He wants to know what's going on and whether you've won the war.

BANCO I understand his impatience. We *have* won.

LADY DUNCAN Bully for you. Rise, my dear Macbett.

BANCO   I'm not Macbett. I'm Banco.

LADY DUNCAN   Excuse me. Rise, my dear Banco.

BANCO   Thank you, madam. (*To the* ORDERLY) What are you gaping at? Get the hell out of here, you stupid bastard.

ORDERLY   Yessir. (*He disappears.*)

BANCO   I apologize for that momentary indiscretion. Swearing like a trooper. Please forgive me, your Highness.

LADY DUNCAN   Of course I forgive you, Banco. It's to be expected in wartime. People are more high strung than in peacetime, obviously. The main thing is to win. If a few rude words are going to help the war effort, that's fine by me. Have you taken Baron Candor prisoner?

BANCO   Of course.

LADY DUNCAN   And Baron Glamiss?

MACBETT'S VOICE   (*coming from the left*)   Banco. Banco. Where are you? Who are you talking to?

BANCO   To her Highness, Lady Duncan, sent by the Archduke himself to gather information. Macbett will tell you about the fate of Glamiss.

MACBETT   (*still offstage*)   I'll be right with you.

BANCO   I'll leave you to Macbett, madam. He'll tell you what's happening to our prisoners and give you a full account.

MACBETT'S VOICE   (*quite near now*)   I'm coming.

BANCO   Excuse me, your Highness. I must go and feed my men. A good general is like a mother to his troops. (*He goes out left.*)

MACBETT'S VOICE   (*nearer still*)   Coming. Coming.

MACBETT *enters left. He greets* LADY DUNCAN.

MACBETT We have served our beloved sovereign well. Candor is in our hands. We've pursued Glamiss to a nearby mountain which you can see in the distance there. He's surrounded. We've got him trapped.

LADY DUNCAN So you're General Macbett, are you?

MACBETT At your command, your Highness.

LADY DUNCAN I remember you looking different. You don't look very much like yourself.

MACBETT My face looks different when I'm tired and I'm afraid I don't look very much like myself. People often take me for my twin brother. Or for Banco's twin brother.

LADY DUNCAN You must get tired quite a lot.

MACBETT War isn't a picnic. But one must learn to take the rough with the smooth. Let's say it's . . .

LADY DUNCAN puts her hand to MACBETT who kneels and kisses it, then gets up quickly.

. . . an occupational hazard.

LADY DUNCAN I'll go and tell the Archduke the good news.

BANCO'S VOICE (*in the wings*) All clear.

LADY DUNCAN goes to the wings stage right and signals with her hand. She returns center stage. Fanfares are heard.

MACBETT His Highness the Archduke!

SOLDIER His Highness the Archduke!

BANCO'S VOICE The Archduke!

LADY DUNCAN Here comes the Archduke!

BANCO'S HEAD (*appearing and disappearing*) The Archduke!

SOLDIER   The Archduke!

MACBETT   The Archduke!

LADY DUNCAN   Here comes the Archduke!

BANCO'S VOICE   The Archduke!

SOLDIER   The Archduke!

MACBETT   The Archduke!

LADY DUNCAN   Here comes the Archduke!

BANCO'S HEAD   The Archduke!

SOLDIER   The Archduke!

MACBETT   The Archduke!

LADY DUNCAN   Here comes the Archduke!

Blazing fanfares. The sound of cheering. DUNCAN
enters right. The fanfares stop.

LADY DUNCAN   The battle is over.

MACBETT   Greetings, your Highness.

BANCO'S HEAD   Greetings, your Highness.

SOLDIER   Greetings, your Highness.

MACBETT   My humble greetings.

DUNCAN   Did we win?

MACBETT   The danger is over.

DUNCAN   Thank God. Has Candor been executed?

MACBETT   No, my good lord. But we've taken him
prisoner.

DUNCAN   Why haven't you killed him? What are you
waiting for?

MACBETT   Your orders, my good lord.

DUNCAN   You have them. Off with his head. Jump to
it. What have you done with Glamiss? Have you torn
him limb from limb?

MACBETT   No, my good lord. But he is surrounded.

Any moment now we'll take him prisoner. There's no cause for alarm, your Majesty.

DUNCAN Well then, well done. I can't thank you enough.

The SOLDIERS *and the crowd shouting "Hurrah!" We don't see them—unless they're projected onto the back.*

MACBETT We're proud and happy to have been of service, my good lord.

BANCO'S HEAD (*appearing and disappearing*) We were only doing our duty, my good lord.

More fanfares which get softer and softer until they become a background accompaniment to the scene.

DUNCAN Thank you, my dear generals, and thank you, my gallant soldiers, who saved my country and my throne. Many of you laid down your lives in the struggle. Thank you all again, dead or alive, for having defended my throne . . . which, of course, is also yours. When you return home, whether it be to your humble villages, your lowly hearths, or your simple but glorious tombs, you will be an example to generations to come, now and in the future and, better still, in the past; they will keep your memory alive for hundreds and hundreds of years, in word and deed, voiceless perhaps but ever present, in fame or anonymity, in the face of an undying yet transient history. Your presence, for even though absent you will be present to those who, whether they can see you or not, shall gaze lovingly at your photographs— your presence will serve as a pointer, tomorrow, and in the future, to all those who are tempted not to follow your example. As for the present, continue as you have done in the past, to earn your daily bread as gallantly as ever by the sweat of your brow, neath the sun's burning rays and under the watchful eye of your lords and masters who love you despite yourselves and whatever your shortcomings have a higher opinion of you than you might imagine. You may go.

Fanfares and hurrahs fainter now.

MACBETT   Bravo!
SOLDIER   Bravo!
DUNCAN   Nicely put, don't you think?
LADY DUNCAN   Bravo, Duncan! (*She applauds.*) That was a marvelous speech.

MACBETT *and the* SOLDIER *applaud.*

BANCO'S VOICE   Bravo!
DUNCAN   They deserved it. In future, my generals and my friends will all share in my glory. And my noble wife. (*He smiles at* LADY DUNCAN *and kisses her hand.*) You can all be proud of yourselves. And now, justice and retribution. Bring in Candor. Where's Banco?
MACBETT   He's with the prisoner.
DUNCAN   He will be the executioner.

MACBETT (*aside*)   That honor should have been mine.

DUNCAN   Let him approach with the traitor. Go and get him.

> The SOLDIER *goes out left. At the same moment* CANDOR *and* BANCO *come on right. Banco's head is covered in a hood. He is wearing a red pullover and carrying an axe.* CANDOR *is handcuffed.*

DUNCAN (*to* CANDOR)   You're going to pay for your treachery.

CANDOR   And pay dearly. I have no illusions. If only I had won. The victor is always right. *Vae victis.* (*To* MACBETT) If you'd fought for me, I'd have rewarded you well. I'd have made you a duke. And you, Banco, I'd have made you a duke, too. You'd both have been loaded with honor and riches.

DUNCAN (*to* CANDOR)   Don't worry. Macbett will be Baron Candor. He'll inherit all your lands, and your wife and daughter, too, if he likes.

MACBETT (*to* DUNCAN)   I'm faithful to you, my lord. I'm faithfulness personified. I was born faithful to you, as a dog or horse is born faithful to its master.

DUNCAN (*to* BANCO)   Don't you worry, either. You've no need to be jealous. Once Glamiss is captured and beheaded, you will be Baron Glamiss and inherit all his property.

MACBETT (*to* DUNCAN)   Thank you, my lord.

BANCO (*to* DUNCAN)   Thank you, my lord.

MACBETT (*to* DUNCAN)   We would have been faithful.

BANCO (*to* DUNCAN)   We would have been faithful.

MACBETT   Even if you hadn't rewarded us.

BANCO   Even if you hadn't rewarded us.

30

MACBETT   Serving you is its own reward.

BANCO   Serving you is its own reward.

MACBETT   But as it is, your bounty well satisfies our natural greed.

BANCO   We thank you from the bottom of our heart.

MACBETT *and* BANCO (MACBETT *drawing his sword and* BANCO *brandishing his cleaver*) . . . from the bottom of our heart. We'd go through Hell for you, your gracious Majesty.

A MAN *crosses the stage from left to right.*

MAN   Rags and bones! Rags and bones.

DUNCAN (*to* CANDOR)   You see how devoted *they* are?

MACBETT *and* BANCO   It's because you are a good king, generous and just.

MAN   Rags and bones! Rags and bones. (*He goes out left. The rag-and-bone* MAN *can be cut or kept in as the director wishes.*)

As he goes out, a SERVANT *comes in carrying armchairs for* DUNCAN, LADY DUNCAN *and the others.*

During the action which follows, he will bring a towel, a basin, and some soap, or perhaps just some eau de cologne for LADY DUNCAN, *who washes her hands—very emphatically, as if trying to get rid of a spot or stain. She should do this in a rather mechanical absent-minded way. Then the same* SERVANT *brings in a table and tea service and serves cups of tea to those present.*

The lights come up on a guillotine, and then gradually a whole forest of guillotines comes into view.

DUNCAN (*to* CANDOR) Have you anything to say? We're listening.

They all settle down to look and listen.

SERVANT (*to* LADY DUNCAN) Tea is served, madam.

CANDOR If I'd been stronger, I'd have been your anointed king. Defeated, I'm a traitor and a coward. If only I'd won. But History was against me. History is right, objectively speaking. I'm just a historical dead end. I hope at least that my fate will serve as an example to you all and to posterity. Throw in your lot with the stronger. But how do you know who the stronger is, before it comes to the crunch? The masses should keep out of it until the fighting is over and then throw in their lot with the winner. The logic of events is the only one that counts. Historical reason is the only reason. There are no transcendental values to set against it. I am guilty. But our rebellion was necessary, if only to prove that I'm a criminal. I shall die happy. My life is an empty husk. My body and those of my followers will fertilize the fields and push up wheat for future harvests. I'm a perfect example of what not to do.

DUNCAN (*quietly to* LADY DUNCAN) This is too long. Aren't you bored? I bet you're excited to see what happens next. No, no, we won't torture him. Just put him to death. Disappointed? I've got a surprise for you, dear. The entertainment will be more lavish than you thought. (*To everybody*) Justice demands that the soldiers of Candor's army be executed along with him. There aren't very many of them.

137,000—not too many, not too few. Let's get a move on. We want to be done by dawn.

Upstage a large red sun slowly sinks. DUNCAN *claps his hands.*

Go on. Off with his head.

CANDOR   Long live the Archduke!

BANCO *has already arranged his head on the guillotine. To do so he has had to get rid of his ax.*

One after another, CANDOR's *soldiers pass in a continuous procession to the guillotine. (The same actors follow each other around.)*

Another way to do it would be to have the scaffold and the guillotine appear as soon as DUNCAN *gives the order.* BANCO *pushes the button and the heads fall.*

BANCO   Hurry, hurry, hurry, hurry!

After each "Hurry" the blade falls. The heads pile up in the basket.

DUNCAN (*to* MACBETT)   Have a seat next to my dear wife.

MACBETT *sits down beside* LADY DUNCAN. *They both need to be clearly visible so that the audience can see what's going on. For example,* LADY DUNCAN *and the others could be sitting with their*

33

backs to the guillotine but still appear to be watching the executions. LADY DUNCAN *is counting heads.*

During the whole of this, the SERVANT *is serving tea to one or other of the characters, offering them buns and so on.*

MACBETT   I'm overwhelmed, madam, to be so close to you.

LADY DUNCAN (*still counting*)   Four, five, six, seven, seventeen, twenty-three, thirty-three, thirty-three— I think I missed one.

Without ever stopping counting, she starts nudging MACBETT *and playing footsy with him—at first discreetly, then more and more obviously until the whole thing becomes excessive and grossly indecent.*

MACBETT *edges away a little. At first he is rather embarrassed and confused. Then gradually, half-frightened, half-pleased, he gives in, eagerly acquiescing.*

DUNCAN (*to* MACBETT)   Now, back to business. I create you Baron Candor. Your comrade Banco will be Baron Glamiss when Glamiss has been executed in his turn.

LADY DUNCAN (*still fondling* MACBETT)   A hundred and sixteen, a hundred and eighteen, what a moving sight.

MACBETT   I'm very grateful to your Highness, my lord.

LADY DUNCAN   Three hundred. I'm getting dizzy. Nine thousand three hundred.

DUNCAN (*to* MACBETT)   Now listen carefully.

> MACBETT *disentangles himself a little from* LADY DUNCAN, *who continues to play with him, rubbing up against him and putting her hand on his knee.*

MACBETT   I'm all ears, my lord.

DUNCAN   I shall keep half of Candor's lands and half of Glamiss's too. They will be added to the crown estates.

LADY DUNCAN   Twenty thousand.

BANCO (*still working the guillotine*)   Thank you, your Highness.

DUNCAN (*to* MACBETT)   There are some things you will have to do for me—both of you—in return. Certain duties, certain obligations, certain taxes to be paid.

> An OFFICER *runs onstage and stops center stage.*

OFFICER   Glamiss has escaped!

DUNCAN   I'll tell you the details later.

OFFICER   My lord, Glamiss has escaped.

DUNCAN (*to the* OFFICER)   What?

OFFICER   Glamiss has escaped. Part of his forces rallied to him.

> BANCO *stops guillotining and comes downstage. The other characters jump up.*

BANCO How could he have escaped? He was surrounded. He was as good as taken. It's a conspiracy.

DUNCAN Damn!

LADY DUNCAN (*still pressing against* MACBETT) Damn!

MACBETT Damn!

DUNCAN (*to* BANCO) Whoever is responsible, you won't be Baron Glamiss nor get half his lands till you bring him before me bound hand and foot. (*Turning to the* OFFICER.) And you're going to have your head cut off for bringing us such disagreeable news.

OFFICER It's not my fault.

> A SOLDIER *drags the* OFFICER *upstage to the guillotine. The* OFFICER *yells. They cut his head off.*

> *Music.* DUNCAN *goes out.* LADY DUNCAN *plays footsy with* MACBETT *and rolls her eyes at him.*

> DUNCAN *comes back on. The music stops.*

> *He addresses* LADY DUNCAN *who is going out backward blowing kisses to* MACBETT.

DUNCAN Come along, madam. (*He drags her off by the scruff of the neck.*)

LADY DUNCAN I wanted to see what was going to happen next.

DUNCAN'S VOICE (*to* BANCO) Bring me Glamiss—by tomorrow.

> *Music.*

BANCO (*going over to* MACBETT) We've got to start all over again. What a disaster.

MACBETT   What a disaster.
BANCO   What a disaster.
MACBETT   What a disaster.

Wind and storm.

The stage is dark. All we can see is Macbett's face—and the faces of the FIRST AND SECOND WITCHES *when they appear.*

Enter MACBETT *and* BANCO

MACBETT   What a storm, Banco. Terrifying. The trees look as if they're trying to pull themselves up by the roots. I just hope they don't topple onto our heads.
BANCO   It's ten miles to the nearest inn and we haven't got a horse.
MACBETT   We didn't realize how far we'd come.
BANCO   And now we're caught in the storm.
MACBETT   Still, we can't stand here all day discussing the weather.
BANCO   I'll go and stand by the road. Perhaps a cart will come along and give us a lift.
MACBETT   I'll wait for you here.

   BANCO *goes out.*

FIRST WITCH   Hail Macbett, thane of Candor.
MACBETT   You frightened me. I didn't know there was anybody there. It's only an old woman. She looks like a witch to me. (*To the* WITCH) How did you know I'm thane of Candor? Has rumor added it's

murmur to the rustling of the forest? Are wind and storm echoing the news abroad?

SECOND WITCH (*to* MACBETT) Hail Macbett, thane of Glamiss.

MACBETT Thane of Glamiss? But Glamiss lives. Besides, Duncan promised his title and his lands to Banco. (*He notices that it was the* SECOND WITCH *who spoke.*) Another one.

FIRST WITCH Glamiss is dead. Drowned. The torrent swept him and his horse away.

MACBETT Is this some kind of joke? I'll have your tongues cut out, you old hags.

FIRST WITCH Duncan is very displeased with Banco for letting Glamiss escape.

MACBETT How do you know?

SECOND WITCH Duncan wants to take advantage of this. He is going to give you the title and keep the lands for himself.

MACBETT Duncan is loyal. He keeps his promises.

FIRST WITCH You will be Archduke and rule the country.

MACBETT You're lying. I'm not ambitious. Or rather my only ambition is to serve my king.

FIRST WITCH You will be king yourself. It is ordained. I can see the star on your forehead.

MACBETT It's impossible. Duncan has a son, Macol, who's studying at Carthage. He is the natural and legitimate heir to the throne.

SECOND WITCH There's another son who's just finishing a post-graduate degree in economics and navigation at Ragusa. He's called Donalbain.

MACBETT Never heard of him.

FIRST WITCH (*to* MACBETT) You can forget about him. He won't interfere. (*To the* SECOND WITCH) It wasn't navigation. It was business studies—though obviously shipping was part of the course.

MACBETT Rubbish. Die. (*He waves his sword and strikes at the air. We hear the Witches' terrifying laughter.*) Hellish creatures.

They have disappeared.

Did I really see them and hear them? They've changed into the wind and storm. Disappeared into the roots of trees.

FIRST WITCH (*now a woman's melodious voice*) I'm not the wind. I'm not a dream, Macbett. I'll soon be back. Then you'll know my power and my charm.

MACBETT Jumping catfish! (*He takes three or four more swipes, then stops.*) I thought I recognized that voice. Who can it be? Voice, have you a body? Have you a face? Where are you?

FIRST WITCH (*melodiously*) Right beside you. Right beside you. And a long way off. Farewell, Macbett. Till we meet again.

MACBETT I'm shivering. It must be the cold. Or the rain. Or is it fear? Or horror? Or some mysterious longing that this voice arouses in me? Am I already under its spell? (*Change of tone.*) Filthy hags. (*Change of tone.*) Banco. Banco. Where can he have got to? Have you found a cart? Where are you? Banco. Banco. (*He goes out right.*)

Pause. The stage is empty. Noise of the storm.

FIRST WITCH (*to the* SECOND WITCH) Here comes Banco.

SECOND WITCH When they're not together, they're either following each other about or looking for each other.

The FIRST WITCH *hides stage right. The* SECOND WITCH *hides stage left.* BANCO *enters upstage.*

BANCO Macbett. Macbett. (*He makes a show of looking for* MACBETT.) Macbett, I've found the cart. (*To himself*) I'm soaked to the skin. Luckily, it's slackening off a bit.

In the distance a voice calling "Banco."

I thought I heard him calling. He should have stayed here. He must have got tired of waiting.

VOICE Banco! Banco!

BANCO Here I am. Where are you?

VOICE (*nearer now, coming from the right*) Banco! Banco!

BANCO Coming. Where are you? (*He runs stage right.*)

ANOTHER VOICE (*different, coming from the left*) Banco!

BANCO Where are you?

FIRST WITCH'S VOICE Banco!

BANCO Is that Macbett?

SECOND WITCH'S VOICE Banco!

BANCO It doesn't sound like him.

The TWO WITCHES *leave their hiding place and close in on* BANCO *from both sides.*

BANCO   What's the meaning of this?

FIRST WITCH   Hail Banco, Macbett's companion.

SECOND WITCH   Hail, General Banco.

BANCO   Who are you? Hideous creatures, what do you want? Lucky for you, you're women—of a kind. Otherwise, I'd have cut your heads off for fooling with me like that.

FIRST WITCH   Now don't get excited, General Banco.

BANCO   How do you know my name?

SECOND WITCH   Hail Banco—who won't be thane of Glamiss.

BANCO   How do you know that title was supposed to be mine? How do you know I won't get it? Has rumor added its murmur to the rustling of the forest? Are wind and storm echoing the news abroad?—Anyway, I can't be thane of Glamiss.

FIRST WITCH   Glamiss is dead. Drowned. The torrent swept him and his horse away.

BANCO   Is this some kind of joke? I'll have your tongues cut out, you old hags.

SECOND WITCH   Duncan is very displeased with you for letting Glamiss escape.

BANCO   How do you know?

FIRST WITCH   He wants to take advantage of this. He's going to give the title, Baron Glamiss, to Macbett. All the estates will revert to the crown.

BANCO   The title alone would have been enough. Why should Duncan wish to deprive me of it? No, Duncan is loyal. He keeps his promises. Why should he give

4 1

the title to Macbett. Why should he punish me? Why should Macbett have all the favors and all the privileges?

SECOND WITCH   Macbett is your rival. Your successful rival.

BANCO   He is my companion. He is my friend. He is my brother. He is loyal.

The WITCHES *withdraw a little and jump up and down.*

THE TWO WITCHES   He thinks he's loyal. He thinks he's loyal. (*They laugh.*)

BANCO (*drawing his sword*)   Monstrous creatures, I know who you are. You're spies. You're working for the enemies of Duncan, our loyal and beloved sovereign.

He tries to run them through. But they escape and run off, FIRST WITCH *to the left,* SECOND WITCH *to the right.*

FIRST WITCH (*before she disappears*)   Macbett will be king. He'll take Duncan's place.

SECOND WITCH   He'll mount the throne.

BANCO *runs backward and forward brandishing his sword, trying to run them through.*

BANCO   Where are you? Accursed gypsies. Hellish creatures. (*He sheathes his sword and returns to center stage.*) Did I really see them and hear them?

They've changed into the wind and storm. They've changed into the roots of trees. Was it all a dream?

SECOND WITCH'S VOICE   Hear me, Banco, hear me. (*The* SECOND WITCH'S VOICE *becomes pleasant and melodious.*) Mark me. You won't be king. But you'll be greater than Macbett. Greater than Macbett. You will found a dynasty which will rule over our country for a thousand years. You will be greater than Macbett—root and father of many kings.

BANCO   I don't believe it . . . I don't believe it. (*He takes three or four more swipes, then stops.*) I thought I recognized that voice. Who can it be? Voice, have you a body? Have you a face? Where are you?

VOICE   Right beside you. And a long way off. You'll see me again soon. Then you'll know my power and my charm. Till then, Banco.

BANCO   I'm shivering. It must be the rain. Or is it fear? Or horror? Or some mysterious longing that this voice arouses in me? Who does it remind me of? Am I already under its spell? (*Change of tone.*) Just ugly old hags, that's all. Spies, intriguers, liars. Father of kings, me? When our beloved sovereign has sons of his own? Macol, who's studying at Carthage, is the natural and legitimate heir to the throne. There's also Donalbain who's just finished a post-graduate degree in business studies at Ragusa. Nonsense, every word of it. I won't give it another thought.

MACBETT'S VOICE   Banco! Banco!

BANCO   It's Macbett's voice. Macbett! Ah, there you are.

MACBETT'S VOICE   Banco!

BANCO Macbett! (*He rushes off left, where* MAC-
BETT'S VOICE *was coming from.*)

Pause. The stage is empty.

*Gradually, the light changes. Upstage a sort of enor-
mous moon, very bright, surrounded by big stars. Perhaps the Milky Way, too, like a big bunch of grapes.*

*During the next scene the setting will gradually become
more specific. Little by little we are able to make out
the outline of a castle. In the middle of it, a small
lighted window. It's important that the sets work with
or without the characters.*

*The following sequence can be kept in or cut as re-
quired.*

DUNCAN *crosses silently right to left.*

When he's gone off left, LADY DUNCAN *appears and follows him across. She disappears.*

MACBETT *crosses silently, going the opposite way. An*
OFFICER *crosses silently from right to left.*

BANCO *crosses silently right to left.*

A WOMAN *crosses slowly and silently in the opposite
direction. (I think the woman, at least, should be kept
in.)*

Pause. The stage is empty. BANCO *enters upstage.*

BANCO Well, how about that then? The witch was
right. Where did she get her information? Does she

have a contact at court? But so quickly. Perhaps she
does have supernatural powers after all. Unusual, to
say the least. Perhaps she's found a way of harness-
ing sound waves. Perhaps she's discovered that channel, mentioned in certain myths, that enables you to
put the person talking in touch with the person listening. Perhaps she's invented mirrors which reflect
distant images as if they were close at hand, as if
they were talking to you six feet away. Perhaps she
has enchanted glasses that enable her to see for
hundreds or thousands of miles. Perhaps she has
instruments for amplifying sound and making the
ear incredibly sensitive. One of the Archduke's officers has just come to tell me of Glamiss's death
and of my being passed over. Did Macbett plot to
gain the title? Could my loyal friend and companion
be a swindler? Is Duncan so ungrateful that he can
disregard my efforts and the risks I've taken, the
dangers I've undergone to defend him and keep him
from harm? Is there no one I can trust? And shall I
then suspect my brother, my faithful dog, the wine I
drink, the very air I breathe? No, no. I know Macbett
too well to be anything but convinced of his loyalty
and his virtue. Duncan's decision is undoubtedly his
own; no prompter but his own nature. It shows him
in his true colors. But Macbett can't have heard yet.
When he does, he'll refuse to have anything to do
with it. (*He begins to go off left, then returns center
stage.*) They have looked into space, these monstrous
daughters of the devil. Can they also look into the
future? They told me I should father a line of kings.
Strange and incredible. I wish they could tell me
more. Perhaps they really do know what will hap-

pen. I wish I could see them but I can't . . . But I did.

He goes out left. MACBETT *enters right. Before he comes on we hear him shouting.*

MACBETT   Banco! Banco! (*He comes on. Shouts again, and again.*) Banco! Where can he have got to? They told me he was hereabouts. I wanted to talk to him. A messenger from the Archduke has summoned me to court. The king tells me Glamiss is dead and that I'm to inherit his title, but not his lands. The witches' prophecies are beginning to come true. I tried to tell Duncan that I didn't want him to dispossess Banco in my favor. I tried to tell him that Banco and I were friends and that Banco hadn't done anything to deserve such treatment, that he had served his sovereign loyally. But he wouldn't listen, hear me. If I accept the title, I might lose the friendship of my dear comrade, Banco. If I refuse, I shall incur the king's displeasure. Have I the right to disobey him? I don't disobey when he sends me to war, so I can't very well disobey when he rewards me. That would be contempt. I must explain to Banco. Anyway, Baron Glamiss—it's only a title. There's no money in it, since Duncan's annexed the lands. Yes, I should like to see Banco, but at the same time perhaps I'd rather wait. It's a tricky situation. How did the witches know about it? Will their other predictions come true? It seems impossible. I'd like to know the logic behind it. How do they explain a chain of cause and effect which will set me on the throne? I'd like to hear what they have to say about it—if only to make fun of them. (*He goes out left.*)

Pause. The stage is empty.

The BUTTERFLY HUNTER *comes on left, butterfly net in hand. He is wearing a pale-colored suit and a boater. He has a little black mustache and pince nez. He chases a couple of butterflies and runs off left in pursuit of a third.*

BANCO (*enter right*)   Where are those witches? They prophesied Glamiss's death. That's come true. They told me I'd be dispossessed of my rightful title, Baron Glamiss. They told me I should father a long line of kings and princes. Will their prophecy about my descendants come true as well? I'd like to know the logic behind it. How do they explain the chain of cause and effect that will set my posterity on the throne? I'd like to know what they have to say about it—if only to make fun of them. (*He goes out left.*)

Pause. The stage is empty. MACBETT *comes on left. The* FIRST WITCH *has taken up her position stage right unseen by the audience.*

FIRST WITCH (*to* MACBETT. *She speaks in a croaking voice.*)   Macbett, you wanted to see me.

Lights up on the WITCH. *She is dressed like a witch, bent double, with a rasping voice. She props herself up on a big stick. She has dirty white unkempt hair.*

47

MACBETT *jumps. His hand goes instinctively to his sword.*

MACBETT   Cursed hag. You were there all the time.

FIRST WITCH   I came when you called.

MACBETT   On the battlefield I've never been afraid. No enemy has ever frightened me. Bullets have whizzed past my head. I've hacked my way through burning forests. When the flagship was sinking, I wasn't afraid. I jumped into the shark-infested sea and slashed their throats with one hand while swimming with the other. But my hair stands on end when I see this woman's shadow or hear her voice. There's a smell of sulphur in the air. I must use my sword—but as a cross not as a weapon. (*To the* WITCH) You guessed I wanted to speak with you.

The SECOND WITCH *appears behind the* FIRST WITCH *during the following exchange. There needs to be a certain distance—not very great—between them.*

The SECOND WITCH *will need to move slowly from stage left to stage right to arrive in the center of the spot, behind the* FIRST WITCH.

The FIRST WITCH *appears suddenly. A spot comes up on her. The* SECOND WITCH *should emerge more slowly into the light, first of all her head, then her shoulders, then the rest of her body, and her stick. Her shadow enlarged by the lighting will be thrown on the back wall.*

FIRST WITCH   I heard you. I can read your thoughts. I know what you're thinking now and what was going through your mind a few moments ago. You pretended you wanted to see me to make fun of me. You admitted you were afraid. Pull yourself together, general, for Hell's sake. What do you want to know?

MACBETT   Don't you know already?

FIRST WITCH   Some things I know, but some things are beyond my power. Our knowledge is limited, but I can see that, whether you are aware of it or not, your ambition has been kindled. Whatever explanations you may give yourself they are false; they only conceal your true intent.

MACBETT   I want only one thing; to serve my sovereign.

FIRST WITCH   Who are you kidding?

MACBETT   You want to make me believe that I'm other than I am—but you won't succeed.

FIRST WITCH   You're useful to him, otherwise he'd have your head.

MACBETT   My life is his to dispose of.

FIRST WITCH   You're his instrument. You saw how he got you to fight against Glamiss and Candor.

MACBETT   He was right. They were rebels.

FIRST WITCH   He took all Glamiss's lands and half of Candor's.

MACBETT   Everything belongs to the king. Equally the king and all he has belong to us. He is looking after it for us.

FIRST WITCH   And his flunkeys are left to carry the can.

SECOND WITCH   He, he, he, he, he!

MACBETT (*noting the* SECOND WITCH) Where did she spring from?

FIRST WITCH He doesn't know how to hold an ax. He doesn't know how to use a scythe.

MACBETT What do you know about it?

FIRST WITCH He can't fight himself—he sends others out to do it for him.

SECOND WITCH He'd be too frightened.

FIRST WITCH He knows how to steal other people's wives.

SECOND WITCH Are they part of the public domain too —the King's property?

FIRST WITCH He demands service from others, although he doesn't know the meaning of the word himself.

MACBETT I didn't come here to listen to your treasonous lies.

FIRST WITCH Why did you come and meet me, if that's all we're good for?

MACBETT I'm beginning to wonder. It was a mistake.

FIRST WITCH Then bugger off . . .

SECOND WITCH If you're not interested . . .

FIRST WITCH You hesitate, I see. So you've decided to stay.

SECOND WITCH If you'd rather . . .

FIRST WITCH If it's easier for you . . .

SECOND WITCH We can disappear.

MACBETT Stay a little, daughters of Satan. I want to know more.

FIRST WITCH Be your own master, instead of taking someone else's orders.

SECOND WITCH Tools he's done with he casts aside. You've outlived your usefulness.

MACBETT

FIRST WITCH He despises those who are faithful to him.

SECOND WITCH He thinks they're cowards.

FIRST WITCH Or fools.

SECOND WITCH He respects those who stand up to him.

MACBETT He fights them, too. He beat the rebels Glamiss and Candor.

FIRST WITCH Macbett beat them, not he.

SECOND WITCH Glamiss and Candor were his faithful generals before you.

FIRST WITCH He hated their independence.

SECOND WITCH He took back what he'd given them.

FIRST WITCH A fine example of his generosity.

SECOND WITCH Glamiss and Candor were proud.

FIRST WITCH And noble. Duncan couldn't stand that.

SECOND WITCH And courageous.

MACBETT I won't be another Glamiss. Or another Candor. This time there won't be a Macbett to beat them.

FIRST WITCH You're beginning to understand.

SECOND WITCH He, he, he, he!

FIRST WITCH If you're not careful, he'll have time to find another.

MACBETT I behaved honorably. I obeyed my sovereign. That's a law of heaven.

SECOND WITCH It wasn't behaving honorably to fight your peers.

FIRST WITCH But their death will be useful to you.

SECOND WITCH He would have used them against you.

FIRST WITCH Now nothing stands in your way.

SECOND WITCH You want the throne. Admit it.

MACBETT No.

FIRST WITCH   It's no good pretending you don't. You're worthy to be king.

SECOND WITCH   You're made for it. It's written in the stars.

MACBETT   You open the slippery slope of temptation before me. Who are you and what do you want? I almost succumbed to your wiles. But I came to my senses in time. Away.

The TWO WITCHES *give ground.*

FIRST WITCH   We're here to open your eyes.

SECOND WITCH   We only want to help you.

FIRST WITCH   It's for your own good.

SECOND WITCH   Justice is all we ask.

FIRST WITCH   True justice.

MACBETT   Stranger and stranger.

SECOND WITCH   He, he, he, he!

MACBETT   Have you really got my interests at heart? Does justice mean so much to you? You old hags, ugly as sin, you shameless old women want to sacrifice your life for my happiness?

SECOND WITCH   Yes, yes, he, he, he, of course.

FIRST WITCH   Because we love you, Macbett. (*Her voice is beginning to alter.*)

SECOND WITCH   It's because she loves you—(*The voice alters.*)—as much as her country, as much as justice, as much as the commonwealth.

FIRST WITCH (*melodious voice*)   It's to help the poor. To bring peace to a country that has known such suffering.

MACBETT   I know that voice.

FIRST WITCH   You know us, Macbett.

MACBETT For the last time, I order you to tell me who you are or I'll cut your throats for you. (*Taking out sword.*)
SECOND WITCH Save yourself the trouble.
FIRST WITCH All in good time, Macbett.
SECOND WITCH Put back your sword.

MACBETT *submits*.

And now, Macbett, I want you to watch closely, very closely. Open your eyes. Pin back your ears.

The SECOND WITCH *circles the* FIRST WITCH *like a conjuror's assistant. Each time she circles, she jumps two or three times. These jumps develop into a gracious dance as the new aspects of the* TWO WITCHES *are unveiled. Toward the end the dance becomes slow.*

SECOND WITCH (*circling the first*) Quis, quid, ubi . . . quibus auxiliis, cur, quomodo, quando. Felix qui potuit regni cognoscere causas. Fiat lux hic et nunc et fiat voluntas tua. Ad augusta per angusta, ad augusta per angusta. (*The* SECOND WITCH *takes the* FIRST WITCH's *stick and throws it away.*) Alter ego surge, alter ego surge.

The FIRST WITCH, *who was bent double, straightens up.*

For this scene—a transformation scene—the FIRST WITCH *is center stage, brilliantly lit.*

The SECOND WITCH *as she circles passes alternately through light and dark areas, depending on*

whether she is downstage or upstage of the FIRST
WITCH.

MACBETT, *standing to one side, is in the shade.
We are vaguely aware of his startled reactions as
the scene progresses.*

The SECOND WITCH *uses her stick like a magic
wand. Each time she touches the* FIRST WITCH
with her wand a transformation takes place.

*Obviously the whole scene should be done to music.
For the beginning at least some staccato would be
most suitable.*

SECOND WITCH (*as before*) Ante, apud, ad, adver-
sus . . .

She touches the FIRST WITCH *with her wand. The*
FIRST WITCH *lets fall her old cloak. Underneath is
another old cloak.*

Circum, circa, citra, cis . . .

She touches the FIRST WITCH, *who sheds her old
cloak. She is still covered by an ancient shawl that
reaches to her feet.*

SECOND WITCH Cotra, erga, extra, infra . . . (*The*
SECOND WITCH *stands up straight.*) Inter, intra,
juxta, ob . . . (*As she passes in front of the* FIRST
WITCH *she pulls off her glasses.*) Penes, pone, post et
praeter . . . (*She pulls off the old shawl. Underneath the shawl a very beautiful dress appears,
covered in spangles and glinting stones.*) Prope,

propter, per, secundum . . . (*Music more legato and melodious. She pulls off the First Witch's pointed chin.*) Supra, versus, ultra, trans . . .

The FIRST WITCH *sings several notes and trills. The light is sufficiently bright for us to see the First Witch's face and mouth as she sings. She stops singing. The* SECOND WITCH, *as she passes behind the* FIRST, *throws away her stick.*

Video, meliora, deteriora sequor.

MACBETT (*trancelike*) Video meliora, deteriora sequor.

The SECOND WITCH *keeps circling.*

MACBETT *and* FIRST WITCH (*together*) Video meliora, deteriora sequor.

FIRST *and* SECOND WITCHES Video meliora, deteriora sequor.

ALL THREE (*together*) Video meliora, deteriora sequor. Video meliora, deteriora sequor. Video meliora, deteriora sequor.

The SECOND WITCH *removes what's left of the First Witch's mask—i.e., the pointed nose and hairpiece.*

Still circling, she puts a scepter in the First Witch's hands and a crown on her head. Under the lights the FIRST WITCH *appears as if surrounded in a halo of light.*

As she passes behind, the SECOND WITCH *removes her face mask and her old clothes in a single go.*

Now revealed in all her beauty, the FIRST WITCH *becomes* LADY DUNCAN.

The SECOND WITCH *becomes her lady in waiting, equally young and beautiful.*

MACBETT   Oh your Majesty. (*He falls to his knees.*)

The SECOND WITCH, *now Lady Duncan's maid, places a step ladder behind the* FIRST WITCH, *now* LADY DUNCAN, *for her to climb.*

If this can't be managed, LADY DUNCAN *walks backward, slowly and majestically, stage right, where there is a ladder which she proceeds to mount.*

MACBETT *gets up and once more throws himself at Lady Duncan's feet.*

MACBETT   Oh mirabile visu! Oh madam!

In one movement, the LADY IN WAITING *tears off Lady Duncan's sumptuous dress.* LADY DUNCAN *stands revealed in a sparkling bikini, a black-and-red cape on her back and holding a scepter in one hand and in the other a dagger which the* LADY IN WAITING *has given her.*

LADY IN WAITING (*pointing to* LADY DUNCAN)   In naturalibus.

MACBETT   Let me be your slave.

LADY DUNCAN (*to* MACBETT, *holding out the dagger to him*)   I'll be yours if you wish. Would you like that? Here is the instrument of your ambition and our rise to power. (*Seductively.*) Take it if that's what you want, if you want me. But act boldly. Hell helps those who help themselves. Look into yourself. You can feel your desire for me growing, your hidden ambition coming into the open, inflaming you. You'll take his place at my side. I'll be your mistress. You'll be my sovereign. An indelible bloodstain will mark this blade—a souvenir of your success and a spur to greater things which we shall accomplish with the same glory. (*She raises him up.*)

MACBETT   Madam, sire, or rather siren . . .

LADY DUNCAN   Still hesitating, Macbett?

LADY IN WAITING (*to* LADY DUNCAN)   Make up his mind for him.

LADY DUNCAN   Make up your mind.

MACBETT   Madam, I have certain scruples . . . can't we just . . .

LADY DUNCAN   I know you're brave. But even brave men have their weaknesses and moments of cowardice. Above all they suffer from guilt—and that's mortal. Pull yourself together. You were never afraid to kill when someone else was giving the orders. If fear now weighs you down, unburden yourself to me. I'll reassure you, promise you that no man of woman born will be able to conquer you. No other army will defeat your army till the forest arms itself to march against you.

LADY IN WAITING   Which is practically impossible. (*To* MACBETT) Remember we want only to save our country. The two of you will build a better society, a brave new world.

The stage grows gradually darker.

MACBETT *rolls at Lady Duncan's feet. All that can be seen is Lady Duncan's glistening body. We hear the voice of the* LADY IN WAITING.

LADY IN WAITING   Omnia vincit amor.

Blackout.

A room in the palace.

In front of the palace, BANCO *and an* OFFICER.

OFFICER His Highness is tired. He can't see you now.

BANCO Does he know what I've come for?

OFFICER I explained everything, but he says it's a *fait accompli.* He's given Glamiss's title to Macbett and he can't very well take it back again. Besides, it's only his word.

BANCO But still . . .

OFFICER That's the way it is.

BANCO Does he know Glamiss is dead, drowned?

OFFICER I told him, but he'd already heard. Lady Duncan knew of it through her Lady in Waiting.

BANCO There's no reason why he shouldn't give me my promised reward. The title or the lands, if not both.

OFFICER What do you want me to do? I've done my best?

BANCO It's impossible. He can't do this to me.

Enter DUNCAN *stage right.*

DUNCAN (*to* BANCO) What's all the fuss about?

BANCO My lord—

DUNCAN I don't like being disturbed. What do you want?

BANCO Didn't you tell me, that when Glamiss had been taken, dead or alive, you'd give me my reward?

DUNCAN Where is he? Dead or alive I don't see him.

BANCO You know very well he's drowned.

DUNCAN That's hearsay. Bring me his body.

BANCO His bloated corpse has been swept out to sea.

DUNCAN Well go and look for it. Take a boat.

BANCO The sharks have eaten it.

DUNCAN Take a knife and cut through the shark's belly.

BANCO Several sharks.

DUNCAN Cut through all their bellies then.

BANCO I risked my life defending you against the rebels.

DUNCAN You've come out of it alive, haven't you?

BANCO I killed all your enemies.

DUNCAN You had that pleasure.

BANCO I could've done without it.

DUNCAN But you didn't

BANCO My lord—

DUNCAN Not another word. Where is Glamiss's body? Show me the *corpus delicti*.

BANCO Glamiss's death is common knowledge. You've given his title to Macbett.

DUNCAN Are you demanding an explanation?

BANCO It's not fair.

DUNCAN I'll be the judge of that. We'll find other rebel barons to dispossess. There's bound to be something for you in the future.

BANCO   I'm afraid I think you're lying.

DUNCAN   How dare you insult me?

BANCO   But . . . but . . .

DUNCAN   Show this gentleman the door.

The OFFICER *appears to be on the point of launching himself violently at* BANCO. *He shouts.*

OFFICER   Out!

DUNCAN   No need for rough stuff. Banco is a good friend of ours. His nerves are a little on edge, that's all. He'll get over it. He'll get his opportunity.

BANCO (*going out*)   What a bloody sauce . . .

DUNCAN (*to the* OFFICER)   I don't know what got into me. I should have made him Baron. But he wanted the money, too, which should rightfully have reverted to me. Well, that's the way it is. But if he gets dangerous, we shall have to be careful—very careful.

OFFICER (*putting his hand on his sword*)   I understand, my lord.

DUNCAN   No, no, not so fast. Not immediately. Later. If he becomes dangerous. Would you like his title and half his lands?

OFFICER (*energetically*)   Yes, my lord. Whatever you say, my lord.

DUNCAN   You're a thrusting little codger, aren't you? I suppose you'd like me to confiscate Macbett's title and fortune and give you a bit of that as well?

OFFICER (*as before*)   Yes, my lord. Whatever you say, my lord.

DUNCAN   Macbett is also becoming dangerous. Very dangerous. Perhaps he'd like to replace me on the throne. That sort of person needs to be watched.

Hoodlums, that's what they are, gangsters. All they think about is money, power, luxury. I wouldn't be surprised if Macbett also had an eye on my wife. Not to mention my courtesans. How about you? Would you like me to lend you my wife?

OFFICER (*protesting energetically*)   Oh no, my lord.

DUNCAN   Don't you fancy her?

OFFICER   She is very beautiful, my lord. But honor, your honor comes first.

DUNCAN   That's a good chap. Thanks. I'll see that you're rewarded.

OFFICER   Whatever you say, my lord.

DUNCAN   I'm surrounded by grasping enemies and fickle friends. Nobody is unselfish. You'd think the prosperity of the kingdom and my personal well-being would satisfy them. They've got no ideals. None at all. We shall be on our guard.

> *Fanfares and music. Something old fashioned and formal.*

A room in the Archduke's Palace. Just a few items, one or two chairs and a different backcloth, will do to establish the locality. Whatever can be set up in a blackout lasting not more than thirty seconds.

Music. DUNCAN *enters right, followed by* LADY DUNCAN. *He is agitated and she has difficulty keeping up with him.*

DUNCAN *comes to a sudden halt center stage. He turns to* LADY DUNCAN.

DUNCAN No. madam, I won't allow it.

LADY DUNCAN So much the worse for you.

DUNCAN I said, I won't allow it.

LADY DUNCAN Why not? Why ever not?

DUNCAN Let me speak frankly, with my customary candor.

LADY DUNCAN Frankly or not it all boils down to the same thing.

DUNCAN What do I care?

LADY DUNCAN You said I could. It's no good denying it.

DUNCAN I shall if I want. I said perhaps.

LADY DUNCAN What about me? What am I supposed to say?

DUNCAN Whatever comes into your head.

LADY DUNCAN I never say whatever comes into my head.

DUNCAN If it isn't in your head how can you say it?

LADY DUNCAN First one thing, then another. Tomorrow it'll be something else again.

DUNCAN I can't help that.

LADY DUNCAN Neither can I.

DUNCAN Stop contradicting.

LADY DUNCAN You're always putting things off.

DUNCAN You've only yourself to blame.

LADY DUNCAN You're such an old fuss-pot.

DUNCAN Madam, madam, madam!

LADY DUNCAN You're being very stubborn. Men are so self-centered.

DUNCAN Let's get back to the subject in hand.

LADY DUNCAN It's no good your getting cross, it only makes me cross as well. The most important thing is done. If you were more objective about it . . . but you aren't. So, let's leave it. It's all your fault.

DUNCAN Hold your tongue, madam. He who laughs last, laughs longest.

LADY DUNCAN Your obsessions, your *idées fixes*.

DUNCAN That'll do.

LADY DUNCAN So you still refuse . . .

DUNCAN You'll regret it.

LADY DUNCAN You can't make an omelette without breaking eggs.

DUNCAN You'll pay dearly.

LADY DUNCAN Are you threatening me?

DUNCAN From top to toe.

LADY DUNCAN Another threat!

DUNCAN One day you'll go too far.

LADY DUNCAN And another!

DUNCAN I won't have it. No, absolutely not. You just wait. The shoe will be on the other foot. I'll tell him. You see if I don't. I'll rub his nose in it.

DUNCAN *goes out quickly, followed by* LADY DUNCAN.

LADY DUNCAN I'll forestall you, Duncan. By the time you find out it'll be too late.

DUNCAN, *still agitated, has gone out left after his last speech.* LADY DUNCAN *follows him out, almost at a run.*

The scene between the two of them should be played as a violent quarrel.

MACBETT *and* BANCO *enter right.* MACBETT *looks worried. He has a serious air about him.*

MACBETT   No, seriously. I thought Lady Duncan was
a shallow woman. I was wrong. She is capable of
deep feeling. She is so vivacious, energetic. She really
is. And intellectual. She has some very profound views
on the future of mankind: though she's by no means
a utopian dreamer.

BANCO   It's possible. I believe you. It's difficult to get
to know people, but once they've opened their hearts
to you . . . (*Pointing to Macbett's belt.*) That's a
handsome dagger that you've got there.

MACBETT   A gift from her. Anyway, I'm glad to have
had a chance to talk with you at long last after all
this chasing about like a dog after its own tail or the
devil chasing his shadow.

BANCO   You can say that again.

MACBETT   She's unhappily married. Duncan is a brute.
He maltreats her. It's very trying. She's very delicate,
you know. And he's peevish and broody. Lady Duncan is like a child—she likes to sport and amuse
herself, play tennis, make love. Of course, it's none
of my business, really.

BANCO   Of course.

MACBETT   Far be it from me to speak ill of the king or
want to run him down.

BANCO   Perish the thought.

MACBETT   The Archduke is a very good man, loyal and
. . . generous. You know how fond I am of him.

BANCO   Me, too.

MACBETT   All in all he's a perfect monarch.

BANCO   Almost perfect.

MACBETT   Obviously, as far as perfection is possible
in this world. It's a perfection that doesn't exclude
certain imperfections.

BANCO An imperfect perfection. But perfection all the same.

MACBETT Personally, I've got nothing against him—though my own opinion doesn't enter into it. He has the good of the country at heart. Yes, he's a good king. Though he should be more appreciative of his impartial advisers—like you, for example.

BANCO Or you.

MACBETT Like you or me.

BANCO Quite.

MACBETT He's a bit autocratic.

BANCO Very autocratic.

MACBETT A real autocrat! Nowadays autocracy isn't always the best way to govern. That's what Lady Duncan thinks anyway. She's very charming, you know, and has a lot of interesting ideas, two qualities that aren't often found together.

BANCO Not often, no.

MACBETT She could give him some good advice, interesting advice, get him to see . . . to understand certain principles of government which, in an impartial way, she would share with us. We ourselves, of course, being quite impartial.

BANCO All the same we've got to live, earn our daily bread.

MACBETT Duncan understands that.

BANCO Yes, he's shown himself very understanding so far as you're concerned. He's showered you with blessings.

MACBETT I didn't ask him to. He paid, he paid well, well more or less—he didn't pay too badly for the services I rendered him—which it was my duty to render, since he is my feudal overlord.

BANCO He didn't pay me at all! As you know. He took Glamiss's lands for himself and gave you the title.

MACBETT I don't know what you're referring to. Duncan do a thing like that? Never—well, hardly ever—well, not very often. He has his lapses. I didn't intrigue for it, I promise.

BANCO I never said you did. I know it's not your fault.

MACBETT It's not my fault. Listen: perhaps we can do something for you. We—Lady Duncan and I that is—we could advise him. We could, for example, advise him to take you on as his adviser.

BANCO Lady Duncan knows about this, does she?

MACBETT She's very concerned about you. She's very upset by the king's thoughtlessness. She wants to make it up to you. She's already put in a word for you with the Archduke, you know. I suggested it to her, and she agreed. We've both intervened on your behalf.

BANCO Why keep on if your attempts have been unsuccessful?

MACBETT We'll use other arguments. More cogent ones. Then perhaps he'll understand. If not . . . we'll try again. With even stronger arguments.

BANCO Duncan is stubborn.

MACBETT Very stubborn. Stubborn . . . (*He looks left and right.*) . . . as stubborn as a mule. Still, even the stubbornest mule can be made to budge.

BANCO Made to, yes.

MACBETT Fair enough, he's given me the estates—but he's reserved the right to hunt on my lands. Apparently, it's for "state expenses."

BANCO So he says . . .

MACBETT He *is* the state.

BANCO   My estates are still the same as ever and he takes from me ten thousand chickens a year and their eggs.

MACBETT   You should complain.

BANCO   I fought for him at the head of my own personal army. Now he wants to merge it with his army. He wants to turn my own men against me.

MACBETT   And me.

BANCO   My ancestors would turn over in their graves . . .

MACBETT   So would mine! And there's all his cronies and parasites.

BANCO   Who fat themselves on the sweat of our brow.

MACBETT   And our chickens.

BANCO   And our sheep.

MACBETT   And our pigs.

BANCO   The swine.

MACBETT   And our bread.

BANCO   The blood we've shed for him.

MACBETT   The dangers we've undergone.

BANCO   Ten thousand chickens, ten thousand horses, ten thousand recruits. What does he do with them? He can't eat them all. The rest just goes bad.

MACBETT   And a thousand young girls.

BANCO   We know what he does with them.

MACBETT   He owes us everything.

BANCO   More than he can pay.

MACBETT   Not to mention the rest.

BANCO   My honor.

MACBETT   My glory.

BANCO   Our ancestral rights.

MACBETT   My property.

BANCO   The right to make more and more money.

MACBETT   Self-rule.

BANCO   To run our own affairs.

MACBETT   We must drive him out.

BANCO   Lock, stock and barrel. Down with Duncan.

MACBETT   Down with Duncan!

BANCO   We must overthrow him.

MACBETT   I was going to suggest . . . we should divide the kingdom. We'll each have our share and I'll take the throne. I'll be king and you can be my chamberlain.

BANCO   Your second-in-command.

MACBETT   Well third, actually. It's a difficult task we've set ourselves and we need all the help we can get. There is a third in this conspiracy—Lady Duncan.

BANCO   Well, well. That's a piece of luck.

MACBETT   She's indispensable.

LADY DUNCAN enters upstage.

BANCO   Madam! What a surprise.

MACBETT   (*to* BANCO)   We're engaged.

BANCO   The future Lady Macbett. Well, well. (*Looking from one to the other.*) Heartiest congratulations. (*He kisses Lady Duncan's hand.*)

LADY DUNCAN   To the death!

They all three draw their daggers and cross them at arm's length.

Let's swear to kill the tyrant!

MACBETT   The usurper.

BANCO   Down with the dictator!

LADY DUNCAN   The despot.

MACBETT   He's a miscreant.

BANCO   An ogre.

LADY DUNCAN   An ass.

MACBETT   A goose.

BANCO   A louse.

LADY DUNCAN   Let's swear to exterminate him.

ALL THREE (*together*)   We swear to exterminate him.

Fanfares. The conspirators go out quickly left.

The ARCHDUKE *comes on right. In this scene, at least at the beginning,* DUNCAN *has real majesty.*

Enter the OFFICER *upstage.*

OFFICER   My lord, it's the first day of the month, the day when the scrofulous, the tubercular, the consumptive, and the hysterical come for you to cure their maladies by your heavenly gift.

A MONK *comes on left.*

MONK   Greetings, my lord.

DUNCAN   Greetings, father.

MONK   God be with you.

DUNCAN   And with you.

MONK   May the lord preserve you. (*He blesses the Archduke, who bows his head.*)

The OFFICER, *carrying the king's purple robe, the crown, and the royal scepter, goes over to the* MONK.

The MONK *blesses the crown and takes it from the* OFFICER. *He goes over to* DUNCAN, *who kneels down, and puts it on his head.*

MONK   In the name of Almighty God, I confirm you in your sovereign power.

DUNCAN   May the lord make me worthy.

The OFFICER *gives the purple cloak to the* MONK *who puts it around Duncan's shoulders.*

MONK   May the Lord bless you and keep you, and may no harm come to you so long as you wear this cloak.

A SERVANT *comes on right carrying the ciborium for communion. He gives it to the* MONK *who offers* DUNCAN *the Host.*

DUNCAN   Domine non sum dignus.

MONK   Corpus Christi.

DUNCAN   Amen.

The MONK *gives the ciborium back to the* SERVANT, *who goes out.*

The OFFICER *hands the* MONK *the scepter.*

MONK   I renew the gift of healing which the Lord God transmits through me, his unworthy servant. May the Lord purge our souls as he heals the sickness of our feeble bodies. May He cure us of jealousy, pride, luxury, our base striving after power, and may He open our eyes to the vanity of worldly goods.

DUNCAN   Hear us, O Lord.

OFFICER (*kneeling*)   Hear us, O Lord.

MONK   Hear us, O Lord. May hatred and anger waft
away like smoke in the wind. Grant that man may
prevail against nature, where suffering and destruc-
tion reign. May love and peace be freed from their
chains, may all destructive forces be chained up that
joy may shine forth in heavenly light. May that light
flood us that we may bathe ourselves in it. Amen.

DUNCAN *and* OFFICER   Amen.

MONK   Take your scepter with my blessing. With it
you are to touch the sick.

> DUNCAN *and the* OFFICER *get up. The* MONK *kneels
> before* DUNCAN *who mounts the throne and sits.
> The* OFFICER *stands on Duncan's left. This scene
> should be played with solemnity.*

DUNCAN   Bring in the patients.

> The MONK *rises and goes and stands on Duncan's
> right.*

> The FIRST SICK MAN *comes in upstage left. He is
> bent double and walks with difficulty. He is wear-
> ing a cape with a hood. His face is a ravaged mask
> —like a leper's.*

Come here. A little nearer. Don't be afraid.

> The SICK MAN *approaches and kneels on one of the
> bottom steps of the throne. He has his back to the
> audience.*

FIRST SICK MAN   Have pity on me, my lord. I've come a long way. On the other side of the ocean, there is a continent and beyond that continent, there are seven countries. And beyond those seven countries there's another sea, and beyond that sea there are mountains. I live on the other side of those mountains in a damp and sunless valley. The damp has eaten away my bones. I'm covered in scrofula, in tumors and pustules which break out everywhere. My body is a running sore. I stink. My wife and children can't bear me to come near them. Save me, lord. Cure me.

DUNCAN   I shall cure you. Believe in me and hope. (*He touches the Sick Man's head with his scepter.*) By the grace of our Lord Jesus Christ, by the gift of the power vested in me this day, I absolve you of the sin which has stained your soul and body. May your soul be as pure as clear water, as the sky on the first day of creation.

The FIRST SICK MAN *stands up and turns toward the audience. He draws himself up to his full height, drops his stick and lifts his hands to heaven.*

His face is clear and smiling. He shouts for joy and runs out left.

The SECOND SICK MAN *enters right and approaches the throne.*

DUNCAN   What is your trouble?

SECOND SICK MAN   My lord, I'm unable to live and I can't die. I can't sit down, I can't lie down, I can't stand still, and I can't run. I burn and itch from the top of my head to the soles of my feet. I can't bear to be indoors or on the street. For me, the universe is a prison. It pains me to look at the world. I can't bear the light nor sit in the shade. Other people fill me with horror, yet I can't bear to be alone. My eyes wander restlessly over trees, sheep, dogs, grass, stars, stones. I have never had a single happy moment. I should like to be able to cry, my lord, and to know joy. (*During this speech, he has come up to the throne and climbed the steps.*)

DUNCAN Forget you exist. Remember that you are.

Pause.

Seen from behind, one can read in the twitching of the Sick Man's shoulders that it's impossible for him to comply.

I order you. Obey.

The SECOND SICK MAN, *who was twisted in agony, relaxes his back and shoulders and appears to be calming down. He gets up slowly, holds out his arms and turns around. The audience can see the contorted face relax and light up.*

He walks off left, jauntily, almost dancing.

OFFICER Next!

A THIRD SICK MAN *approaches* DUNCAN, *who cures him in the same way. Then in quick succession a Fourth, Fifth, Sixth . . . Tenth, Eleventh come on stage right and go out left after having been touched by Duncan's scepter.*

Before each entrance, the OFFICER *shouts "Next!"*

Some of the Patients are on crutches or in wheel-chairs.

All this should be properly controlled and toward the end should be accompanied by music which gradually gets faster and faster.

While this is going on, the MONK *has slowly dropped away till he is sitting rather than kneeling on the floor. He looks poised.*

After the Eleventh SICK MAN, *the tempo becomes slower and the music fades into the distance.*

Two last patients come in, one from the left, the other from the right. They are wearing long capes with hoods that come down over their faces. The OFFICER *who shouted "Next" fails to notice the last patient, who creeps up behind him.*

Suddenly the music cuts out. At the same moment, the MONK *throws back his hood or takes off his mask, and we see that it's* BANCO *in disguise. He pulls out a long dagger.*

DUNCAN (*to* BANCO) You?

At the same moment, LADY DUNCAN *throws off her disguise and stabs the* OFFICER *in the back. He falls.*

DUNCAN (*to* LADY DUNCAN) You, madam?

*The other beggar—*MACBETT*—also pulls out a dagger.*

DUNCAN Murderers!
BANCO (*to* DUNCAN) Murderer!
MACBETT (*to* DUNCAN) Murderer!

> DUNCAN *dodges* BANCO *and comes face to face with* MACBETT. *He tries to go out left but his escape is cut off by* LADY DUNCAN, *who holds out her arms to stop him. She has a dagger in one hand.*

LADY DUNCAN (*to* DUNCAN) Murderer!
DUNCAN (*to* LADY DUNCAN) Murderess! (*He runs left, meets* MACBETT.)
MACBETT Murderer!
DUNCAN Murderer! (*He runs right.* BANCO *cuts him off.*)
BANCO (*to* DUNCAN) Murderer!
DUNCAN (*to* BANCO) Murderer!

> DUNCAN *backs toward the throne. The three others close in on him, slowly drawing their circle tighter.*

> As DUNCAN *mounts the first step,* LADY DUNCAN *snatches off his cloak.* DUNCAN *backs up the steps trying to cover his body with his arms. Without his cloak he feels naked and exposed.*

> *He doesn't get very far, however, for the others are after him. His scepter falls one way, his crown*

the other. MACBETT *pulls at him and brings him down.*

DUNCAN   Murderers!

He rolls on the ground. BANCO *strikes the first blow, shouting.*

BANCO   Murderer!
MACBETT (*stabbing him a second time*)   Murderer!
LADY DUNCAN (*stabbing him a third time*)   Murderer!

The three of them get up and stand over him.

DUNCAN   Murderers! (*Quieter.*) Murderers! (*Feebly.*) Murderers!

The three conspirators draw apart. LADY DUNCAN *stays by the body, looking down.*

LADY DUNCAN   He was my husband, after all. Now that he's dead, he looks just like my father. I couldn't stand my father.

Blackout.

A room in the palace. In the distance we can hear the crowd shouting, "Long live Macbett! Long live his bride! Long live Macbett! Long live his bride!"

Two SERVANTS *enter upstage, one from one side, one from the other. They meet downstage center. They can be played by two men, or a man and a woman, possibly even two women.*

SERVANTS (*looking at each other*) They're coming.

> *They go and hide upstage. Enter left Duncan's widow, the future* LADY MACBETT, *followed by* MACBETT. *They have not as yet acquired the regal attributes.*
>
> *The cheering and shouts of "Long live Macbett and his bride" are louder.*
>
> *They go to the exit stage left.*

LADY DUNCAN Thank you for bringing me to my apartments. I'm going to lie down. I'm quite tired after my exertions.

MACBETT Yes, you could do with a rest. I'll come and
pick you up at ten o'clock for the marriage ceremony.
The coronation is at midday. In the afternoon, at
five o'clock, there will be a banquet—our wedding
feast.

LADY DUNCAN (*giving her hand to* MACBETT *to be
kissed*) Till tomorrow then, Macbett.

She goes out. MACBETT *crosses to go out right.
The sound of scattered cheering.*

The two SERVANTS *who had hidden reappear and
come downstage.*

FIRST SERVANT Everything is ready for the wedding
ceremony and the breakfast afterward.

SECOND SERVANT Wines from Italy and Samoa.

FIRST SERVANT Bottles of beer coming by the dozen.

SECOND SERVANT And gin.

FIRST SERVANT Oxen.

SECOND SERVANT Herds of deer.

FIRST SERVANT Roebuck to be barbecued.

SECOND SERVANT They've come from France, from
the Ardennes.

FIRST SERVANT Fishermen have risked their lives to
provide sharks. They'll eat the fins.

SECOND SERVANT They killed a whale for oil to dress
the salad.

FIRST SERVANT There'll be Pernod from Marseille.

SECOND SERVANT Vodka from the Urals.

FIRST SERVANT A giant omelette containing a hundred and thirty thousand eggs.

SECOND SERVANT Chinese pancakes.

FIRST SERVANT Spanish melons from Africa.

SECOND SERVANT   There's never been anything like it.

FIRST SERVANT   Viennese pastries.

SECOND SERVANT   Wine will flow like water in the streets.

FIRST SERVANT   To the sound of a dozen gypsy orchestras.

SECOND SERVANT   Better than Christmas.

FIRST SERVANT   A thousand times better.

SECOND SERVANT   Everyone in the country will get two hundred and forty-seven black sausages.

FIRST SERVANT   And a ton of mustard.

SECOND SERVANT   Frankfurters.

FIRST SERVANT   And sauerkraut.

SECOND SERVANT   And more beer.

FIRST SERVANT   And more wine.

SECOND SERVANT   And more gin.

FIRST SERVANT   I'm drunk already, just thinking about it.

SECOND SERVANT   Just thinking about it I can feel my belly bursting.

FIRST SERVANT   My liver swelling. (*They throw their arms around each other's necks and stagger out drunkenly, shouting "Long live Macbett and his bride."*)

BANCO *enters right. He crosses to stage center and stops, facing the audience. He appears to reflect for a moment.* MACBETT *appears upstage left.*

MACBETT   Ah, it's Banco. What's he doing here all by himself? I'll hide and overhear him. (*He pretends to pull invisible curtains.*)

BANCO   So Macbett is to be king; Baron Candor, Baron

Glamiss, then king—as from tomorrow. One by one the witches' predictions have come true. One thing they didn't mention was the murder of Duncan, in which I had a hand. But how would Macbett have come to power unless Duncan had died or abdicated in his favor—which is constitutionally impossible? You have to take the throne by force. Another thing they didn't mention was that Lady Duncan would be Lady Macbett. So Macbett gets everything—while I get nothing. What an extraordinarily successful career—wealth, fame, power, a wife. He's got everything a man could possibly want. I struck down Duncan because I had a grudge against him. But what good has it done me? True, Macbett has given me his word. He said I could be chamberlain. But will he keep his promise? I doubt it. Didn't he promise to be faithful to Duncan—and then kill him? People will say I did the same. I can't say I didn't. I can't get it out of my mind. I'm sorry now—and I haven't any of Macbett's advantages, his success, his fame, to stifle my remorse. The witches told me I shouldn't be archduke or king, but they said I should father a whole line of kings, princes, presidents, and dictators. That's some consolation. They said it would happen, yes, they said it would happen. They've proved conclusively that they can see into the future. Before I met them I had no desire, no ambition beyond that of serving my king. Now I'm consumed with envy and jealousy. They've taken the lid off my ambition and here I am carried away by a force I can't control—grasping, avid, insatiable. I shall father dozens of kings. That's something. But yet I have no sons or daughters. And I'm not married.

Whom shall I marry? The Lady in Waiting is rather
sexy. I'll ask her to marry me. She's a bit spooky but
so much the better. She'll be able to see danger coming and we can take steps to avoid it. Once I'm married, once I've started a family, once I'm chamberlain, I'll curtail Macbett's powers. I'll be his *éminence
gris*. Who knows, perhaps the witches will reconsider
their predictions. Perhaps I will reign in my own lifetime after all. (*He goes out right.*)

MACBETT   I heard every word, the traitor! So that's all
the thanks I get for promising to make him chamberlain. I didn't know my wife and her maid had
told him that he'd be father to a line of kings. Funny
she never mentioned it. It's disturbing to think she
kept it from me. Who are they trying to fool, me or
Banco? Why? Banco father to a line of kings. Have
I killed Duncan to put Banco's issue on the throne?
It's all a sinister plot. Well, we'll soon see about that.
We'll soon see if my initiative can foil the snares of
destiny the devil has set for me. Let's destroy his
issue at the fountainhead—that is, Banco himself.
(*He crosses right and calls.*) Banco! Banco!

BANCO'S VOICE   Coming, Macbett. Coming. (BANCO
comes on.) What do you want?

MACBETT   Coward, so that is how you repay me for
all the favors I was going to grant you. (*He stabs*
BANCO *in the heart.*)

BANCO (*falling*)   Oh my God! Have mercy.

MACBETT   Where are all those kings now? They're going to rot with you and in you, nipped in the bud.
(*He goes.*)

Blackout.

Lights up.

Shouts of "Long live Macbett! Long live Lady Macbett! Long live our beloved king! Long live the bride!"

MACBETT *and* LADY MACBETT *come on right. They are in robes of state. They wear crowns and purple robes.*

MACBETT *is carrying his scepter. Sound of bells ringing and the enthusiastic cheering of the crowd.* MACBETT *and* LADY MACBETT *stop center stage with their backs to the audience and wave left and right to the crowd.*

Noise of the crowd: "Hurrah! Long live the Archduke! Long live the Archduchess!"

MACBETT *and* LADY MACBETT *turn and salute the audience, waving and blowing kisses. They turn and face each other.*

MACBETT   We'll discuss it later.

LADY MACBETT   I can explain everything, dear.

MACBETT   Well, I've canceled your prediction. I've nipped it in the bud. You've no longer got the upper hand. I discovered your little arrangements and took steps accordingly.

LADY MACBETT   I didn't mean to hide anything from you, love. As I said, I can explain everything. But not in public.

MACBETT   We'll discuss it later.

MACBETT takes her hand and they go out right, smiling at the crowd. The cheering continues.

Pause. The stage is empty. LADY MACBETT comes on with her LADY IN WAITING. She is in the same costume as in the previous scene.

LADY IN WAITING   It suits you, being a bride. The crowd cheering. The way you held yourself. Such grace. Such majesty. He cut a fine figure, too. He's looking much younger. You made a lovely couple.

LADY MACBETT   He's gone to sleep. He had a few too many after the ceremony. And there's still the wedding feast to come. Let's make the most of it. Hurry up.

LADY IN WAITING   Yes, ma'am. (*She collects a case from offstage right.*)

LADY MACBETT   Away with this sacred and anointed crown. (*She throws the crown away. She takes off the necklace with a cross on it which she had been wearing.*) This cross has been burning me. I've got a wound, here on my chest. But I've doused it with curses.

Meanwhile the LADY IN WAITING has been opening the case and taking out her witch's costume. She proceeds to dress LADY MACBETT in it.

The cross symbolizes the struggle of two forces,
heaven and hell. Which will prove the stronger?
Within this small compass a universal warfare is
condensed. Help me. Undo my white dress. Quickly,
take it off. It's burning me as well. And I spit out the
Host which fortunately stuck in my throat. Give me
the flask of spiced and magic vodka. Alcohol 90 proof
is like mineral water to me. Twice I nearly fainted
when they held up the icons for me to touch. But I
carried it off. I even kissed one of them. Pouah, it
was disgusting.

During all this, the LADY IN WAITING *is undressing
her.*

Hurry up. I hear something.

LADY IN WAITING   Yes, ma'am. I'm doing my best.

LADY MACBETT   Hurry, hurry, hurry. Give me my rags,
my smelly old dress. My apron covered in vomit. My
muddy boots. Take this wig off. Where's my dirty
gray hair? Give me my chin. Here, take these teeth.
My pointed nose, and my stick tipped with poisoned
steel.

The LADY IN WAITING *picks up one of the sticks
left by the pilgrims.*

As LADY MACBETT *issues her orders, "Unhook my
white dress!" etc., the* LADY IN WAITING *carries
them out.*

*As indicated in the text, she puts on her smelly
old dress, her apron covered in vomit, her dirty*

gray hair, takes out her teeth, shows the plate to audience, puts on her pointed nose, etc.

FIRST WITCH   Hurry! Faster!
SECOND WITCH   I am hurrying, my dear.
FIRST WITCH   They are waiting for us.

The SECOND WITCH *produces a long shawl from the case and puts it around her shoulders, at the same time pulling on a dirty gray wig.*

The two WITCHES *are bent double and sniggering.*

I feel much more at home, dressed like this.
SECOND WITCH   He, he, he, he!

She shuts the case. They both sit astride it.

FIRST WITCH   Well, that's that, then.
SECOND WITCH   A job well done.
FIRST WITCH   We've mixed it nicely.
SECOND WITCH   He, he, he, he. Macbett won't be able to get out of it now.
FIRST WITCH   The boss will be pleased.
SECOND WITCH   We'll tell him all about it.
FIRST WITCH   He'll be waiting to send us on another mission.
SECOND WITCH   Let's skedaddle. Suitcase, fly!
FIRST WITCH   Fly! Fly! Fly!

The FIRST WITCH, *who is sitting in front of the case, mimes a steering wheel. It's a very noisy engine. The* SECOND WITCH *spreads her arms, like wings.*

MACBETT

Blackout. Spotlight on the case which appears to be flying.

The main hall of the palace. Upstage, the throne. Downstage and a little to the left, a table with stools. Four GUESTS are already seated.

Four or five life-size dolls represent the other GUESTS. Upstage, other tables and other GUESTS projected onto the back wall on either side of the throne.

MACBETT *comes on left.*

MACBETT   Don't get up, my friends.

FIRST GUEST   Long live the Archduke!

SECOND GUEST   Long live our sovereign!

THIRD GUEST   Long live Macbett!

FOURTH GUEST   Long live our guide! Our great captain! Our Macbett!

MACBETT   Thank you, friends.

FIRST GUEST   Glory and honor and health to our beloved sovereign, Lady Macbett!

FOURTH GUEST   Her beauty and her grace make her worthy of your highness. May you live and prosper. May the state flourish under your wise and powerful rule, guided and helped by your lady wife.

MACBETT   Accept my thanks for both. She should have been here by now.

SECOND GUEST   Her Highness is never late normally.

MACBETT   I left her only a few minutes ago. She and her maid were right behind me.

THIRD GUEST   Has she taken ill? I'm a doctor.

MACBETT   She's gone to her room to put on some lipstick, a dab of powder, and a new necklace. In the meanwhile, don't stop drinking. I'll come and join you.

A SERVANT *comes on.*

There's not enough wine. More wine there!

SERVANT   I'll go and get some, my lord.

MACBETT   Your health, my friends. How happy I am to be with you. I feel surrounded by the warmth of your affection. If you knew how much I need your friendship—as much as a plant needs water or a man wine. I find it consoling, soothing, reassuring, having you around me. Ah, if only you knew . . . But I mustn't let myself go. It's not the moment for confessions. You set out to do something and end up doing something quite different, which you didn't intend at all. History is full of tricks like that. Everything slips through your fingers. We unleash forces that we cannot control and which end up by turning against us. Everything turns out the opposite of what you wanted. Man doesn't rule events, events rule him. I was happy when I was serving Duncan faithfully. I hadn't a care in the world.

The SERVANT *comes in.* MACBETT *turns toward him.*

Quickly, we're dying of thirst. (*Looking at a portrait —it could just as easily be an empty frame.*) Who put Duncan's picture in my place? Is this someone's idea of a joke?

SERVANT I don't know, my lord. I didn't see anything, my lord.

MACBETT How dare you. (*He takes the* SERVANT *by the throat, then lets him go again. He goes to un-hook the portrait—which could equally well be an empty frame or invisible.*)

FIRST GUEST But that's your picture, my lord.

SECOND GUEST They put your picture where Duncan's was, not vice versa.

MACBETT It does look like him though.

THIRD GUEST Your eyes are affected, my lord.

FOURTH GUEST (*to the* FIRST GUEST) I wonder if myopia is brought on by power?

FIRST GUEST (*to the* FOURTH GUEST) I shouldn't have thought so—not necessarily.

SECOND GUEST Oh yes, it happens quite frequently.

As soon as MACBETT *lets go of his throat, the* SER-VANT *goes off right.*

MACBETT Perhaps I'm mistaken. (*To the others, who had got up at the same time as he did.*) Sit down, friends. A little wine will clear my head. Anyway, whoever it looks like, Duncan or me, let's smash that picture. Then we'll all have a few drinks. (*He sits down and drinks.*) Why are you looking at me like that? Sit down, I said. We'll all have a few drinks to-gether. (*He stands up and pounds on the table with his fist.*) Sit down!

The GUESTS *sit down.* MACBETT *sits down too.*

Drink, gentlemen, drink. You must admit, I'm a better king than Duncan was.

THIRD GUEST   Hear, hear, my lord!

MACBETT   This country needs a younger man at the helm, braver and more energetic. I can assure you, you haven't lost in the exchange.

FOURTH GUEST   That's what we think, your Highness.

MACBETT   Think! What did you think of Duncan, when he was alive? Did you tell him what you thought? Did you tell him he was the bravest? The most energetic commander? Or did you tell him I should take his place? That I should be king instead of him?

FIRST GUEST   My lord—

MACBETT   I thought he was more suited to it myself. Do you agree? Or do you think differently? Answer me!

SECOND GUEST   My lord—

MACBETT   My lord, my lord, my lord . . . well, what then? You've lost your voice, have you? Anyone who thinks I'm not the best possible ruler, past, present and to come, get up and say so. You don't dare. (*Pause.*) You don't dare. And the greatest. And the most just. You miserable specimens. Go on, get drunk.

The lights go out upstage. The other lot of tables that were projected on the back or reflected by means of mirrors disappear.

BANCO suddenly appears. When he starts speaking he is framed in the doorway, stage right. He moves forward.

BANCO   I dare, Macbett.

MACBETT   Banco!

BANCO   I dare tell you you're a traitor, a swindler, and a murderer.

MACBETT (*giving ground*)   You're not dead after all.

The four GUESTS *have risen.* MACBETT *continues to give ground as* BANCO *comes forward.*

Banco! (*He half draws his dagger.*) Banco!

FIRST GUEST (*to* MACBETT)   It's not Banco, my lord.

MACBETT   I tell you it is.

SECOND GUEST   It's not Banco in flesh and blood. It's only his ghost.

MACBETT   His ghost? (*He laughs.*) Yes, it's only a ghost. I can see through it, put my hand through it. So you are dead after all. You don't frighten me. A pity I can't kill you a second time. This is no place for you here.

THIRD GUEST   He's come from Hell.

MACBETT   You've come from Hell and must return. How did you manage it? Show me the pass that Satan's lieutenant gave you. Have you got till midnight? Sit down. In the place of honor. Poor ghost. You can neither eat nor drink. Sit down among my guests here.

The GUESTS *are frightened and draw back.*

What are you worried about? Go up to him. Give him the illusion he exists. He'll despair even more when he returns to his dark abode . . . either too hot or too wet.

BANCO   Scum! All I can do now is curse you.

MACBETT   You can't make me feel any remorse. If I hadn't killed you first, you'd have killed me—as you did Duncan. You struck the first blow, remember? I was going to make you chamberlain, but you wanted to rule in my place.

BANCO   As you took Duncan's place, who made you Baron twice over.

MACBETT (*to the* GUESTS)   There's no cause for alarm. What are you so frightened of? To think I choose my generals from among these crybabies.

BANCO   I trusted you, I followed you, then you and the witches put a spell on me.

MACBETT   You wanted to substitute your progeny for mine. Well, you didn't get very far. All your children, your grandchildren, your great-grandchildren, died in your seed before being born. Why call me names? I just got there first, that's all.

BANCO   You're in for some surprises, Macbett. Make no mistake. You'll pay for this.

MACBETT   He makes me laugh. I say *he:* really all there is are a few odds and ends, the remains of his old personality—leftovers, a robot.

BANCO *disappears.*

At practically the same moment, DUNCAN *appears, mounting the throne.*

FOURTH GUEST   The Archduke! Look, look! The Archduke!

SECOND GUEST   The Archduke!

MACBETT   I'm the only Archduke around here. Look at me, can't you, when you speak to me.

THIRD GUEST   The Archduke! (*He points.*)

MACBETT (*turning*)   Is this some kind of reunion or something?

The GUESTS go cautiously up to DUNCAN, but stop a certain distance away. The FIRST and SECOND GUESTS kneel to the right and left of the throne. The two others, further off, are on either side of MACBETT, though a certain distance away.

The three of them, MACBETT and the two GUESTS, have their backs to the audience. The first two are in profile. DUNCAN, on his throne, faces straight out.

FIRST *and* THIRD GUESTS (*to the* ARCHDUKE)   My lord—

MACBETT   You didn't believe Banco was real, but you seem to believe that Duncan exists all right and is sitting there on the throne. Is it because he was your sovereign that you've grown used to paying him homage and holding him in awe? Now it's my turn to say, "It's only a ghost." (*To* DUNCAN) As you can see, I've taken your throne. And I've taken your wife. All the same, I served you well and you distrusted me. (*To his* GUESTS) Get back to your places. (*He draws his dagger.*) Quickly. You have no king here but me. You pay homage to me now.

The GUESTS retreat, terrified.

And call me "My Lord." Say . . .

GUESTS (*bowing and scraping*)   We hear and obey, my lord. Our happiness is to submit.

FOURTH GUEST   Our greatest happiness is to do what you say.

MACBETT   I see you understand. (*To* DUNCAN) I don't want to see you again till you've been forgiven by the thousands of soldiers I slaughtered in your name, and till they have been pardoned in their turn by the thousands of women that they raped, and by the thousands of children and peasants they killed.

DUNCAN   I've killed or had killed tens of thousands of men and women, soldiers and civilians alike. I've had thousands of homesteads burnt to the ground. True. Very true. But there is one thing that you haven't got quite right. You didn't steal my wife. (*He laughs sardonically.*)

MACBETT   Are you mad? (*To the four* GUESTS) His death has made him balmy—isn't that right, gentlemen?

GUESTS (*one after the other*)   Yes, my lord.

MACBETT (*to* DUNCAN)   Go on, shoo! you silly old ghost.

DUNCAN *disappears behind the throne. He had already stood up to prepare his exit.*

MAID   My lord, my lord! She's disappeared!

MACBETT   Who?

MAID   Your noble wife, my lord. Lady Macbett.

MACBETT   What did you say?

MAID   I went into her room. It was empty. Her things were gone and so was her maid.

MACBETT   Go and find her and bring her to me. She had a headache. She's gone for a walk in the grounds

to get a breath of fresh air before coming in to dinner.

MAID We've looked everywhere. We've cried out her
name. But only our echoes answered.

MACBETT (*to the four* GUESTS) Scour the forests!
Scour the countryside! Bring her to me! (*To the*
MAID) Go and look in the attic, in the dungeons, in
the cellar. Perhaps she got shut in by mistake.
Quickly. Jump to it.

The MAID *goes out.*

And you. Jump to it. Take police dogs. Search every
house. Have them close the frontiers. Have patrol
boats comb the seas, even outside our territorial
waters. Have powerful searchlights sweep the waves.
Make contact with our neighboring states to have
her expelled and brought back home. If they invoke
the right of asylum or say they haven't signed a
treaty of extradition, declare war on them. I want
reports every quarter of an hour. And arrest all old
women who look as if they might be witches. I want
all the caves searched.

The MAID *comes in upstage.*

The four GUESTS, *who were feverishly grabbing
swords off the wall and buckling them on and
getting tangled up in the process, stop suddenly in
the midst of all this activity and turn to face the*
MAID.

MAID Lady Macbett is coming.

LADY DUNCAN *enters.*

She was just on her way up from the cellar, coming up the stairs. (*The* MAID *goes out.*)

LADY MACBETT, *or rather* LADY DUNCAN, *is rather different from when she last appeared. She is no longer wearing her crown. Her dress is a bit rumpled.*

FIRST *and* SECOND GUESTS (*together*) Lady Macbett!
THIRD *and* FOURTH GUESTS (*together*) Lady Macbett!
FOURTH GUEST Lady Macbett!
MACBETT You're rather late, madam. I've turned the whole country upside down, looking for you. Where have you been all this time? I'd like an explanation— but not just now. (*To the four* GUESTS) Sit down, gentlemen. Our wedding feast can now begin. Let's eat, drink, and be merry. (*To* LADY MACBETT) Let's forget our little difference. You've come back, my darling, that's the main thing. Let's feast and enjoy ourselves in the company of our dear friends here, who love you as dearly as I do and who have been waiting eagerly for you to arrive.

Upstage the projection or the mirrors with the other GUESTS *and tables appear again.*

FIRST *and* SECOND GUESTS Long live Lady Macbett!
THIRD *and* FOURTH GUESTS Long live Lady Macbett!
MACBETT (*to* LADY MACBETT) Take the place of honor.

FOURTH GUEST Lady Macbett, our beloved sovereign!

LADY MACBETT *or* LADY DUNCAN Beloved or not, I am your sovereign. But I'm not Lady Macbett, I'm Lady Duncan—the unhappy but faithful widow of your rightful king, the Archduke Duncan.

MACBETT (*to* LADY DUNCAN) Are you mad?

Song. Opera.

FIRST GUEST She is mad.

SECOND GUEST Is she mad?

THIRD GUEST She's off her head.

FOURTH GUEST She's out of her mind.

FIRST GUEST We were at her wedding!

MACBETT (*to* LADY DUNCAN) You're my wife. Surely you can't have forgotten. They were all there at the wedding.

LADY DUNCAN Not my marriage, no. What you saw was Macbett being married to a sorceress who had taken my face, my voice, my body. She threw me in the palace dungeons and chained me up. Just now my chains fell and the bolts drew back as if by magic. I want nothing to do with you, Macbett. I'm not your accomplice. You murdered your master and your friend. Usurper, imposter.

MACBETT Then how do you know what's been going on?

FIRST GUEST (*singing*) Yes, how does she know?

SECOND GUEST (*singing*) She couldn't have known. She was shut up.

THIRD GUEST (*singing*) She couldn't have known.

GUESTS (*singing*) She couldn't have known.

LADY DUNCAN (*speaking*) I heard all about it on the

prison telegraph. My neighbors tapped out the message on the wall in code. I knew everything there was to know. Well, go and look for her—your beautiful wife, the old hag.

MACBETT (*singing*)   Alas, alas, alas! This time it's not a ghost, it's not a ghost this time.

End of Macbett's sung section.

Yes, I'd like to meet that old hag again. She took the way you look and the way you move and made them still more beautiful. She had a more beautiful voice than yours. Where can I find her? She must have disappeared into mist or into thin air. We have no flying machines to track her down, no devices for tracing unidentified flying objects.

GUESTS (*singing together*)   Long live Macbett, down with Macbett. Long live Macbett, down with Macbett! Long live Lady Duncan, down with Lady Duncan! Long live Lady Duncan, down with Lady Duncan!

LADY DUNCAN (*to* MACBETT)   It doesn't look as if your witch is going to help you any more. Unluckily for you, she's abandoned you.

MACBETT   Unluckily? Aren't I lucky to be king of this country? I don't need anyone's help. (*To the* GUESTS) Get out, you slaves.

They go out.

LADY DUNCAN   You won't get off so lightly. You won't be king for long. Macol, Duncan's son, has just come back from Carthage. He has mustered a large and

powerful army. The whole country is against you.
You've run out of friends, Macbett. (LADY MACBETT
disappears.)

Shouts of "Down with Macbett! Long live Macol!
Down with Macbett! Long live Macol!"

Fanfares. MACOL *enters.*

MACBETT   I fear no one.

MACOL   So I've found you at last. Lowest of the low,
despicable, ignoble, abject creature. Monster, villain,
scum, murderer. Moral imbecile. Slimy snake. Acro-
chord. Horned adder. Foul toad. Filthy slob.

MACBETT   Not very impressive. A foolish boy playing
at being an avenger. Psychosomatic cripple. Ridiculous imbecile. Heroic puppy. Infatuated idiot. Pre-
sumptuous upstart. Greenhorn ninny.

LADY DUNCAN (*to* MACOL, *indicating* MACBETT)   Kill
this unclean man, then throw away your tainted
sword.

MACBETT   Silly little sod. Shoo! I killed your fool of a
father. I wouldn't like to have to kill you, too. It's no
good. You can't hurt me. No man of woman born
can harm Macbett.

MACOL   They've pulled the wool over your eyes. They
were putting you on.

LADY DUNCAN (*to* MACBETT)   Macol isn't my son.
Duncan adopted him. Banco was his father, his
mother was a gazelle that a witch transformed into
a woman. After bringing Macol into the world, she
changed back into a gazelle again. I left the court
secretly before he was born so that no one would

know that I wasn't pregnant. Everyone took him for my son and Duncan's. He wanted an heir, you see.

MACOL   I shall resume my father's name and found a dynasty that will last for centuries.

LADY DUNCAN   No, Macol. Duncan looked after you. He sent you to Carthage University. You must carry on the family name.

MACBETT   Accursed hags. The most cruelly ironic fate since Oedipus.

MACOL   I'll kill two birds with one stone—revenge both my natural and adoptive fathers. But I won't give up my name.

LADY DUNCAN   Ungrateful boy. You have certain obligations to the memory of Duncan. The whole world is ass-backward. The good behave worse than the bad.

MACOL   (*drawing his sword, to* MACBETT)   We have some old scores to settle between us. You're not going to draw your stinking breath one moment longer.

MACBETT   On your own head be it. You're making a bad mistake. I can only be beaten when the forest marches against me.

> MEN *and* WOMEN *approach* MACBETT *and* MACOL *who are center stage. Each of them is carrying a placard with a tree drawn on it—branches would do as well.*
>
> *Recourse should be had to these two solutions only when there are inadequate technical resources. What should really happen is that the whole set, or at least the upstage part of it, should lumber forward to encircle* MACBETT.

MACOL   Look behind you. The forest is on the march.

MACBETT *turns.*

MACBETT   Shit!

MACOL *stabs* MACBETT *in the back.* MACBETT *falls.*

MACOL   Take away this carrion.

Noises off. Shouts of "Long live Macol! Long live Macol! The tyrant is dead! Long live Macol, our beloved sovereign! Long live Macol!"

And bring me a throne.

Two GUESTS *take up Macbett's body. At the same time the throne is brought on.*

GUEST   Please be seated, my lord.

The other GUESTS *arrive. Some of them put up placards reading "Macol is always right."*

GUESTS   Long live Macol! Long live Banco's dynasty! Long live the king!

Sound of bells. MACOL *is by the throne. The* BISHOP *comes on right.*

MACOL (*to the* BISHOP)   You've come to crown me?
BISHOP   Yes, your Highness.

A poor WOMAN *comes on left.*

WOMAN   May your reign be a happy one!

SECOND WOMAN (*coming on right*)   Spare a thought for the poor!

MAN (*coming on right*)   No more injustice.

SECOND MAN   Hate has destroyed our house. Hate has poisoned our souls.

THIRD MAN   May your reign usher in a time of peace, harmony and concord.

FIRST WOMAN   May your reign be blessed.

SECOND WOMAN   A time of joy.

MAN   A time of love.

ANOTHER MAN   Let us embrace, my brothers.

BISHOP   And I will give you my blessing.

MACOL (*standing in front of the throne*)   Silence!

FIRST WOMAN   He's going to speak.

FIRST MAN   The king is going to speak.

SECOND WOMAN   Let's listen to what he has to say.

SECOND MAN   We're listening, my lord. We'll drink your words.

ANOTHER MAN   God bless you.

BISHOP   God bless you.

MACOL   Quiet, I say. Don't all talk at once. I'm going to make an announcement. Nobody move. Nobody breathe. Now get this into your heads. Our country sank beneath the yoke, each day a new gash was added to her wounds. But I have trod upon the tyrant's head and now wear it on my sword.

A MAN *comes on with Macbett's head on the end of a pike.*

MACBETT

THIRD MAN   You got what was coming to you.

SECOND WOMAN   He got what was coming to him.

FOURTH MAN   I hope God doesn't forgive him.

FIRST WOMAN   Let him be damned eternally.

FIRST MAN   Let him burn in Hell.

SECOND MAN   I hope they torture him.

THIRD MAN   I hope he doesn't get a moment's peace.

FOURTH MAN   I hope he repents in the flames and God refuses him.

FIRST WOMAN   I hope they tear his tongue out and it grows again, and they pull it out again twenty times a day.

SECOND MAN   I hope they roast him on a spit. I hope they impale him. I hope he can see how happy we are. I hope our laughter deafens him.

SECOND WOMAN   I've got my knitting needles. Let's put his eyes out.

MACOL   If you don't shut up at once, I'll set my soldiers and dogs on you.

A forest of guillotines appears upstage as in the First Scene.

MACOL   Now that the tyrant is dead and curses his mother for bringing him into the world, I'll tell you this: My poor country shall have more vices than it had before, more suffer and more sundry ways than ever by me that do succeed.

As Macol's announcement continues, there are murmurs of discontent, amazement and despair from the crowd. At the end of the speech, MACOL is left alone.

EUGÈNE IONESCO

In me I know
All the particulars of vice so grafted
That, when they shall be opened, black
Macbett will seem as pure as snow and the
  poor state
Esteem him as a lamb, being compared
With my confineless harms. I grant him bloody.
Luxurious, avaricious, false, deceitful,
Sudden, malicious, smacking of every sin
That has a name: but there's no bottom, none,
In my voluptuousness. Your wives, your daughters,
Your matrons, and your maids, cannot fill up
The cistern of my lust, and my desire
All continent impediments shall o'erbear
That do oppose my will. Better Macbett,
Than such a one to reign. With this there grows
In my most ill-composed affection, such
a staunchless avarice, that now I'm king
I shall cut off the nobles from their lands,
Desire his jewels, and this other's house,
And my more-having will be as a sauce
To make my hunger more, that I shall forge
Quarrels unjust against the good and loyal,
Destroying them for wealth. The king—
  becoming graces
As justice, verity, temp'rance, stableness,
Bounty, perseverance, mercy, lowliness.
Devotion, patience, courage, fortitude,
I have no relish of them, but abound
In the division of each several crime,
Acting it many ways.

MACBETT

The BISHOP, *who was the only one left, goes dejectedly out right.*

Now I have power, I shall
Pour the sweet milk of concord into Hell,
Uproar the universal peace, confound
All unity on earth.
First I'll make this Archduchy a kingdom—
and me the king. An empire—and me the
emperor. Super-highness, super-king,
super-majesty, emperor of emperors.

He disappears in the mist.

The mist clears. The BUTTERFLY HUNTER *crosses the stage.*

Selected Grove Press Theater Paperbacks

17061-X ARDEN, JOHN / Plays: One (Serjeant Musgrave's Dance; The Workhouse Donkey; Armstrong's Last Goodnight) / $4.95

17083-0 AYCKBOURN, ALAN / Absurd Person Singular, Absent Friends, Bedroom Farce: Three Plays / $6.95

17208-6 BECKETT, SAMUEL / Endgame / $3.95

17233-7 BECKETT, SAMUEL / Happy Days / $4.95

62061-5 BECKETT, SAMUEL / Ohio Impromptu, Catastrophe, and What Where: Three Plays / $4.95

17204-3 BECKETT, SAMUEL / Waiting for Godot / $4.95

13034-8 BRECHT, BERTOLT / Galileo / $4.95

17472-0 BRECHT, BERTOLT / The Threepenny Opera / $3.95

17411-9 CLURMAN, HAROLD / Nine Plays of the Modern Theater (Waiting for Godot by Samuel Beckett; The Visit by Friedrich Durrenmatt; Tango by Slawomir Mrozek; The Caucasian Chalk Circle by Bertolt Brecht; The Balcony by Jean Genet; Rhinoceros by Eugene Ionesco; American Buffalo by David Mamet; The Birthday Party by Harold Pinter; and Rosencrantz and Guildenstern Are Dead by Tom Stoppard) / $15.95

17535-2 COWARD, NOEL / Three Plays (Private Lives; Hay Fever; Blithe Spirit) / $7.95

17239-6 DURRENMATT, FRIEDRICH / The Visit / $5.95

17214-0 GENET, JEAN / The Balcony / $7.95

17390-2 GENET, JEAN / The Maids and Deathwatch: Two Plays / $8.95

17022-9 HAYMAN, RONALD / How to Read a Play / $6.95

17075-X INGE, WILLIAM / Four Plays (Come Back, Little Sheba; Picnic; Bus Stop; The Dark at the Top of the Stairs) / $8.95

62199-9 IONESCO, EUGENE / Exit the King, The Killer and Macbett / $9.95

17209-4 IONESCO, EUGENE / Four Plays (The Bald Soprano; The Lesson; The Chairs; Jack or The Submission) $6.95

17226-4 IONESCO, EUGENE / Rhinoceros and Other Plays (The Leader; The Future Is in Eggs; or It Takes All Sorts to Make a World) / $6.95

17485-2 JARRY, ALFRED / The Ubu Plays (Ubu Rex; Ubu Cuckolded; Ubu Enchained) / $9.95

17744-4 KAUFMAN, GEORGE and HART, MOSS / Three Plays (Once in a Lifetime; You Can't Take It With You; The Man Who Came to Dinner) / $8.95

17016-4 MAMET, DAVID / American Buffalo / $5.95

62049-6 MAMET, DAVID / Glengarry Glen Ross / $6.95

17040-7 MAMET, DAVID / A Life in the Theatre / $9.95
17043-1 MAMET, DAVID / Sexual Perversity in Chicago and The Duck Variations / $7.95
17264-7 MROZEK, SLAWOMIR / Tango / $3.95
17092-X ODETS, CLIFFORD / Six Plays (Waiting for Lefty; Awake and Sing; Golden Boy; Rocket to the Moon; Till the Day I Die; Paradise Lost) / $7.95
17001-6 ORTON, JOE / The Complete Plays (The Ruffian on the Stair; The Good and Faithful Servant; The Erpingham Camp; Funeral Games; Loot; What the Butler Saw; Entertaining Mr. Sloan) / $9.95
17084-9 PINTER, HAROLD / Betrayal / $6.95
17019-9 PINTER, HAROLD / Complete Works: One (The Birthday Party; The Room; The Dumb Waiter; A Slight Ache; A Night Out; The Black and White; The Examination) $8.95
17020-2 PINTER, HAROLD / Complete Works: Two (The Caretaker; Night School; The Dwarfs; The Collection; The Lover; Five Revue Sketches) / $6.95
17051-2 PINTER, HAROLD / Complete Works: Three (The Homecoming; Landscape; Silence; The Basement; Six Revue Sketches; Tea party [play]; Tea Party [short story]; Mac) / $6.95
17950-1 PINTER, HAROLD / Complete Works: Four (Old Times; No Man's Land; Betrayal; Monologue; Family Voices) / $5.95
17251-5 PINTER, HAROLD / The Homecoming / $5.95
17885-8 PINTER, HAROLD / No Man's Land / $7.95
17539-5 POMERANCE, BERNARD / The Elephant Man / $5.95
17743-6 RATTIGAN, TERENCE / Plays: One (French Without Tears; The Winslow Boy; Harlequinade; The Browning Version) / $5.95
62040-2 SETO, JUDITH ROBERTS / The Young Actor's Workbook / $8.95
17948-X SHAWN, WALLACE and GREGORY, ANDRÉ / My Dinner with André / $6.95
13033-X STOPPARD, TOM / Rosencrantz and Guildenstern Are Dead / $4.95
17884-X STOPPARD, TOM / Travesties / $4.95
17206-X WALEY, ARTHUR, tr. and ed. / The Nō Plays of Japan / $7.95

GROVE PRESS, 841 Broadway, New York, N.Y. 10003